What Readers Are Saying About
Practical Programming, Second Edition

I wish I could go back in time and give this book to my 10-year-old self when I first learned programming! It's so much more engaging, practical, and accessible than the dry introductory programming books that I tried (and often failed) to comprehend as a kid. I love the authors' hands-on approach of mixing explanations with code snippets that students can type into the Python prompt.

➤ **Philip Guo**
Creator of Online Python Tutor (www.pythontutor.com), Assistant Professor, Department of Computer Science, University of Rochester

Practical Programming delivers just what it promises: a clear, readable, usable introduction to programming for beginners. This isn't just a guide to hacking together programs. The book provides foundations to lifelong programming skills: a crisp, consistent, and visual model of memory and execution and a design recipe that will help readers produce quality software.

➤ **Steven Wolfman**
Senior Instructor, Department of Computer Science, University of British Columbia

The second edition of this excellent text reflects the authors' many years of experience teaching Python to beginning students. Topics are presented so that each leads naturally to the next, and common novice errors and misconceptions are explicitly addressed. The exercises at the end of each chapter invite interested students to explore computer science and programming language topics.

➤ **Kathleen Freeman**
  Director of Undergraduate Studies, Department of Computer and Information Science, University of Oregon

Practical Programming, 2nd Edition

An Introduction to Computer Science Using Python 3

Paul Gries
Jennifer Campbell
Jason Montojo

The Pragmatic Bookshelf

Dallas, Texas • Raleigh, North Carolina

Many of the designations used by manufacturers and sellers to distinguish their products are claimed as trademarks. Where those designations appear in this book, and The Pragmatic Programmers, LLC was aware of a trademark claim, the designations have been printed in initial capital letters or in all capitals. The Pragmatic Starter Kit, The Pragmatic Programmer, Pragmatic Programming, Pragmatic Bookshelf, PragProg and the linking *g* device are trademarks of The Pragmatic Programmers, LLC.

Every precaution was taken in the preparation of this book. However, the publisher assumes no responsibility for errors or omissions, or for damages that may result from the use of information (including program listings) contained herein.

Our Pragmatic courses, workshops, and other products can help you and your team create better software and have more fun. For more information, as well as the latest Pragmatic titles, please visit us at *http://pragprog.com*.

The team that produced this book includes:

Lynn Beighley (editor)
Potomac Indexing, LLC (indexer)
Molly McBeath (copyeditor)
David J Kelly (typesetter)
Janet Furlow (producer)
Juliet Benda (rights)
Ellie Callahan (support)

Printed in the United States of America.
ISBN-13: 978-1-93778-545-1
Printed on acid-free paper.
Book version: P3.0—January 2016

Contents

Acknowledgments

This book would be confusing and riddled with errors if it weren't for a bunch of awesome people who patiently and carefully read our drafts.

We had a great team of people provide technical reviews: (in no particular order) Steve Wolfman, Adam Foster, Owen Nelson, Arturo Martínez Peguero, C. Keith Ray, Michael Szamosi, David Gries, Peter Beens, Edward Branley, Paul Holbrook, Kristie Jolliffe, Mike Riley, Sean Stickle, Tim Ottinger, Bill Dudney, Dan Zingaro, and Justin Stanley. We also appreciate all the people who reported errata as we went through the beta phases: your feedback was invaluable.

Greg Wilson started us on this journey when he proposed that we write a textbook, and he was our guide and mentor as we worked together to create the first edition of this book.

Last and foremost is our awesome editor, Lynn Beighley, who never once scolded us, even though we thoroughly deserved it many times. Lynn, we can't imagine having anyone better giving us feedback and guidance. Thank you so much.

Preface

This book uses the Python programming language to teach introductory computer science topics and a handful of useful applications. You'll certainly learn a fair amount of Python as you work through this book, but along the way you'll also learn about issues that every programmer needs to know: ways to approach a problem and break it down into parts, how and why to document your code, how to test your code to help ensure your program does what you want it to, and more.

We chose Python for several reasons:

- *It is free and well documented.* In fact, Python is one of the largest and best-organized open source projects going.

- *It runs everywhere.* The reference implementation, written in C, is used on everything from cell phones to supercomputers, and it's supported by professional-quality installers for Windows, Mac OS X, and Linux.

- *It has a clean syntax.* Yes, every language makes this claim, but during the several years that we have been using it at the University of Toronto, we have found that students make noticeably fewer "punctuation" mistakes with Python than with C-like languages.

- *It is relevant.* Thousands of companies use it every day: it is one of the languages used at Google, Industrial Light & Magic uses it extensively, and large portions of the game EVE Online are written in Python. It is also widely used by academic research groups.

- *It is well supported by tools.* Legacy editors like vi and Emacs all have Python editing modes, and several professional-quality IDEs are available. (We use IDLE, the free development environment that comes with a standard Python installation.)

Our Approach

We use an "objects first, classes second" approach: students are shown how to *use* objects from the standard library early on but do not create their own classes until after they have learned about flow control and basic data structures. This allows students to get familiar with what a type is (in Python, all types, including integers and floating-point numbers, are classes) before they have to write their own types.

We have organized the book into two parts. The first covers fundamental programming ideas: elementary data types (numbers, strings, lists, sets, and dictionaries), modules, control flow, functions, testing, debugging, and algorithms. Depending on the audience, this material can be covered in a couple of months.

The second part of the book consists of more or less independent chapters on more advanced topics that assume all the basic material has been covered. The first of these chapters shows students how to create their own classes and introduces encapsulation, inheritance, and polymorphism (courses for computer science majors should probably include this material). The other chapters cover testing, databases, and GUI construction; these will appeal to both computer science majors and students from the sciences and will allow the book to be used for both.

Further Reading

Lots of other good books on Python programming exist. Some are accessible to novices, such as *Introduction to Computing and Programming in Python: A Multimedia Approach [GE13]* and *Python Programming: An Introduction to Computer Science [Zel03]*; others are for anyone with any previous programming experience (*How to Think Like a Computer Scientist: Learning with Python [DEM02]*, *Object-Oriented Programming in Python [GL07]* and *Learning Python [Lut13]*). You may also want to take a look at *Python Education Special Interest Group (EDU-SIG) [Pyt11]*, the special interest group for educators using Python.

Python Resources

Information about a variety of Python books and other resources is available at http://wiki.python.org/moin/FrontPage.

Learning a second programming language can be enlightening. There are many possiblities, such as well-known languages like C, Java, C#, and Ruby. Python is similar in concept to those languages. However, you will likely learn more and become a better programmer if you learn a programming language that requires a different mindset, such as Racket,[1] Erlang,[2] or Haskell.[3] In any case, we strongly recommend learning a second programming language.

What You'll See

In this book, we'll do the following:

- We'll show you how to develop and use programs that solve real-world problems. Most of the examples will come from science and engineering, but the ideas can be applied to any domain.

- We'll start by teaching you the core features of Python. These features are included in every modern programming language, so you can use what you learn no matter what you work on next.

- We'll also teach you how to think methodically about programming. In particular, we will show you how to break complex problems into simple ones and how to combine the solutions to those simpler problems to create complete applications.

- Finally, we'll introduce some tools that will help make your programming more productive, as well as some others that will help your applications cope with larger problems.

Online Resources

All the source code, errata, discussion forums, installation instructions, and exercise solutions are available at http://pragprog.com/book/gwpy2/practical-programming.

---

1. http://www.ccs.neu.edu/home/matthias/HtDP2e/index.html
2. http://learnyousomeerlang.com
3. http://learnyouahaskell.com

## CHAPTER 1

What's Programming?

(Photo credit: NASA/Goddard Space Flight Center Scientific Visualization Studio)

Take a look at the pictures above. The first one shows forest cover in the Amazon basin in 1975. The second one shows the same area twenty-six years later. Anyone can see that much of the rainforest has been destroyed, but how much is "much"?

Now look at this:

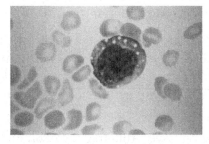

(Photo credit: CDC)

Are these blood cells healthy? Do any of them show signs of leukemia? It would take an expert doctor a few minutes to tell. Multiply those minutes by the number of people who need to be screened. There simply aren't enough human doctors in the world to check everyone.

This is where computers come in. Computer programs can measure the differences between two pictures and count the number of oddly shaped platelets in a blood sample. Geneticists use programs to analyze gene sequences; statisticians, to analyze the spread of diseases; geologists, to predict the effects of earthquakes; economists, to analyze fluctuations in the stock market; and climatologists, to study global warming. More and more scientists are writing programs to help them do their work. In turn, those programs are making entirely new kinds of science possible.

Of course, computers are good for a lot more than just science. We used computers to write this book. You probably used one today to chat with friends, find out where your lectures are, or look for a restaurant that serves pizza *and* Chinese food. Every day, someone figures out how to make a computer do something that has never been done before. Together, those "somethings" are changing the world.

This book will teach you how to make computers do what *you* want them to do. You may be planning to be a doctor, a linguist, or a physicist rather than a full-time programmer, but whatever you do, being able to program is as important as being able to write a letter or do basic arithmetic.

We begin in this chapter by explaining what programs and programming are. We then define a few terms and present a few useful bits of information for course instructors.

1.1 Programs and Programming

A *program* is a set of instructions. When you write down directions to your house for a friend, you are writing a program. Your friend "executes" that program by following each instruction in turn.

Every program is written in terms of a few basic operations that its reader already understands. For example, the set of operations that your friend can understand might include the following: "Turn left at Darwin Street," "Go forward three blocks," and "If you get to the gas station, turn around—you've gone too far."

Computers are similar but have a different set of operations. Some operations are mathematical, like "Take the square root of a number," while others include "Read a line from the file named data.txt" and "Make a pixel blue."

The most important difference between a computer and an old-fashioned calculator is that you can "teach" a computer new operations by defining them in terms of old ones. For example, you can teach the computer that "Take the average" means "Add up the numbers in a sequence and divide by the sequence's size." You can then use the operations you have just defined to create still more operations, each layered on top of the ones that came before. It's a lot like creating life by putting atoms together to make proteins and then combining proteins to build cells, combining cells to make organs, and combining organs to make a creature.

Defining new operations and combining them to do useful things is the heart and soul of programming. It is also a tremendously powerful way to think about other kinds of problems. As Professor Jeannette Wing wrote in *Computational Thinking [Win06]*, computational thinking is about the following:

- *Conceptualizing, not programming.* Computer science isn't computer programming. Thinking like a computer scientist means more than being able to program a computer: it requires thinking at multiple levels of abstraction.

- *A way that humans, not computers, think.* Computational thinking is a way humans solve problems; it isn't trying to get humans to think like computers. Computers are dull and boring; humans are clever and imaginative. We humans make computers exciting. Equipped with computing devices, we use our cleverness to tackle problems we wouldn't dare take on before the age of computing and build systems with functionality limited only by our imaginations.

- *For everyone, everywhere.* Computational thinking will be a reality when it becomes so integral to human endeavors it disappears as an explicit philosophy.

We hope that by the time you have finished reading this book, you will see the world in a slightly different way.

1.2 What's a Programming Language?

Directions to the nearest bus station can be given in English, Portuguese, Mandarin, Hindi, and many other languages. As long as the people you're talking to understand the language, they'll get to the bus station.

In the same way, there are many programming languages, and they all can add numbers, read information from files, and make user interfaces with windows and buttons and scroll bars. The instructions look different, but they accomplish the same task. For example, in the Python programming language, here's how you add 3 and 4:

```
3 + 4
```

But here's how it's done in the Scheme programming language:

```
(+ 3 4)
```

They both express the same idea—they just look different.

Every programming language has a way to write mathematical expressions, repeat a list of instructions a number of times, choose which of two instructions to do based on the current information you have, and much more. In this book, you'll learn how to do these things in the Python programming language. Once you understand Python, learning the next programming language will be much easier.

1.3 What's a Bug?

Pretty much everyone has had a program crash. A standard story is that you were typing in a paper when, all of a sudden, your word processor crashed. You had forgotten to save, and you had to start all over again. Old versions of Microsoft Windows used to crash more often than they should have, showing the dreaded "blue screen of death." (Happily, they've gotten a *lot* better in the past several years.) Usually, your computer shows some kind of cryptic error message when a program crashes.

What happened in each case is that the people who wrote the program told the computer to do something it couldn't do: open a file that didn't exist, perhaps, or keep track of more information than the computer could handle, or maybe repeat a task with no way of stopping other than by rebooting the computer. (Programmers don't mean to make these kinds of mistakes, but they are *very* hard to avoid.)

Worse, some bugs don't cause a crash; instead, they give incorrect information. (This is worse because at least with a crash you'll notice that there's a problem.) As a real-life example of this kind of bug, the calendar program that one of the authors uses contains an entry for a friend who was born in 1978. That friend, according to the calendar program, had his 5,875,542nd birthday this past February. It's entertaining, but it can also be tremendously frustrating.

Every piece of software that you can buy has bugs in it. Part of your job as a programmer is to minimize the number of bugs and to reduce their severity. In order to find a bug, you need to track down where you gave the wrong instructions, then you need to figure out the right instructions, and then you need to update the program without introducing other bugs. This is a hard, hard task that requires a lot of planning and care.

Every time you get a software update for a program, it is for one of two reasons: new features were added to a program or bugs were fixed. It's always a game of economics for the software company: are there few enough bugs, and are they minor enough or infrequent enough in order for people to pay for the software?

In this book, we'll show you some fundamental techniques for finding and fixing bugs and also show you how to prevent them in the first place.

1.4 The Difference Between Brackets, Braces, and Parentheses

One of the pieces of terminology that causes confusion is what to call certain characters. The Python style guide (and several dictionaries) use these names, so this book does too:

()   Parentheses

[]   Brackets

{}   Braces (Some people call these *curly brackets* or *curly braces*, but we'll stick to just *braces*.)

1.5 Installing Python

Installation instructions and use of the IDLE programming environment are available on the book's website: http://pragprog.com/titles/gwpy2/practical-programming.

## CHAPTER 2

Hello, Python

Programs are made up of commands that tell the computer what to do. These commands are called *statements*, which the computer executes. This chapter describes the simplest of Python's statements and shows how they can be used to do arithmetic, which is one of the most common tasks for computers and also a great place to start learning to program. It's also the basis of almost everything that follows.

2.1 How Does a Computer Run a Python Program?

In order to understand what happens when you're programming, you need to have a basic understanding of how a computer executes a program. The computer is assembled from pieces of hardware, including a *processor* that can execute instructions and do arithmetic, a place to store data such as a *hard drive*, and various other pieces, such as a computer monitor, a keyboard, a card for connecting to a network, and so on.

To deal with all these pieces, every computer runs some kind of *operating system*, such as Microsoft Windows, Linux, or Mac OS X. An operating system, or OS, is a program; what makes it special is that it's the only program on the computer that's allowed direct access to the hardware. When any other application (such as your browser, a spreadsheet program, or a game) wants to draw on the screen, find out what key was just pressed on the keyboard, or fetch data from the hard drive, it sends a request to the OS (see Figure 1, *Talking to the operating system*, on page 8).

This may seem like a roundabout way of doing things, but it means that only the people writing the OS have to worry about the differences between one graphics card and another and whether the computer is connected to a network through ethernet or wireless. The rest of us—everyone analyzing scientific data or creating 3D virtual chat rooms—only have to learn our way

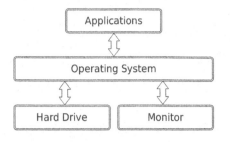

Figure 1—Talking to the operating system

around the OS, and our programs will then run on thousands of different kinds of hardware.

Twenty-five years ago that's how most programmers worked. Today, though, it's common to add another layer between the programmer and the computer's hardware. When you write a program in Python, Java, or Visual Basic, it doesn't run directly on top of the OS. Instead, another program, called an *interpreter* or *virtual machine*, takes your program and runs it for you, translating your commands into a language the OS understands. It's a lot easier, more secure, and more portable across operating systems than writing programs directly on top of the OS:

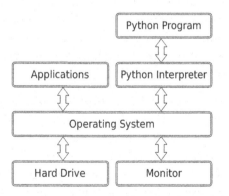

There are two ways to use the Python interpreter. One is to tell it to execute a Python program that is saved in a file with a .py extension. Another is to interact with it in a program called a *shell*, where you type statements one at a time. The interpreter will execute each statement when you type it, do what the statement says to do, and show any output as text, all in one window. We will explore Python in this chapter using a Python shell.

Install Python Now (If You Haven't Already)

If you haven't yet installed Python 3, please do so now. (Python 2 won't do; there are significant differences between Python 2 and Python 3, and this book uses Python 3.) Locate installation instructions on the book's website: http://pragprog.com/titles/gwpy2/practical-programming.

Programming requires practice: you won't learn how to program just by reading this book, much like you wouldn't learn how to play guitar just by reading a book on how to play guitar.

Python comes with a program called IDLE, which we use to write Python programs. IDLE has a Python shell that communicates with the Python interpreter and also allows you to write and run programs that are saved in a file.

We *strongly* recommend that you open IDLE and follow along with our examples. Typing in the code in this book is the programming equivalent of repeating phrases back to an instructor as you're learning to speak a new language.

2.2 Expressions and Values: Arithmetic in Python

You're familiar with mathematical expressions like 3 + 4 ("three plus four") and 2 - 3 / 5 ("two minus three divided by five"); each expression is built out of *values* like 2, 3, and 5 and *operators* like + and -, which combine their *operands* in different ways. In the expression 4 / 5, the operator is "/" and the operands are 4 and 5.

Expressions don't have to involve an operator: a number by itself is an expression. For example, we consider 212 to be an expression as well as a value.

Like any programming language, Python can *evaluate* basic mathematical expressions. For example, the following expression adds 4 and 13:

```
>>> 4 + 13
17
```

The >>> symbol is called a *prompt*. When you opened IDLE, a window should have opened with this symbol shown; you don't type it. It is prompting you to type something. Here we typed 4 + 13, and then we pressed the Return (or Enter) key in order to signal that we were done entering that *expression*. Python then evaluated the expression.

When an expression is evaluated, it produces a single value. In the previous expression, the evaluation of 4 + 13 produced the value 17. When typed in the shell, Python shows the value that is produced.

Subtraction and multiplication are similarly unsurprising:

```
>>> 15 - 3
12
>>> 4 * 7
28
```

The following expression divides 5 by 2:

```
>>> 5 / 2
2.5
```

The result has a decimal point. In fact, the result of division always has a decimal point even if the result is a whole number:

```
>>> 4 / 2
2.0
```

Types

Every value in Python has a particular *type*, and the types of values determine how they behave when they're combined. Values like 4 and 17 have type int (short for *integer*), and values like 2.5 and 17.0 have type float. The word *float* is short for *floating point*, which refers to the decimal point that moves around between digits of the number.

An expression involving two floats produces a float:

```
>>> 17.0 - 10.0
7.0
```

When an expression's operands are an int and a float, Python automatically converts the int to a float. This is why the following two expressions both return the same answer:

```
>>> 17.0 - 10
7.0
>>> 17 - 10.0
7.0
```

If you want, you can omit the zero after the decimal point when writing a floating-point number:

```
>>> 17 - 10.
7.0
>>> 17. - 10
7.0
```

However, most people think this is bad style, since it makes your programs harder to read: it's very easy to miss a dot on the screen and see '17' instead of '17.'.

Integer Division, Modulo, and Exponentiation

Every now and then, we want only the integer part of a division result. For example, we might want to know how many 24-hour days there are in 53 hours (which is two 24-hour days plus another 5 hours). To calculate the number of days, we can use *integer division*:

```
>>> 53 // 24
2
```

We can find out how many hours are left over using the *modulo* operator, which gives the remainder of the division:

```
>>> 53 % 24
5
```

Python doesn't round the result of integer division. Instead, it takes the *floor* of the result of the division, which means that it rounds down to the nearest integer:

```
>>> 17 // 10
1
```

Be careful about using % and // with negative operands. Because Python takes the floor of the result of an integer division, the result is one smaller than you might expect if the result is negative:

```
>>> -17 // 10
-2
```

When using modulo, the sign of the result matches the sign of the divisor (the second operand):

```
>>> -17 % 10
3
>>> 17 % -10
-3
```

For the mathematically inclined, the relationship between // and % comes from this equation, for any two non-zero numbers a and b:

```
(b * (a // b) + a % b) is equal to a
```

For example, because -17 // 10 is -2, and -17 % 10 is 3; then 10 * (-17 // 10) + -17 % 10 is the same as 10 * -2 + 3, which is -17.

Floating-point numbers can be operands for // and % as well. With //, the result is rounded down to the nearest whole number, although the type is a floating-point number:

```
>>> 3.3 // 1
3.0
>>> 3 // 1.0
3.0
>>> 3 // 1.1
2.0
>>> 3.5 // 1.1
3.0
>>> 3.5 // 1.3
2.0
```

The following expression calculates 3 raised to the 6th power:

```
>>> 3 ** 6
729
```

Operators that have two operands are called *binary operators*. Negation is a *unary operator* because it applies to one operand:

```
>>> -5
-5
>>> --5
5
>>> ---5
-5
```

2.3 What *Is* a Type?

We've now seen two types of numbers (integers and floating-point numbers), so we ought to explain what we mean by a *type*. In computing, a type consists of two things:

- a set of values, and
- a set of operations that can be applied to those values.

For example, in type int, the values are ..., -3, -2, -1, 0, 1, 2, 3, ... and we have seen that these operators can be applied to those values: +, -, *, /, //, %, and **.

The values in type float are a subset of the real numbers, and it happens that the same set of operations can be applied to float values. If an operator can be applied to more than one type of value, it is called an *overloaded operator*. We can see what happens when these are applied to various values in Table 1, *Arithmetic Operators*, on page 13.

Finite Precision

Floating-point numbers are not exactly the fractions you learned in grade school. For example, look at Python's version of the fractions $\frac{2}{3}$ and $\frac{5}{3}$:

Symbol	Operator	Example	Result
-	Negation	-5	-5
+	Addition	11 + 3.1	14.1
-	Subtraction	5 - 19	-14
*	Multiplication	8.5 * 4	34.0
/	Division	11 / 2	5.5
//	Integer Division	11 // 2	5
%	Remainder	8.5 % 3.5	1.5
**	Exponentiation	2 ** 5	32

Table 1—Arithmetic Operators

```
>>> 2 / 3
0.6666666666666666
>>> 5 / 3
1.6666666666666667
```

The first value ends with a 6, and the second with a 7. This is fishy: both of them should have an infinite number of 6s after the decimal point. The problem is that computers have a finite amount of memory, and (to make calculations fast and memory efficient) most programming languages limit how much information can be stored for any single number. The number 0.6666666666666666 turns out to be the closest value to $\frac{2}{3}$ that the computer can actually store in that limited amount of memory, and 1.6666666666666667 is as close as we get to the real value of $\frac{5}{3}$.

Operator Precedence

Let's put our knowledge of ints and floats to use in converting Fahrenheit to Celsius. To do this, we subtract 32 from the temperature in Fahrenheit and then multiply by $\frac{5}{9}$:

```
>>> 212 - 32 * 5 / 9
194.22222222222223
```

Python claims the result is 194.22222222222223 degrees Celsius, when in fact it should be 100. The problem is that multiplication and division have higher *precedence* than subtraction; in other words, when an expression contains a mix of operators, the * and / are evaluated before the - and +. This means that what we actually calculated was 212 - ((32 * 5) / 9): the *subexpression* 32 * 5 is evaluated before the division is applied, and that division is evaluated before the subtraction occurs.

More on Numeric Precision

Integers (values of type int) in Python can be as large or as small as you like. However, float values are only *approximations* to real numbers. For example, $\frac{1}{4}$ can be stored exactly, but as we've already seen, $\frac{2}{3}$ cannot. Using more memory won't solve the problem, though it will make the approximation closer to the real value, just as writing a larger number of 6s after the 0 in 0.666... doesn't make it exactly equal to $\frac{2}{3}$.

The difference between $\frac{2}{3}$ and 0.6666666666666666 may look tiny. But if we use 0.6666666666666666 in a calculation, then the error may get compounded. For example, if we add 1 to $\frac{2}{3}$, the resulting value ends in ...6665, so in many programming languages, $1 + \frac{2}{3}$ is not equal to $\frac{5}{3}$:

```
>>> 2 / 3 + 1
1.6666666666666665
>>> 5 / 3
1.6666666666666667
```

As we do more calculations, the rounding errors can get larger and larger, particularly if we're mixing very large and very small numbers. For example, suppose we add 10000000000 (ten billion) and 0.00000000001 (there are 10 zeros after the decimal point):

```
>>> 10000000000 + 0.00000000001
10000000000.0
```

The result ought to have twenty zeros between the first and last significant digit, but that's too many for the computer to store, so the result is just 10000000000—it's as if the addition never took place. Adding lots of small numbers to a large one can therefore have no effect at all, which is *not* what a bank wants when it totals up the values of its customers' savings accounts.

It's important to be aware of the floating-point issue. There is no magic bullet to solve it, because computers are limited in both memory and speed. *Numerical analysis*, the study of algorithms to approximate continuous mathematics, is one of the largest subfields of computer science and mathematics.

Here's a tip: if you have to add up floating-point numbers, add them from smallest to largest in order to minimize the error.

We can alter the order of precedence by putting parentheses around subexpressions:

```
>>> (212 - 32) * 5 / 9
100.0
```

Table 2, *Arithmetic Operators Listed by Precedence from Highest to Lowest*, on page 15 shows the order of precedence for arithmetic operators.

Operators with higher precedence are applied before those with lower precedence. Here is an example that shows this:

```
>>> -2 ** 4
-16
>>> -(2 ** 4)
-16
>>> (-2) ** 4
16
```

Because exponentiation has higher precedence than negation, the subexpression 2 ** 4 is evaluated before negation is applied.

Precedence	Operator	Operation
Highest	**	Exponentiation
	-	Negation
	*, /, //, %	Multiplication, division, integer division, and remainder
Lowest	+, -	Addition and subtraction

Table 2—Arithmetic Operators Listed by Precedence from Highest to Lowest

Operators on the same row have equal precedence and are applied left to right, except for exponentiation, which is applied right to left. So, for example, because binary operators + and - are on the same row, 3 + 4 - 5 is equivalent to (3 + 4) - 5, and 3 - 4 + 5 is equivalent to (3 - 4) + 5.

It's a good rule to parenthesize complicated expressions even when you don't need to, since it helps the eye read things like 1 + 1.7 + 3.2 * 4.4 - 16 / 3. On the other hand, it's a good rule to *not* use parentheses in simple expressions such as 3.1 * 5.

2.4 Variables and Computer Memory: Remembering Values

Like mathematicians, programmers frequently name values so that they can use them later. A name that refers to a value is called a *variable*. In Python, variable names can use letters, digits, and the underscore symbol (but they can't start with a digit). For example, X, species5618, and degrees_celsius are all allowed, but 777 isn't (it would be confused with a number), and neither is no-way! (it contains punctuation).

You create a new variable by *assigning* it a value:

```
>>> degrees_celsius = 26.0
```

This statement is called an *assignment statement*; we say that degrees_celsius is *assigned* the value 26.0. That makes degrees_celsius refer to the value 26.0. We can use variables anywhere we can use values. Whenever Python sees a variable in an expression, it substitutes the value to which the variable refers:

```
>>> degrees_celsius = 26.0
>>> degrees_celsius
26.0
>>> 9 / 5 * degrees_celsius + 32
78.80000000000001
>>> degrees_celsius / degrees_celsius
1.0
```

Variables are called *variables* because their values can vary as the program executes. We can assign a new value to a variable:

```
>>> degrees_celsius = 26.0
>>> 9 / 5 * degrees_celsius + 32
78.80000000000001
>>> degrees_celsius = 0.0
>>> 9 / 5 * degrees_celsius + 32
32.0
```

Assigning a value to a variable that already exists doesn't create a second variable. Instead, the existing variable is reused, which means that the variable no longer refers to its old value.

We can create other variables; this example calculates the difference between the boiling point of water and the temperature stored in degrees_celsius:

```
>>> degrees_celsius = 15.5
>>> difference = 100 - degrees_celsius
>>> difference
84.5
```

Warning: = Is Not Equality in Python!

In mathematics, = means "the thing on the left is equal to the thing on the right." In Python, it means something quite different. Assignment is not symmetric: x = 12 assigns the value 12 to variable x, but 12 = x results in an error. Because of this, we never describe the statement x = 12 as "x equals 12." Instead, we read this as "x gets 12" or "x is assigned 12."

Values, Variables, and Computer Memory

We're going to develop a model of computer memory—a *memory model*—that will let us trace what happens when Python executes a Python program. This memory model will help us accurately predict and explain what Python does when it executes code, a skill that is a requirement for becoming a good programmer.

Every location in the computer's memory has a *memory address*, much like an address for a house on a street, that uniquely identifies that location.

The Online Python Tutor

Philip Guo wrote a web-based memory visualizer that matches our memory model pretty well. Here's the URL: http://pythontutor.com/visualize.html. It can trace both Python 2 and Python 3 code; make sure you select the correct version. The settings that most closely match our memory model are these:

- Hide frames of exited functions
- Render all objects on the heap
- Hide environment parent pointers
- Use text labels for references

We strongly recommend that you use this visualizer whenever you want to trace execution of a Python program.

In case you find it motivating, we weren't aware of Philip's visualizer when we developed our memory model (and vice versa), and yet they match extremely closely.

We're going to mark our memory addresses with an *id* prefix (short for *identifier*) so that they look different from integers: *id1*, *id2*, *id3*, and so on.

Here is how we draw the floating-point value 26.0 using the memory model:

id1:float

```
  26.0
```

This picture shows the value 26.0 at the memory address *id1*. We will always show the type of the value as well—in this case, float. We will call this box an *object*: a value at a memory address with a type. During execution of a program, every value that Python keeps track of is stored inside an object in computer memory.

In our memory model, a variable contains the memory address of the object to which it refers:

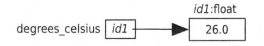

In order to make the picture easier to interpret, we will usually draw arrows from variables to their objects.

We use the following terminology:

- Value 26.0 has the memory address *id1*.
- The object at the memory address *id1* has type float and the value 26.0.
- Variable degrees_celsius *contains* the memory address *id1*.
- Variable degrees_celsius *refers* to the value 26.0.

Whenever Python needs to know which value degree_celsius refers to, it looks at the object at the memory address that degree_celsius contains. In this example, that memory address is *id1*, so Python will use the value at the memory address *id1*, which is 26.0.

Assignment Statement

Here is the general form of an assignment statement:

«variable» = *«expression»*

This is executed as follows:

1. Evaluate the expression on the right of the = sign to produce a value. This value has a memory address.
2. Store the memory address of the value in the variable on the left of the =. Create a new variable if that name doesn't already exist; otherwise, just reuse the existing variable, replacing the memory address that it contains.

Consider this example:

```
>>> degrees_celsius = 26.0 + 5
>>> degrees_celsius
31.0
```

Here is how Python executes the statement degrees_celsius = 26.0 + 5:

1. Evaluate the expression on the right of the = sign: 26.0 + 5. This produces the value 31.0, which has a memory address. (Remember that Python stores all values in computer memory.)
2. Make the variable on the left of the = sign, degrees_celsius, refer to 31.0 by storing the memory address of 31.0 in degrees_celsius.

Reassigning to Variables

Consider this code:

```
>>> difference = 20
>>> double = 2 * difference
>>> double
40
>>> difference = 5
>>> double
40
```

This code demonstrates that assigning to a variable *does not change any other variable*. We start by assigning value 20 to variable difference, and then we assign the result of evaluating 2 * difference (which produces 40) to variable double.

Next, we assign value 5 to variable difference, but when we examine the value of double, it still refers to 40.

Here's how it works according to our rules. The first statement, difference = 20, is executed as follows:

1. Evaluate the expression on the right of the = sign: 20. This produces the value 20, which we'll put at memory address *id1*.
2. Make the variable on the left of the = sign, difference, refer to 20 by storing *id1* in difference.

Here is the current state of the memory model. (Variable double has not yet been created because we have not yet executed the assignment to it.)

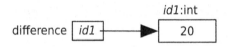

The second statement, double = 2 * difference, is executed as follows:

1. Evaluate the expression on the right of the = sign: 2 * difference. As we see in the memory model, difference refers to the value 20, so this expression is equivalent to 2 * 20, which produces 40. We'll pick the memory address *id2* for the value 40.
2. Make the variable on the left of the = sign, double, refer to 40 by storing *id2* in double.

Here is the current state of the memory model:

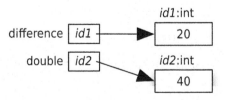

When Python executes the third statement, double, it merely looks up the value that double refers to (40) and displays it.

The fourth statement, difference = 5, is executed as follows:

1. Evaluate the expression on the right of the = sign: 5. This produces the value 5, which we'll put at the memory address *id3*.
2. Make the variable on the left of the = sign, difference, refer to 5 by storing *id3* in difference.

Here is the current state of the memory model:

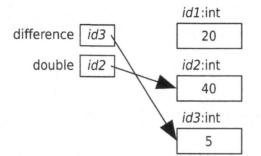

Variable double still contains *id2*, so it still refers to 40. Neither variable refers to 20 anymore.

The fifth and last statement, double, merely looks up the value that double refers to, which is still 40, and displays it.

We can even use a variable on both sides of an assignment statement:

```
>>> number = 3
>>> number
3
>>> number = 2 * number
>>> number
6
>>> number = number * number
>>> number
36
```

We'll now explain how Python executes this code, but we won't explicitly mention memory addresses. Trace this on a piece of paper while we describe what happens; make up your own memory addresses as you do this.

Python executes the first statement, number = 3, as follows:

1. Evaluate the expression on the right of the = sign: 3. This one is easy to evaluate: 3 is produced.

2. Make the variable on the left of the = sign, number, refer to 3.

Python executes the second statement, number = 2 * number, as follows:

1. Evaluate the expression on the right of the = sign: 2 * number. number currently refers to 3, so this is equivalent to 2 * 3, so 6 is produced.

2. Make the variable on the left of the = sign, number, refer to 6.

Python executes the third statement, number = number * number, as follows:

1. Evaluate the expression on the right of the = sign: number * number. number currently refers to 6, so this is equivalent to 6 * 6, so 36 is produced.

2. Make the variable on the left of the = sign, number, refer to 36.

Augmented Assignment

In this example, the variable score appears on both sides of the assignment statement:

```
>>> score = 50
>>> score
50
>>> score = score + 20
>>> score
70
```

This is so common that Python provides a shorthand notation for this operation:

```
>>> score = 50
>>> score
50
>>> score += 20
>>> score
70
```

An *augmented assignment* combines an assignment statement with an operator to make the statement more concise. An augmented assignment statement is executed as follows:

1. Evaluate the expression on the right of the = sign to produce a value.

2. Apply the operator attached to the = sign to the variable on the left of the = and the value that was produced. This produces another value. Store the memory address of that value in the variable on the left of the =.

Note that the operator is applied *after* the expression on the right is evaluated:

```
>>> d = 2
>>> d *= 3 + 4
>>> d
14
```

All the operators (except for negation) in Table 2, *Arithmetic Operators Listed by Precedence from Highest to Lowest*, on page 15, have shorthand versions. For example, we can square a number by multiplying it by itself:

```
>>> number = 10
>>> number *= number
>>> number
100
```

This code is equivalent to this:

```
>>> number = 10
>>> number = number * number
>>> number
100
```

Table 3, *Augmented Assignment Operators*, contains a summary of the augmented operators you've seen plus a few more based on arithmetic operators you learned about in Section 2.2, *Expressions and Values: Arithmetic in Python*, on page 9.

Symbol	Example	Result
+=	x = 7 x += 2	x refers to 9
-=	x = 7 x -= 2	x refers to 5
*=	x = 7 x *= 2	x refers to 14
/=	x = 7 x /= 2	x refers to 3.5
//=	x = 7 x //= 2	x refers to 3
%=	x = 7 x %= 2	x refers to 1
**=	x = 7 x **= 2	x refers to 49

Table 3—Augmented Assignment Operators

2.5 How Python Tells You Something Went Wrong

Broadly speaking, there are two kinds of errors in Python: *syntax errors*, which happen when you type something that isn't valid Python code, and *semantic errors*, which happen when you tell Python to do something that it just can't do, like divide a number by zero or try to use a variable that doesn't exist.

Here is what happens when we try to use a variable that hasn't been created yet:

```
>>> 3 + moogah
Traceback (most recent call last):
  File "<stdin>", line 1, in <module>
NameError: name 'moogah' is not defined
```

This is pretty cryptic; Python error messages are meant for people who already know Python. (You'll get used to them and soon find them helpful.) The first two lines aren't much use right now, though they'll be indispensable when we start writing longer programs. The last line is the one that tells us what went wrong: the name moogah wasn't recognized.

Here's another error message you might sometimes see:

```
>>> 2 +
  File "<stdin>", line 1
    2 +
      ^
SyntaxError: invalid syntax
```

The rules governing what is and isn't legal in a programming language are called its *syntax*. The message tells us that we violated Python's syntax rules—in this case, by asking it to add something to 2 but not telling it what to add.

Earlier, in *Warning: = Is Not Equality in Python!*, on page 16, we claimed that 12 = x results in an error. Let's try it:

```
>>> 12 = x
  File "<stdin>", line 1
SyntaxError: can't assign to literal
```

A *literal* is any value, like 12 and 26.0. This is a SyntaxError because when Python examines that assignment statement, it knows that you can't assign a value to a number even before it tries to execute it; you can't change the value of 12 to anything else. 12 is just 12.

2.6 A Single Statement That Spans Multiple Lines

Sometimes statements get pretty intricate. The recommended Python style is to limit lines to 80 characters, including spaces, tabs, and other *whitespace* characters, and that's a common limit throughout the programming world.

Here's what to do when lines get too long or when you want to split it up for clarity.

In order to split up a statement into more than one line, you need to do one of two things:

1. Make sure your line break occurs inside parentheses, or
2. Use the line-continuation character, which is a backslash, \.

Note that the line-continuation character is a backslash (\), not the division symbol (/).

Here are examples of both:

```
>>> (2 +
... 3)
5
>>> 2 + \
... 3
5
```

Notice how we don't get a SyntaxError. Each triple-dot prompt in our examples indicates that we are in the middle of entering an expression; we use them to make the code line up nicely. You do not type the dots any more than you type the greater-than signs in the usual >>> prompt, and if you are using IDLE, you won't see them at all.

Here is a more realistic (and tastier) example: let's say we're baking cookies. The authors live in Canada, which uses Celsius, but we own cookbooks that use Fahrenheit. We are wondering how long it will take to preheat our oven. Here are our facts:

• The room temperature is 20 degrees Celsius.
• Our oven controls use Celsius, and the oven heats up at 20 degrees per minute.
• Our cookbook uses Fahrenheit, and it says to preheat the oven to 350 degrees.

We can convert t degrees Fahrenheit to t degrees Celsius like this: $(t - 32) * 5 / 9$. Let's use this information to try to solve our problem.

```
>>> room_temperature_c = 20
>>> cooking_temperature_f = 350
>>> oven_heating_rate_c = 20
>>> oven_heating_time = (
... ((cooking_temperature_f - 32) * 5 / 9) - room_temperature_c) / \
... oven_heating_rate_c
>>> oven_heating_time
7.833333333333333
```

Not bad—just under eight minutes to preheat.

The assignment statement to variable oven_heating_time spans three lines. The first line ends with an open parenthesis, so we do not need a line continuation character. The second ends *outside* the parentheses, so we need the line-continuation character. The third line completes the assignment statement.

That's still hard to read. Once we've continued an expression on the next line, we can indent (by typing the tab key or by typing the space bar a bunch) to our heart's content to make it clearer:

```
>>> oven_heating_time = (
...     ((cooking_temperature_f - 32) * 5 / 9) - room_temperature_c) / \
...     oven_heating_rate_c
```

Or even this—notice how the two subexpressions involved in the subtraction line up:

```
>>> oven_heating_time = (
...     ((cooking_temperature_f - 32) * 5 / 9) -
...      room_temperature_c) / \
...     oven_heating_rate_c
```

In the previous example, we clarified the expression by working with indentation. However, we could have made this process even clearer by converting the cooking temperature to Celsius before calculating the heating time:

```
>>> room_temperature_c = 20
>>> cooking_temperature_f = 350
>>> cooking_temperature_c = (cooking_temperature_f - 32) * 5 / 9
>>> oven_heating_rate_c = 20
>>> oven_heating_time = (cooking_temperature_c - room_temperature_c) / \
...     oven_heating_rate_c
>>> oven_heating_time
7.833333333333333
```

The message to take away here is that well-named temporary variables can make code much clearer.

2.7 Describing Code

Programs can be quite complicated and are often thousands of lines long. It can be helpful to write a *comment* describing parts of the code so that when you or someone else reads it they don't have to spend much time figuring out why the code is there.

In Python, any time the # character is encountered, Python will ignore the rest of the line. This allows you to write English sentences:

```
>>> # Python ignores this sentence because of the # symbol.
```

The # symbol does not have to be the first character on the line; it can appear at the end of a statement:

```
>>> (212 - 32) * 5 / 9 # Convert 212 degrees Fahrenheit to Celsius.
100.0
```

Notice that the comment doesn't describe how Python works. Instead, it is meant for humans reading the code to help them understand why the code exists.

2.8 Making Code Readable

Much like there are spaces in English sentences to make the words easier to read, we use spaces in Python code to make it easier to read. In particular, we always put a space before and after every binary operator. For example, we write v = 4 + -2.5 / 3.6 instead of v=4+-2.5/3.6. There are situations where it may not make a difference, but that's a detail we don't want to fuss about, so we always do it: it's almost never *harder* to read if there are spaces.

Psychologists have discovered that people can keep track of only a handful of things at any one time (*Forty Studies That Changed Psychology [Hoc04]*). Since programs can get quite complicated, it's important that you choose names for your variables that will help you remember what they're for. id1, X2, and blah won't remind you of anything when you come back to look at your program next week: use names like celsius, average, and final_result instead.

Other studies have shown that your brain automatically notices differences between things—in fact, there's no way to stop it from doing this. As a result, the more inconsistencies there are in a piece of text, the longer it takes to read. (JuSt thInK a bout how long It w o u l d tAKE you to rEa d this cHaPTer iF IT wAs fORmaTTeD like thIs.) It's therefore also important to use consistent names for variables. If you call something maximum in one place, don't call it max_val in another; if you use the name max_val, don't also use the name maxVal, and so on.

These rules are so important that many programming teams require members to follow a style guide for whatever language they're using, just as newspapers and book publishers specify how to capitalize headings and whether to use a comma before the last item in a list. If you search the Internet for *programming style guide* (https://www.google.com/search?q=programming+style+guide), you'll discover links to hundreds of examples. In this book, we follow the style guide for Python from http://www.python.org/dev/peps/pep-0008/.

You will also discover that lots of people have wasted many hours arguing over what the "best" style for code is. Some of your classmates (and your instructors) may have strong opinions about this as well. If they do, ask them what data they have to back up their beliefs. Strong opinions need strong evidence to be taken seriously.

2.9   The Object of This Chapter

In this chapter, you learned the following:

- An operating system is a program that manages your computer's hardware on behalf of other programs. An interpreter or virtual machine is a program that sits on top of the operating system and runs your programs for you. The Python shell is an interpreter, translating your Python statements into language the operating system understands and translating the results back so you can see and use them.

- Programs are made up of statements, or instructions. These can be simple expressions like 3 + 4 and assignment statements like celsius = 20 (which create new variables or change the values of existing ones). There are many other kinds of statements in Python, and we'll introduce them throughout the book.

- Every value in Python has a specific type, which determines what operations can be applied to it. The two types used to represent numbers are int and float. Floating-point numbers are approximations to real numbers.

- Python evaluates an expression by applying higher-precedence operators before lower-precedence operators. You can change that order by putting parentheses around subexpressions.

- Python stores every value in computer memory. A memory location containing a value is called an object.

- Variables are created by executing assignment statements. If a variable already exists because of a previous assignment statement, Python will use that one instead of creating a new one.

- Variables contain memory addresses of values. We say that variables refer to values.

- Variables must be assigned values before they can be used in expressions.

2.10   Exercises

Here are some exercises for you to try on your own. Solutions are available at http://pragprog.com/titles/gwpy2/practical-programming.

1. For each of the following expressions, what value will the expression give? Verify your answers by typing the expressions into Python.

    a. 9 - 3
    b. 8 * 2.5
    c. 9 / 2
    d. 9 / -2
    e. 9 // -2
    f. 9 % 2
    g. 9.0 % 2
    h. 9 % 2.0
    i. 9 % -2
    j. -9 % 2
    k. 9 / -2.0
    l. 4 + 3 * 5
    m. (4 + 3) * 5

2. Unary minus negates a number. Unary plus exists as well; for example, Python understands +5. If x has the value -17, what do you think +x should do? Should it leave the sign of the number alone? Should it act like absolute value, removing any negation? Use the Python shell to find out its behavior.

3. Write two assignment statements that do the following.

    a. Create a new variable, temp, and assign it the value 24.

    b. Convert the value in temp from Celsius to Fahrenheit by multiplying by 1.8 and adding 32; make temp refer to the resulting value.

    What is temp's new value?

4. For each of the following expressions, in which order are the subexpressions evaluated?

    a. 6 * 3 + 7 * 4
    b. 5 + 3 / 4
    c. 5 - 2 * 3 ** 4

5. a. Create a new variable x, and assign it the value 10.5.

    b. Create a new variable y, and assign it the value 4.

    c. Sum x and y, and make x refer to the resulting value. After this statement has been executed, what are x and y's values?

6. Write a bullet list description of what happens when Python evaluates the statement x += x - x when x has the value 3.

7. When a variable is used before it has been assigned a value, a NameError occurs. In the Python shell, write an expression that results in a NameError.

8. Which of the following expressions results in SyntaxErrors?

    a. 6 * -----------8

    b. 8 = people

    c. ((((4 ** 3))))

    d. (-(-(-(-5))))

    e. 4 += 7 / 2

CHAPTER 3

Designing and Using Functions

Mathematicians create *functions* to make calculations (such as Fahrenheit to Celsius conversions) easy to reuse and to make other calculations easier to read because they can use those functions instead of repeatedly writing out equations. Programmers do this too, at least as often as mathematicians. In this chapter we will explore several of the built-in functions that come with Python, and we'll also show you how to define your own functions.

3.1 Functions That Python Provides

Python comes with many *built-in functions* that perform common operations. One example is abs, which produces the absolute value of a number:

```
>>> abs(-9)
9
>>> abs(3.3)
3.3
```

Each of these statements is a *function call*.

Keep Your Shell Open

As a reminder, we recommend that you have IDLE open (or another Python editor) and that you try all the code under discussion: this is a good way to cement your learning.

The general form of a function call is as follows:

«*function_name*»(«*arguments*»)

An *argument* is an expression that appears between the parentheses of a function call. In abs(-9), the argument is -9.

Here, we calculate the difference between a day temperature and a night temperature, as might be seen on a weather report (a warm weather system moved in overnight):

```
>>> day_temperature = 3
>>> night_temperature = 10
>>> abs(day_temperature - night_temperature)
7
```

In this call on function abs, the argument is day_temperature - night_temperature. Because day_temperature refers to 3 and night_temperature refers to 10, Python evaluates this expression to -7. This value is then *passed* to function abs, which then *returns*, or produces, the value 7.

Here are the rules to executing a function call:

1. Evaluate each argument one at a time, working from left to right.
2. Pass the resulting values into the function.
3. Execute the function. When the function call finishes, it produces a value.

Because function calls produce values, they can be used in expressions:

```
>>> abs(-7) + abs(3.3)
10.3
```

We can also use function calls as arguments to other functions:

```
>>> pow(abs(-2), round(4.3))
16
```

Python sees the call on pow and starts by evaluating the arguments from left to right. The first argument is a call on function abs, so Python executes it. abs(-2) produces 2, so that's the first value for the call on pow. Then Python executes round(4.3), which produces 4.

Now that the arguments to the call on function pow have been evaluated, Python finishes calling pow, sending in 2 and 4 as the argument values. That means that pow(abs(-2), round(4.3)) is equivalent to pow(2, 4), and 2^4 is 16.

Here is a diagram indicating the order in which the various pieces of this expression are evaluated by Python.

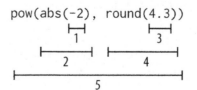

We have underlined each subexpression and given it a number to indicate when Python executes or evaluates that subexpression.

Some of the most useful built-in functions are ones that convert from one type to another. Type names int and float can be used as functions:

```
>>> int(34.6)
34
>>> int(-4.3)
-4
>>> float(21)
21.0
```

In this example, we see that when a floating-point number is converted to an integer, it is truncated, not rounded.

If you're not sure what a function does, try calling built-in function help, which shows documentation for any function:

```
>>> help(abs)
Help on built-in function abs in module builtins:

abs(...)
    abs(number) -> number

    Return the absolute value of the argument.
```

The first line states which function is being described and which *module* it belongs to. Modules are an organizational tool in Python and are discussed in Chapter 6, *A Modular Approach to Program Organization*, on page 99.

The next part describes how to call the function. The arguments are described within the parentheses—here, *number* means that you can call abs with either an int or a float. After the -> is the *return type*, which again is either an int or a float. After that is an English description of what the function does when it is called.

Another built-in function is round, which rounds a floating-point number to the nearest integer:

```
>>> round(3.8)
4
>>> round(3.3)
3
>>> round(3.5)
4
>>> round(-3.3)
-3
>>> round(-3.5)
-4
```

Function round can be called with one or two arguments. If called with one, as we've been doing, it rounds to the nearest integer. If called with two, it rounds to a floating-point number, where the second argument indicates the precision:

```
>>> round(3.141592653, 2)
3.14
```

The documentation for round indicates that the second argument is optional by surrounding it with brackets:

```
>>> help(round)
Help on built-in function round in module builtins:

round(...)
    round(number[, ndigits]) -> number

    Round a number to a given precision in decimal digits (default 0 digits).
    This returns an int when called with one argument, otherwise the
    same type as the number. ndigits may be negative.
```

Let's explore built-in function pow by starting with its help documentation:

```
>>> help(pow)
Help on built-in function pow in module builtins:

pow(...)
    pow(x, y[, z]) -> number

    With two arguments, equivalent to x**y.  With three arguments,
    equivalent to (x**y) % z, but may be more efficient (e.g. for longs).
```

This shows that function pow can be called with either two or three arguments. The English description mentions that when called with two arguments it is equivalent to $x ** y$. Let's try it:

```
>>> pow(2, 4)
16
```

This call calculates 2^4. So far, so good. How about with three arguments?

```
>>> pow(2, 4, 3)
1
```

We know that 2^4 is 16, and evaluation of 16 % 3 produces 1.

3.2 Memory Addresses: How Python Keeps Track of Values

Back in *Values, Variables, and Computer Memory*, on page 16, you learned that Python keeps track of each value in a separate object and that each object has a memory address. You can discover the actual memory address of an object using built-in function id:

```
>>> help(id)
Help on built-in function id in module builtins:

id(...)
    id(object) -> integer

    Return the identity of an object.  This is guaranteed to be unique among
    simultaneously existing objects.  (Hint: it's the object's memory
    address.)
```

How cool is that? Let's try it:

```
>>> id(-9)
4301189552
>>> id(23.1)
4298223160
>>> shoe_size = 8.5
>>> id(shoe_size)
4298223112
>>> fahrenheit = 77.7
>>> id(fahrenheit)
4298223064
```

The addresses you get will probably be different from what's listed above since values get stored wherever there happens to be free space. Function objects also have memory addresses:

```
>>> id(abs)
4297868712
>>> id(round)
4297871160
```

3.3 Defining Our Own Functions

The built-in functions are useful but pretty generic. Often there aren't built-in functions that do what we want, such as calculate mileage or play a game of cribbage. When we want functions to do these sorts of things, we have to write them ourselves.

Because we live in Toronto, Canada, we often deal with our neighbor to the south. The United States typically uses Fahrenheit, so we convert from Fahrenheit to Celsius and back a lot. It sure would be nice to be able to do this:

```
>>> convert_to_celsius(212)
100.0
>>> convert_to_celsius(78.8)
26.0
>>> convert_to_celsius(10.4)
-12.0
```

Python Remembers and Reuses Some Objects

A *cache* is a collection of data. Because small integers—up to about 250 or so, depending on the version of Python you're using—are so common, Python creates those objects as it starts up and reuses the same objects whenever it can. This speeds up operations involving these values. Function id reveals this:

```
>>> i = 3
>>> j = 3
>>> k = 4 - 1
>>> id(i)
4296861792
>>> id(j)
4296861792
>>> id(k)
4296861792
```

What that means is that variables i, j, and k refer to the exact same object. This is called *aliasing*.

Larger integers and all floating-point values aren't necessarily cached:

```
>>> i = 30000000000
>>> j = 30000000000
>>> id(i)
4301190928
>>> id(j)
4302234864
>>> f = 0.0
>>> g = 0.0
>>> id(f)
4298223040
>>> id(g)
4298223016
```

Python decides for itself when to cache a value. The only reason you need to be aware of it is so that you aren't surprised when it happens: the output of your program is not affected by when Python decides to cache.

However, function convert_to_celsius doesn't exist yet, so instead we see this (focus only on the last line of the error message for now):

```
>>> convert_to_celsius(212)
Traceback (most recent call last):
  File "<stdin>", line 1, in <module>
NameError: name 'convert_to_celsius' is not defined
```

To fix this, we have to write a *function definition* that tells Python what to do when the function is called.

We'll go over the syntax of function definitions soon, but we'll start with an example:

```
>>> def convert_to_celsius(fahrenheit):
...     return (fahrenheit - 32) * 5 / 9
...
```

The *function body* is indented. Here, we indent four spaces, as the Python style guide recommends. If you forget to indent, you get this error:

```
>>> def convert_to_celsius(fahrenheit):
... return (fahrenheit - 32) * 5 / 9
  File "<stdin>", line 2
    return (fahrenheit - 32) * 5 / 9
         ^
IndentationError: expected an indented block
```

Now that we've defined function convert_to_celsius, our earlier function calls will work. We can even use built-in function help on it:

```
>>> help(convert_to_celsius)
Help on function convert_to_celsius in module __main__:

convert_to_celsius(fahrenheit)
```

This shows the first line of the function definition, which we call the *function header*. (Later in this chapter, we'll show you how to add more help documentation to a function.)

Here is a quick overview of how Python executes the following code:

```
>>> def convert_to_celsius(fahrenheit):
...     return (fahrenheit - 32) * 5 / 9
...
>>> convert_to_celsius(80)
26.666666666666668
```

1. Python executes the function definition, which creates the function object (but doesn't execute it yet).

2. Next, Python executes function call convert_to_celsius(80). To do this, it assigns 80 to fahrenheit (which is a variable). For the duration of this function call, fahrenheit refers to 80.

3. Python now executes the return statement. fahrenheit refers to 80, so the expression that appears after return is equivalent to (80 - 32) * 5 / 9. When Python evaluates that expression, 26.666666666666668 is produced. We use the word return to tell Python what value to produce as the result of the function call, so the result of calling convert_to_celsius(80) is 26.666666666666668.

4. Once Python has finished executing the function call, it returns to the place where the function was originally called.

Here is a picture showing this sequence:

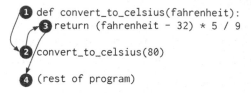

```
1  def convert_to_celsius(fahrenheit):
   3  return (fahrenheit - 32) * 5 / 9

2  convert_to_celsius(80)

4  (rest of program)
```

A function definition is a kind of Python statement. The general form of a function definition is as follows:

```
def «function_name»(«parameters»):
    «block»
```

Keywords Are Words That Are Special to Python

Keywords are words that Python reserves for its own use. We can't use them except as Python intends. Two of them are def and return. If we try to use them as either variable names or as function names (or anything else), Python produces an error:

```
>>> def = 3
  File "<stdin>", line 1
    def = 3
        ^
SyntaxError: invalid syntax
>>> def return(x):
  File "<stdin>", line 1
    def return(x):
           ^
SyntaxError: invalid syntax
```

Here is a complete list of Python keywords. We'll encounter most of them in this book.

False	assert	del	for	in	or	while
None	break	elif	from	is	pass	with
True	class	else	global	lambda	raise	yield
and	continue	except	if	nonlocal	return	
as	def	finally	import	not	try	

The function header (that's the first line of the function definition) starts with def, followed by the name of the function, then a comma-separated list of *parameters* within parentheses, and then a colon. A parameter is a variable.

You can't have two functions with the same name; it isn't an error, but if you do it, the second function definition replaces the first one, much like assigning a value to a variable a second time replaces the first value.

Below the function header and indented (four spaces, as per Python's style guide) is a block of statements called the *function body*. The function body must contain at least one statement.

Most function definitions will include a return statement that, when executed, ends the function and produces a value. The general form of a return statement is as follows:

```
return «expression»
```

When Python executes a return statement, it evaluates the expression and then produces the result of that expression as the result of the function call.

3.4 Using Local Variables for Temporary Storage

Some computations are complex, and breaking them down into separate steps can lead to clearer code. Here, we break down the evaluation of the quadratic polynomial $ax^2 + bx + c$ into several steps (notice that all the statements inside the function are indented the same amount of spaces in order to be aligned with each other):

```
>>> def quadratic(a, b, c, x):
...     first = a * x ** 2
...     second = b * x
...     third = c
...     return first + second + third
...
>>> quadratic(2, 3, 4, 0.5)
6.0
>>> quadratic(2, 3, 4, 1.5)
13.0
```

Variables like first, second, and third that are created within a function are called *local variables*. Local variables get created each time that function is called, and they are erased when the function returns. Because they only exist when the function is being executed, they can't be used outside of the function. This means that trying to access a local variable from outside the function is an error, just like trying to access a variable that has never been defined is an error:

```
>>> quadratic(2, 3, 4, 1.3)
11.280000000000001
>>> first
Traceback (most recent call last):
  File "<stdin>", line 1, in <module>
NameError: name 'first' is not defined
```

A function's parameters are also local variables, so we get the same error if we try to use them outside of a function definition:

```
>>> a
Traceback (most recent call last):
  File "<stdin>", line 1, in <module>
NameError: name 'a' is not defined
```

The area of a program that a variable can be used in is called the variable's *scope.* The scope of a local variable is from the line in which it is defined up until the end of the function.

As you might expect, if a function is defined to take a certain number of parameters, a call on that function must have the same number of arguments:

```
>>> quadratic(1, 2, 3)
Traceback (most recent call last):
  File "<stdin>", line 1, in <module>
TypeError: quadratic() takes exactly 4 arguments (3 given)
```

Remember that you can call built-in function help to find out information about the parameters of a function.

3.5 Tracing Function Calls in the Memory Model

Read the following code. Can you predict what it will do when we run it?

```
>>> def f(x):
...       x = 2 * x
...       return x
...
>>> x = 1
>>> x = f(x + 1) + f(x + 2)
```

That code is confusing, in large part because x is used all over the place. However, it *is* pretty short and it only uses Python features that we have seen so far: assignment statements, expressions, function definitions, and function calls. We're missing some information: Are all the x's the same variable? Does Python make a new x for each assignment? For each function call? For each function definition?

Here's the answer: whenever Python executes a function call, it creates a *namespace* (literally, a space for names) in which to store local variables for that call. You can think of a namespace as a scrap piece of paper: Python writes down the local variables on that piece of paper, keeps track of them as long as the function is being executed, and throws that paper away when the function returns.

Separately, Python keeps another namespace for variables created in the shell. That means that the x that is a parameter of function f is a different variable than the x in the shell!

Let's refine our rules from Section 3.1, *Functions That Python Provides,* on page 31, for executing a function call to include this namespace creation:

Reusing Variable Names Is Common

Using the same name for local variables in different functions is quite common. For example, imagine a program that deals with distances—converting from meters to other units of distance, perhaps. In that program, there would be several functions that all deal with these distances, and it would be entirely reasonable to use meters as a parameter name in many different functions.

1. Evaluate the arguments left to right.

2. Create a namespace to hold the function call's local variables, including the parameters.

3. Pass the resulting argument values into the function by assigning them to the parameters.

4. Execute the function body. As before, when a return statement is executed, execution of the body terminates and the value of the expression in the return statement is used as the value of the function call.

From now on in our memory model, we will draw a separate box for each namespace to indicate that the variables inside it are in a separate area of computer memory. The programming world calls this box a *frame*. We separate the frames from the objects by a vertical dotted line:

Frames	Objects
Frames for namespaces go here	*Objects go here*

Using our newfound knowledge, let's trace that confusing code. At the beginning, no variables have been created; Python is about to execute the function definition. We have indicated this with an arrow:

```
>>> def f(x):
...     x = 2 * x
...     return x
...
>>> x = 1
>>> x = f(x + 1) + f(x + 2)
```

As you've seen in this chapter, when Python executes that function definition, it creates a variable f in the frame for the shell's namespace plus a function object. (Python didn't execute the body of the function; that won't happen until the function is called.) Here is the result:

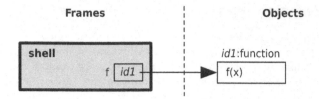

Now we are about to execute the first assignment to x in the shell.

```
>>> def f(x):
...     x = 2 * x
...     return x
...
>>> x = 1
>>> x = f(x + 1) + f(x + 2)
```

Once that assignment happens, both f and x are in the frame for the shell:

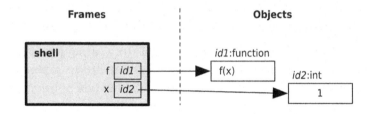

Now we are about to execute the second assignment to x in the shell:

```
>>> def f(x):
...     x = 2 * x
...     return x
...
>>> x = 1
>>> x = f(x + 1) + f(x + 2)
```

Following the rules for executing an assignment from *Assignment Statement,* on page 18, we first evaluate the expression on the right of the =, which is f(x + 1) + f(x + 2). Python evaluates the left function call first: f(x + 1).

Following the rules for executing a function call, Python evaluates the argument, x + 1. In order to find the value for x, Python looks in the current frame. The current frame is the frame for the shell, and its variable x refers to 1, so x + 1 evaluates to 2.

Now we have evaluated the argument to f. The next step is to create a namespace for the function call. We draw a frame, write in parameter x, and assign 2 to that parameter:

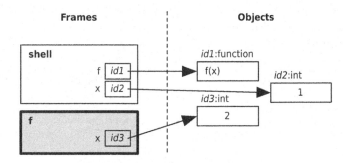

Notice that there are two variables called x, and they refer to different values. Python will always look in the current frame, which we will draw with a thicker border.

We are now about to execute the first statement of function f:

```
>>> def f(x):
...     x = 2 * x
...     return x
...
>>> x = 1
>>> x = f(x + 1) + f(x + 2)
```

x = 2 * x is an assignment statement. The right side is the expression 2 * x. Python looks up the value of x in the current frame and finds 2, so that expression evaluates to 4. Python finishes executing that assignment statement by making x refer to that 4:

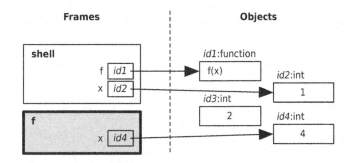

We are now about to execute the second statement of function f:

```
>>> def f(x):
...     x = 2 * x
...     return x
...
>>> x = 1
>>> x = f(x + 1) + f(x + 2)
```

This is a return statement, so we evaluate the expression, which is simply x. Python looks up the value for x in the current frame and finds 4, so that is the return value:

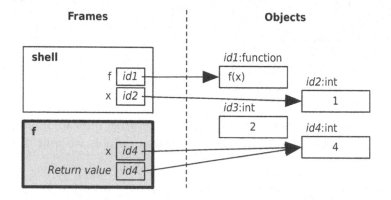

When the function returns, Python comes back to this expression: f(x + 1) + f(x + 2). Python just finished executing f(x + 1), which produced the value 4. It then executes the right function call: f(x + 2).

Following the rules for executing a function call, Python evaluates the argument, x + 2. In order to find the value for x, Python looks in the current frame. The call on function f has returned, so that frame is erased: the only frame left is the frame for the shell, and its variable x still refers to 1, so x + 2 evaluates to 3.

Now we have evaluated the argument to f. The next step is to create a namespace for the function call. We draw a frame, write in the parameter x, and assign 3 to that parameter:

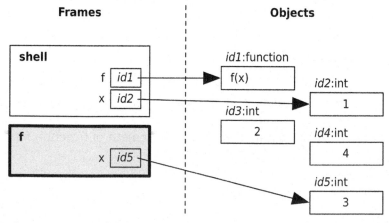

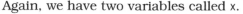
Again, we have two variables called x.

We are now about to execute the first statement of function f:

```
>>> def f(x):
...     x = 2 * x
...     return x
...
>>> x = 1
>>> x = f(x + 1) + f(x + 2)
```

x = 2 * x is an assignment statement. The right side is the expression 2 * x. Python looks up the value of x in the current frame and finds 3, so that expression evaluates to 6. Python finished executing that assignment statement by making x refer to that 6:

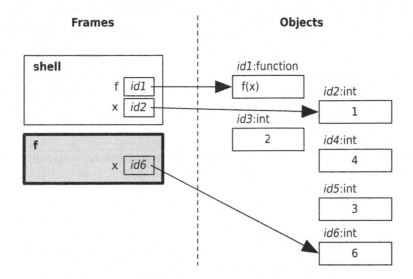

We are now about to execute the second statement of function f:

```
>>> def f(x):
...     x = 2 * x
...     return x
...
>>> x = 1
>>> x = f(x + 1) + f(x + 2)
```

This is a return statement, so we evaluate the expression, which is simply x. Python looks up the value for x in the current frame and finds 6, so that is the return value:

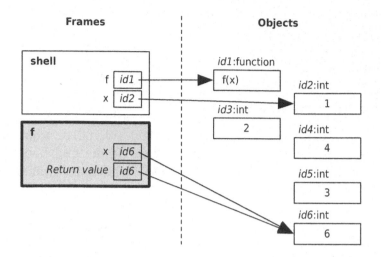

When the function returns, Python comes back to this expression: f(x + 1) + f(x + 2). Python just finished executing f(x + 2), which produced the value 6. Both function calls have been executed, so Python applies the + operator to 4 and 6, giving us 10.

We have now evaluated the right side of the assignment statement; Python completes it by making the variable on the left side, x, refer to 10:

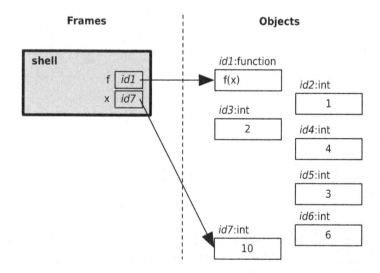

Phew! That's a lot to keep track of. Python does all that bookkeeping for us, but to become a good programmer it's important to understand each individual step.

3.6   Designing New Functions: A Recipe

Writing a good essay requires planning: deciding on a topic, learning the background material, writing an outline, and then filling in the outline until you're done.

Writing a good function also requires planning. You have an idea of what you want the function to do, but you need to decide on the details: What do you name the function? What are the parameters? What does it return?

This section describes a step-by-step recipe for designing and writing a function. Part of the outcome will be a working function, but almost as important is the *documentation* for the function. Python uses three double quotes to start and end this documentation; everything in between is meant for humans to read. This notation is called a *docstring*, which is short for *documentation string*.

Here is an example of a completed function. We'll show you how we came up with this using a function design recipe (FDR), but it helps to see a completed example first:

```
>>> def days_difference(day1, day2):
...     """ (int, int) -> int
...
...     Return the number of days between day1 and day2, which are
...     both in the range 1-365 (thus indicating the day of the
...     year).
...
...     >>> days_difference(200, 224)
...     24
...     >>> days_difference(50, 50)
...     0
...     >>> days_difference(100, 99)
...     -1
...     """
...     return day2 - day1
...
```

Here are the parts of the function, including the docstring:

- The first line is the function header.

- The second line has three double quotes to start the docstring. The (int, int) part describes the types of values expected to be passed to parameters day1 and day2, and the int after the -> is the type of value the function will return.

- After that is a description of what the function will do when it is called. It mentions both parameters and describes what the function returns.

- Next are some example calls and return values as we would expect to see in the Python shell. (We chose the first example because that made day1 smaller than day2, the second example because the two days are equal, and the third example because that made day1 bigger than day2.)

- The last line is the body of the function.

There are six steps to the function design recipe. It may seem like a lot of work at first, but this recipe can save you hours of time when you're working on more complicated functions.

1. *Examples.* The first step is to figure out what arguments you want to give to your function and what information it will return. Pick a name (often a verb or verb phrase): this name is often a short answer to the question, "What does your function do?" Type a couple of example calls and return values.

   We start with the examples because they're the easiest: before we write *anything*, we need to decide what information we have (the argument values) and what information we want the function to produce (the return value). Here are the examples from days_difference:

   ```
   ...        >>> days_difference(200, 224)
   ...        24
   ...        >>> days_difference(50, 50)
   ...        0
   ...        >>> days_difference(100, 99)
   ...        -1
   ```

2. *Type Contract.* The second step is to figure out the types of information your function will handle: Are you giving it integers? Floating-point numbers? Maybe both? We'll see a lot of other types in the upcoming chapters, so practicing this step now while you only have a few choices will help you later. If the answer is, "Both integers and floating-point numbers," then use the word *number*.

   Also, what type of value is returned? An integer, a floating-point number, or possibly either one of them?

   This is called a *contract* because we are claiming that if you call this function with the right types of values, we'll give you back the right type of value. (We're not saying anything about what will happen if we get the *wrong* kind of values.) Here is the type contract from days_difference:

   ```
   ...        """ (int, int) -> int
   ```

3. *Header.* Write the function header. Pick meaningful parameter names to make it easy for other programmers to understand what information to give to your function. Here is the header from days_difference:

```
>>> def days_difference(day1, day2):
```

4. *Description.* Write a short paragraph describing your function: this is what other programmers will read in order to understand what your function does, so it's important to practice this! Mention every parameter in your description and describe the return value. Here is the description from days_difference:

```
...     Return the number of days between day1 and day2, which are
...     both in the range 1-365 (thus indicating the day of the
...     year).
```

5. *Body.* By now, you should have a good idea of what you need to do in order to get your function to behave properly. It's time to write some code! Here is the body from days_difference:

```
...     return day2 - day1
```

6. *Test.* Run the examples to make sure your function body is correct. Feel free to add more example calls if you happen to think of them. For days_difference, we copy and paste our examples into the shell and compare the results to what we expected:

```
>>> days_difference(200, 224)
24
>>> days_difference(50, 50)
0
>>> days_difference(100, 99)
-1
```

Designing Three Birthday-Related Functions

We'll now apply our function design recipe to solve this problem: Which day of the week will a birthday fall upon, given what day of the week it is today and what day of the year the birthday is on? For example, if today is the third day of the year and it's a Thursday, and a birthday is on the 116th day of the year, what day of the week will it be on that birthday?

We'll design three functions that together will help us do this calculation. We'll write them in the same file; until we get to Chapter 6, *A Modular Approach to Program Organization*, on page 99, we'll need to put functions that we write in the same file if we want to be able to have them call one another.

We will represent the day of the week using 1 for Sunday, 2 for Monday, and so on:

Day of the Week	Number
Sunday	1
Monday	2
Tuesday	3
Wednesday	4
Thursday	5
Friday	6
Saturday	7

We are using these numbers simply because we don't yet have the tools to easily convert between days of the week and their corresponding numbers. We'll have to do that translation in our heads.

For the same reason, we will also ignore months and use the numbers 1 through 365 to indicate the day of the year. For example, we'll represent February 1st as 32, since it's the thirty-second day of the year.

How Many Days Difference?

We'll start by seeing how we came up with function days_difference. Here are the function design recipe steps. (Try following along in the Python shell.)

1. *Examples.* We want a clear name for the difference in days; we'll use days_difference. In our examples, we want to call this function and state what it returns. If we want to know how many days there are between the 200th day of the year and the 224th day, we can hope that this will happen:

```
>>> days_difference(200, 224)
24
```

What if the two days are the same? How about if the second one is before the first?

```
>>> days_difference(50, 50)
0
>>> days_difference(100, 99)
-1
```

Now that we have a few examples, we can move on to the next step.

2. *Type Contract.* The arguments in our function call examples are all integers, and the return value is an integer too, so here's our type contract:

```
(int, int) -> int
```

3. *Header.* We have a couple of example calls, and we know what types the parameters are, so we can now write the header. Both arguments are day numbers, so we'll use day1 and day2:

```
def days_difference(day1, day2):
```

4. *Description.* We'll now describe what a call on the function will do. Because the documentation should completely describe the behavior of the function, we need to make sure that it's clear what the parameters mean:

```
Return the number of days between day1 and day2, which are both
in the range 1-365 (thus indicating a day of the year).
```

5. *Body.* We've laid everything out. Looking at the examples, we see that we can implement this using subtraction. Here is the whole function again, including the body:

```
>>> def days_difference(day1, day2):
...     """ (int, int) -> int
...
...     Return the number of days between day1 and day2, which are
...     both in the range 1-365 (thus indicating the day of the
...     year).
...
...     >>> days_difference(200, 224)
...     24
...     >>> days_difference(50, 50)
...     0
...     >>> days_difference(100, 99)
...     -1
...     """
...     return day2 - day1
...
```

6. *Test.* To test it, we fire up the Python shell and copy and paste the calls into the shell, checking that we get back what we expect:

```
>>> days_difference(200, 224)
24
>>> days_difference(50, 50)
0
>>> days_difference(100, 99)
-1
```

Here's something really cool. Now that we have a function with a docstring, we can call help on that function:

```
>>> help(days_difference)
Help on function days_difference in module __main__:

days_difference(day1, day2)
    (int, int) -> int

    Return the number of days between day1 and day2, which are both
    in the range 1-365 (thus indicating the day of the year).

    >>> days_difference(200, 224)
    24
    >>> days_difference(50, 50)
    0
    >>> days_difference(100, 99)
    -1
```

What Day Will It Be in the Future?

It will help our birthday calculations if we write a function to calculate what day of the week it will be given the current weekday and how many days ahead we're interested in. Remember that we're using the numbers 1 through 7 to represent Sunday through Saturday.

Again, we'll follow the function design recipe:

1. *Examples.* We want a short name for what it means to calculate what weekday it will be in the future. We could choose something like which_weekday or what_day; we'll use get_weekday. There are lots of choices.

   We'll start with an example that asks what day it will be if today is Tuesday (day 3 of the week) and we want to know what tomorrow will be (1 day ahead):

   ```
   >>> get_weekday(3, 1)
   4
   ```

   Whenever we have a function that should return a value in a particular range, we should write example calls where we expect either end of that range as a result.

   What if it's Friday (day 6)? If we ask what day it will be tomorrow, we expect to get Saturday (day 7):

   ```
   >>> get_weekday(6, 1)
   7
   ```

What if it's Saturday (day 7)? If we ask what day it will be tomorrow, we expect to get Sunday (day 1):

```
>>> get_weekday(7, 1)
1
```

We'll also try asking about 0 days in the future as well as a week ahead; both of these cases should give back the day of the week we started with:

```
>>> get_weekday(1, 0)
1
>>> get_weekday(4, 7)
4
```

Let's also try 10 weeks and 2 days in the future so we have a case where there are several intervening weeks:

```
>>> get_weekday(7, 72)
2
```

2. *Type Contract.* The arguments in our function call examples are all integers, and the return values are integers too, so here's our type contract:

```
(int, int) -> int
```

3. *Header.* We have a couple of example calls, and we know what types the parameters are, so we can now write the header. The function name is clear, so we'll stick with it.

The first argument is the current day of the week, so we'll use current_weekday. The second argument is how many days from now to calculate. We'll pick days_ahead, although days_from_now would also be fine:

```
def get_weekday(current_weekday, days_ahead):
```

4. *Description.* We need a complete description of what this function will do. We'll start with a sentence describing what the function does, and then we'll describe what the parameters mean:

```
Return which day of the week it will be days_ahead days
from current_weekday.

current_weekday is the current day of the week and is in
the range 1-7, indicating whether today is Sunday (1),
Monday (2), ..., Saturday (7).

days_ahead is the number of days after today.
```

Notice that our first sentence uses both parameters and also describes what the function will return.

5. *Body.* Looking at the examples, we see that we can solve the first example with this: return current_weekday + days_ahead. That, however, won't work for all of the examples; we need to wrap around from day 7 (Saturday) back to day 1 (Sunday). When you have this kind of wraparound, usually the remainder operator, %, will help. Notice that evaluation of (7 + 1) % 7 produces 1, (7 + 2) % 7 produces 2, and so on.

Let's try taking the remainder of the sum: return current_weekday + days_ahead % 7. Here is the whole function again, including the body:

```
>>> def get_weekday(current_weekday, days_ahead):
...     """ (int, int) -> int
...
...     Return which day of the week it will be days_ahead days from
...     current_weekday.
...
...     current_weekday is the current day of the week and is in the
...     range 1-7, indicating whether today is Sunday (1), Monday (2),
...     ..., Saturday (7).
...
...     days_ahead is the number of days after today.
...
...     >>> get_weekday(3, 1)
...     4
...     >>> get_weekday(6, 1)
...     7
...     >>> get_weekday(7, 1)
...     1
...     >>> get_weekday(1, 0)
...     1
...     >>> get_weekday(4, 7)
...     4
...     >>> get_weekday(7, 72)
...     2
...     """
...     return current_weekday + days_ahead % 7
...
```

6. *Test.* To test it, we fire up the Python shell and copy and paste the calls into the shell, checking that we get back what we expect:

```
>>> get_weekday(3, 1)
4
>>> get_weekday(6, 1)
7
>>> get_weekday(7, 1)
8
```

Wait, that's not right. We expected a 1 on that third example, not an 8, because 8 isn't a valid number for a day of the week. We should have wrapped around to 1.

Taking another look at our function body, we see that because % has higher precedence than +, we need parentheses:

```
>>> def get_weekday(current_weekday, days_ahead):
...     """ (int, int) -> int
...
...     Return which day of the week it will be days_ahead days
...     from current_weekday.
...
...     current_weekday is the current day of the week and is in
...     the range 1-7, indicating whether today is Sunday (1),
...     Monday (2), ..., Saturday (7).
...
...     days_ahead is the number of days after today.
...
...     >>> get_weekday(3, 1)
...     4
...     >>> get_weekday(6, 1)
...     7
...     >>> get_weekday(7, 1)
...     1
...     >>> get_weekday(1, 0)
...     1
...     >>> get_weekday(4, 7)
...     4
...     >>> get_weekday(7, 72)
...     2
...     """
...     return (current_weekday + days_ahead) % 7
...
```

Testing again, we see that we've fixed that bug in our code, but now we're getting the wrong answer for the second test!

```
>>> get_weekday(3, 1)
4
>>> get_weekday(6, 1)
0
>>> get_weekday(7, 1)
1
```

The problem here is that when current_weekday + days_ahead evaluates to a multiple of 7, then (current_weekday + days_ahead) % 7 will evaluate to 0, not 7. All the other results work well; it's just that pesky 7.

Because we want a number in the range 1 through 7 but we're getting an answer in the range 0 through 6 and all the answers are correct except that we're seeing a 0 instead of a 7, we can use this trick:

a. Subtract 1 from the expression: current_weekday + days_ahead - 1.

b. Take the remainder.

c. Add 1 to the entire result: (current_weekday + days_ahead - 1) % 7 + 1.

Let's test it again:

```
>>> get_weekday(3, 1)
4
>>> get_weekday(6, 1)
7
>>> get_weekday(7, 1)
1
>>> get_weekday(1, 0)
1
>>> get_weekday(4, 7)
4
>>> get_weekday(7, 72)
2
```

We've passed all the tests, so we can now move on.

What Day Is My Birthday On?

We now have two functions related to day-of-year calculations. One of them calculates the difference between two days of the year. The other calculates the weekday for a day in the future given the weekday today. We can use these two functions to help figure out what day of the week a birthday falls on given what day of the week it is today, what the current day of the year is, and what day of the year the birthday falls on.

Again, we'll follow the function design recipe:

1. *Examples.* We want a name for what it means to calculate what weekday a birthday will fall on. Once more, there are lots of choices; we'll use get_birthday_weekday.

    If today is a Thursday (day 5 of the week), and today is the third day of the year, what day will it be on the fourth day of the year? Hopefully Friday:

    ```
    >>> get_birthday_weekday(5, 3, 4)
    6
    ```

What if it's the same day (Thursday, the 3rd day of the year), but the birthday is the 116th day of the year? For now, we can verify externally (looking at a calendar) that it turns out to be a Friday.

```
>>> get_birthday_weekday(5, 3, 116)
6
```

What if today is Friday, 26 April, the 116th day of the year, but the birthday we want is the 3rd day of the year? This is interesting because the birthday is a couple months before the current day:

```
>>> get_birthday_weekday(6, 116, 3)
5
```

2. *Type Contract.* The arguments in our function call examples are all integers, and the return values are integers too, so here's our type contract:

```
(int, int, int) -> int
```

3. *Header.* We have a couple of example calls, and we know what types the parameters are, so we can now write the header. We're happy enough with the function name so again we'll stick with it.

The first argument is the current day of the week, so we'll use current_weekday, as we did for the previous function. (It's a good idea to be consistent with naming when possible.) The second argument is what day of the year it is today, and we'll choose current_day. The third argument is the day of the year the birthday is, and we'll choose birthday_day:

```
def get_birthday_weekday(current_weekday, current_day, birthday_day):
```

4. *Description.* We need a complete description of what this function will do. We'll start with a sentence describing what the function does, and then we'll describe what the parameters mean:

```
Return the day of the week it will be on birthday_day, given that
the day of the week is current_weekday and the day of the year is
current_day.

current_weekday is the current day of the week and is in the range 1-7,
indicating whether today is Sunday (1), Monday (2), ..., Saturday (7).

current_day and birthday_day are both in the range 1-365.
```

Again, notice that our first sentence uses all parameters and also describes what the function will return. If it gets more complicated, we'll start to write multiple sentences to describe what the function does, but we managed to squeeze it in here.

5. *Body.* It's time to write the body of the function. We have a puzzle:

   a. Using `days_difference`, we can figure out how many days there are between two days.

      Using `get_weekday`, we can figure out what day of the week it will be given the current day of the week and the number of days away.

   We'll start by figuring out how many days from now the birthday falls:

   ```
   days_diff = days_difference(current_day, birthday_day)
   ```

   Now that we know that, we can use it to solve our problem: given the current weekday and that number of days ahead, we can call function `get_weekday` to get our answer:

   ```
   return get_weekday(current_weekday, days_diff)
   ```

   Let's put it all together:

   ```
   >>> def get_birthday_weekday(current_weekday, current_day,
   ...                          birthday_day):
   ...     """ (int, int, int) -> int
   ...
   ...     Return the day of the week it will be on birthday_day,
   ...     given that the day of the week is current_weekday and the
   ...     day of the year is current_day.
   ...
   ...     current_weekday is the current day of the week and is in
   ...     the range 1-7, indicating whether today is Sunday (1),
   ...     Monday (2), ..., Saturday (7).
   ...
   ...     current_day and birthday_day are both in the range 1-365.
   ...
   ...     >>> get_birthday_weekday(5, 3, 4)
   ...     6
   ...     >>> get_birthday_weekday(5, 3, 116)
   ...     6
   ...     >>> get_birthday_weekday(6, 116, 3)
   ...     5
   ...     """
   ...     days_diff = days_difference(current_day, birthday_day)
   ...     return get_weekday(current_weekday, days_diff)
   ...
   ```

6. *Test.* To test it, we fire up the Python shell and copy and paste the calls into the shell, checking that we get back what we expect:

   ```
   >>> get_birthday_weekday(5, 3, 4)
   6
   >>> get_birthday_weekday(5, 3, 116)
   ```

```
6
>>> get_birthday_weekday(6, 116, 3)
5
```

And we're done!

3.7 Writing and Running a Program

So far, we have used the shell to investigate Python. As you have seen, the shell will show you the result of evaluating an expression:

```
>>> 3 + 5 / abs(-2)
5.5
```

In a program that is supposed to interact with a human, showing the result of every expression is probably not desirable behavior. (Imagine if your web browser showed you the result of every calculation it performed.)

Section 2.1, *How Does a Computer Run a Python Program?*, on page 7, explained that in order to save code for later use, you can put it in a file with a .py extension. You can then tell Python to run the code in that file rather than type commands in at the interactive prompt.

Here is a program that we wrote using IDLE and saved in a file called temperature.py. This program consists of a function definition for convert_to_celsius (from earlier in the chapter) and three calls on that function that convert three different Fahrenheit temperatures to their Celsius equivalents.

```
temperature.py - /Users/campbell/temperature.py
def convert_to_celsius(fahrenheit):
    """ (number) -> float

    Return the number of Celsius degrees equivalent to fahrenheit degrees.

    >>> convert_to_celsius(75)
    23.88888888888889
    """

    return (fahrenheit - 32.0) * 5.0 / 9.0


convert_to_celsius(80)
convert_to_celsius(78.8)
convert_to_celsius(10.4)
```
Ln: 15 Col: 24

Notice that there is no >>> prompt. This never appears in a Python program; it is used exclusively in the shell.

Now open IDLE, select File→New Window, and type this program in. (Either that or download the code from the book website and open the file.)

To run the program in IDLE, select Run→Run Module. This will open the Python shell and show the results of running the program. Here is our result.

(The line containing RESTART is letting us know that the shell has restarted, wiping out any previous work done in the shell.)

```
⊖ ○ ○                              Python Shell
Python 3.3.0 (v3.3.0:bd8afb90ebf2, Sep 29 2012, 02:56:36)
[GCC 4.2.1 (Apple Inc. build 5577)] on darwin
Type "copyright", "credits" or "license()" for more information.
>>> =============================== RESTART ===============================
>>>
>>> |
                                                                    Ln: 6 Col: 4
```

Notice that no values are shown, unlike in Section 3.3, *Defining Our Own Functions*, on page 35, when we typed the equivalent code into the shell. In order to have a program print the value of an expression, we use built-in function print. Here is the same program but with calls on function print.

```
⊖ ○ ○          temperature.py – /Users/campbell/temperature.py
def convert_to_celsius(fahrenheit):
    """ (number) -> float

    Return the number of Celsius degrees equivalent to fahrenheit degrees.

    >>> convert_to_celsius(75)
    23.88888888888889
    """

    return (fahrenheit - 32.0) * 5.0 / 9.0

print(convert_to_celsius(80))
print(convert_to_celsius(78.8))
print(convert_to_celsius(10.4))
                                                                    Ln: 15 Col: 31
```

And here is what happens when we run this program:

```
⊖ ○ ○                              Python Shell
Python 3.3.0 (v3.3.0:bd8afb90ebf2, Sep 29 2012, 02:56:36)
[GCC 4.2.1 (Apple Inc. build 5577)] on darwin
Type "copyright", "credits" or "license()" for more information.
>>> =============================== RESTART ===============================
>>>
26.666666666666668
26.0
-12.0
>>> |
                                                                    Ln: 9 Col: 4
```

3.8   Omitting a Return Statement: None

If you don't have a return statement in a function, nothing is produced:

```
>>> def f(x):
...         x = 2 * x
...
>>> res = f(3)
>>> res
>>>
```

Wait, that can't be right—if res doesn't have a value, shouldn't we get a NameError? Let's poke a little more:

```
>>> print(res)
None
>>> id(res)
1756120
```

Variable res has a value: it's None! And None has a memory address. If you don't have a return statement in your function, your function will return None. You can return None yourself if you like:

```
>>> def f(x):
...     x = 2 * x
...     return None
...
>>> print(f(3))
None
```

The value None is used to signal the absence of a value. We'll see some uses for it later in the book.

3.9 Dealing with Situations That Your Code Doesn't Handle

You'll often write a function that only works in some situations. For example, you might write a function that takes as a parameter a number of people who want to eat a pie and returns the percentage of the pie that each person gets to eat. If there are five people, each person gets 20% of the pie; if there are two people, each person gets 50%; if there is one person, that person gets 100%; but if there are zero people, what should the answer be?

Here is an implementation of this function:

```
def pie_percent(n):
    """ (int) -> int

    Assuming there are n people who want to eat a pie, return the percentage
    of the pie that each person gets to eat.

    >>> pie_percent(5)
    20
    >>> pie_percent(2)
    50
    >>> pie_percent(1)
    100
    """

    return int(100 / n)
```

Reading the code, if someone calls pie(0), then you probably see that this will result in a ZeroDivisionError. There isn't anything that anyone can do about this situation: there isn't a sensible answer.

As a programmer, you warn other people about situations that your function isn't set up to handle by describing your assumptions in a *precondition*. Here is the same function with a precondition:

```
def pie_percent(n):
    """ (int) -> int

    Precondition: n > 0

    Assuming there are n people who want to eat a pie, return the percentage
    of the pie that each person gets to eat.

    >>> pie_percent(5)
    20
    >>> pie_percent(2)
    50
    >>> pie_percent(1)
    100
    """

    return int(100 / n)
```

Whenever you write a function and you've assumed something about the parameter values, write a precondition that lets other programmers know your assumptions. If they ignore your warning and call it with invalid values, the fault does not lie with you!

3.10 What Did You Call That?

- A function definition introduces a new variable that refers to a function object. The return statement describes the value that will be produced as a result of the function when this function is done being executed.

- A parameter is a variable that appears between the parentheses of a function header.

- A local variable is a variable that is used in a function definition to store an intermediate result in order to make code easier to write and read.

- A function call tells Python to execute a function.

- An argument is an expression that appears between the parentheses of a function call. The value that is produced when Python evaluates the expression is assigned to the corresponding parameter.

- If you made assumptions about the values of parameters or you know that your function won't work with particular values, write a precondition to warn other programmers.

3.11 Exercises

Here are some exercises for you to try on your own. Solutions are available at http://pragprog.com/titles/gwpy2/practical-programming.

1. Two of Python's built-in functions are min and max. In the Python shell, execute the following function calls:

    a. min(2, 3, 4)
    b. max(2, -3, 4, 7, -5)
    c. max(2, -3, min(4, 7), -5)

2. For the following function calls, in what order are the subexpressions evaluated?

    a. min(max(3, 4), abs(-5))
    b. abs(min(4, 6, max(2, 8)))
    c. round(max(5.572, 3.258), abs(-2))

3. Following the function design recipe, define a function that has one parameter, a number, and returns that number tripled.

4. Following the function design recipe, define a function that has two parameters, both of which are numbers, and returns the absolute value of the difference of the two. Hint: Call built-in function abs.

5. Following the function design recipe, define a function that has one parameter, a distance in kilometers, and returns the distance in miles. (There are 1.6 kilometers per mile.)

6. Following the function design recipe, define a function that has three parameters, grades between 0 and 100 inclusive, and returns the average of those grades.

7. Following the function design recipe, define a function that has four parameters, all of them grades between 0 and 100 inclusive, and returns the average of the *best 3* of those grades. Hint: Call the function that you defined in the previous exercise.

8. Complete the examples in the docstring and then write the body of the following function:

```
def weeks_elapsed(day1, day2):
    """ (int, int) -> int

    day1 and day2 are days in the same year. Return the number of full weeks
    that have elapsed between the two days.

    >>> weeks_elapsed(3, 20)
    2
    >>> weeks_elapsed(20, 3)
    2
    >>> weeks_elapsed(8, 5)

    >>> weeks_elapsed(40, 61)

    """
```

9. Consider this code:

```
def square(num):
    """ (number) -> number

    Return the square of num.

    >>> square(3)
    9
    """
```

In the table below, fill in the Example column by writing square, num, square(3), and 3 next to the appropriate description.

Description	Example
Parameter	
Argument	
Function name	
Function call	

10. Write the body of the square function from the previous exercise.

## CHAPTER 4

Working with Text

From email readers and web browsers to calendars and games, text plays a central role in computer programs. This chapter introduces a non-numeric data type that represents text, such as the words in this sentence or the sequence of bases in a strand of DNA. Along the way, we will see how to make programs a little more interactive by printing messages to our programs' users and getting input from them.

4.1 Creating Strings of Characters

Computers may have been invented to do arithmetic, but these days, most of them spend a lot of their time processing text. Many programs create text, store it, search it, and move it from one place to another.

In Python, text is represented as a *string*, which is a sequence of *characters* (letters, digits, and symbols). The type whose values are sequences of characters is str. The characters consist of those from the Latin alphabet found on most North American keyboards, as well as Chinese morphograms, chemical symbols, musical symbols, and much more.

In Python, we indicate that a value is a string by putting either single or double quotes around it. As we will see in Section 4.2, *Using Special Characters in Strings*, on page 68, single and double quotes are equivalent except for strings that contain quotes. You can use whichever you prefer. (For docstrings, the Python style guidelines say that double quotes are preferred.)

Here are two examples:

```
>>> 'Aristotle'
'Aristotle'
>>> "Isaac Newton"
'Isaac Newton'
```

The opening and closing quotes must match:

```
>>> 'Charles Darwin"
  File "<stdin>", line 1
    'Charles Darwin"
                   ^
SyntaxError: EOL while scanning string literal
```

EOL stands for "end of line." The error above indicates that the end of the line was reached before the end of the string (which should be marked with a closing single quote) was found.

Strings can contain any number of characters, limited only by computer memory. The shortest string is the *empty string*, containing no characters at all:

```
>>> ''
''
>>> ""
''
```

Operations on Strings

Python has a built-in function, len, that returns the number of characters between the opening and closing quotes:

```
>>> len('Albert Einstein')
15
>>> len('123!')
4
>>> len(' ')
1
>>> len('')
0
```

We can add two strings using the + operator, which produces a new string containing the same characters as in the two operands:

```
>>> 'Albert' + ' Einstein'
'Albert Einstein'
```

When + has two string operands, it is referred to as the *concatenation operator*. Operator + is probably the most overloaded operator in Python. So far, we've applied it to integers, floating-point numbers, and strings, and we'll apply it to several more types in later chapters.

As the following example shows, adding an empty string to another string produces a new string that is just like the nonempty operand:

```
>>> "Alan Turing" + ''
'Alan Turing'
>>> "" + 'Grace Hopper'
'Grace Hopper'
```

Here is an interesting question: Can operator + be applied to a string and a numeric value? If so, would addition or concatenation occur? We'll give it a try:

```
>>> 'NH' + 3
Traceback (most recent call last):
  File "<stdin>", line 1, in <module>
TypeError: Can't convert 'int' object to str implicitly
```

This is the second time that we have encountered a type error. The first time, in Section 3.4, *Using Local Variables for Temporary Storage*, on page 39, the problem was that we didn't pass the right number of parameters to a function. Here, Python took exception to our attempts to combine values of different data types because it didn't know which version of + we want: the one that adds numbers or the one that concatenates strings. Because the first operand was a string, Python expected the second operand to also be a string but instead it was an integer. Now consider this example:

```
>>> 9 + ' planets'
Traceback (most recent call last):
  File "<stdin>", line 1, in <module>
TypeError: unsupported operand type(s) for +: 'int' and 'str'
```

Here, because Python saw a 9 first, it expected the second operand to also be numeric. The order of the operands affects the error message.

The concatenation operator must be applied to two strings. If you want to join a string with a number, function str can be applied to the number to get a string representation of it, and then the concatenation can be done:

```
>>> 'Four score and ' + str(7) + ' years ago'
'Four score and 7 years ago'
```

Function int can be applied to a string whose contents look like an integer, and float can be applied to a string whose contents are numeric:

```
>>> int('0')
0
>>> int("11")
11
>>> int('-324')
-324
>>> float('-324')
-324.0
>>> float("56.34")
56.34
```

It isn't always possible to get an integer or a floating-point representation of a string; and when an attempt to do so fails, an error occurs:

```
>>> int('a')
Traceback (most recent call last):
  File "<stdin>", line 1, in <module>
ValueError: invalid literal for int() with base 10: 'a'
>>> float('b')
Traceback (most recent call last):
  File "<stdin>", line 1, in <module>
ValueError: could not convert string to float: 'b'
```

In addition to +, len, int, and float, operator * can be applied to strings. A string can be repeated using operator * and an integer, like this:

```
>>> 'AT' * 5
'ATATATATAT'
>>> 4 * '-'
'----'
```

If the integer is less than or equal to zero, the operator yields the empty string (a string containing no characters):

```
>>> 'GC' * 0
''
>>> 'TATATATA' * -3
''
```

Strings are values, so you can assign a string to a variable. Also, operations on strings can be applied to those variables:

```
>>> sequence = 'ATTGTCCCCC'
>>> len(sequence)
10
>>> new_sequence = sequence + 'GGCCTCCTGC'
>>> new_sequence
'ATTGTCCCCCGGCCTCCTGC'
>>> new_sequence * 2
'ATTGTCCCCCGGCCTCCTGCATTGTCCCCCGGCCTCCTGC'
```

4.2 Using Special Characters in Strings

Suppose you want to put a single quote inside a string. If you write it directly, an error occurs:

```
>>> 'that's not going to work'
  File "<stdin>", line 1
    'that's not going to work'
         ^
SyntaxError: invalid syntax
```

When Python encounters the second quote—the one that is intended to be part of the string—it thinks the string is ended. Then it doesn't know what to do with the text that comes after the second quote.

One simple way to fix this is to use double quotes around the string; we can also put single quotes around a string containing a double quote:

```
>>> "that's better"
"that's better"
>>> 'She said, "That is better."'
'She said, "That is better."'
```

If you need to put a double quote in a string, you can use single quotes around the string. But what if you want to put both kinds of quote in one string? You could do this:

```
>>> 'She said, "That' + "'" + 's hard to read."'
'She said, "That\'s hard to read."'
```

The result is a valid Python string. The backslash is called an *escape character*, and the combination of the backslash and the single quote is called an *escape sequence*. The name comes from the fact that we're "escaping" from Python's usual syntax rules for a moment. When Python sees a backslash inside a string, it means that the next character represents something that Python uses for other purposes, such as marking the end of a string.

The escape sequence \' is indicated using two symbols, but those two symbols represent a single character. The length of an escape sequence is one:

```
>>> len('\'')
1
>>> len('it\'s')
4
```

Python recognizes several escape sequences. In order to see how they are used, we will introduce multiline strings and also revisit built-in function print. Here are some common escape sequences:

Escape Sequence	Description
\'	Single quote
\"	Double quote
\\	Backslash
\t	Tab
\n	Newline
\r	Carriage return

Table 4—Escape Sequences

4.3 Creating a Multiline String

If you create a string using single or double quotes, the whole string must fit onto a single line.

Here's what happens when you try to stretch a string across multiple lines:

```
>>> 'one
  File "<stdin>", line 1
    'one
      ^
SyntaxError: EOL while scanning string literal
```

As we saw in Section 4.1, *Creating Strings of Characters*, on page 65, EOL stands for "end of line"; so in this error report, Python is saying that it reached the end of the line before it found the end of the string.

To span multiple lines, put three single quotes or three double quotes around the string instead of one of each. The string can then span as many lines as you want:

```
>>> '''one
... two
... three'''
'one\ntwo\nthree'
```

Notice that the string Python creates contains a \n sequence everywhere our input started a new line. As programmers, we see escape sequences in strings. In Section 4.4, *Printing Information*, on page 70, we show that when strings are printed, users see the properly rendered strings rather than the escape sequences. That is, they see a tab or a quote rather than \t or \'.

Normalizing Line Endings

In reality, each of the three major operating systems uses a different set of characters to indicate the end of a line. This set of characters is called a *newline*. On Linux and Mac OS X, a newline is one '\n' character; on version 9 and earlier of Mac OS, it is one '\r'; and on Windows, the ends of lines are marked with both characters as '\r\n'.

Python always uses a single \n to indicate a newline, even on operating systems like Windows that do things other ways. This is called *normalizing* the string; Python does this so that you can write exactly the same program no matter what kind of machine you're running on.

4.4 Printing Information

In Section 3.7, *Writing and Running a Program*, on page 59, built-in function print was used to print values to the screen. We will use print to print messages to the users of our program. Those messages may include the values that expressions produce and the values that the variables refer to. Here are two examples of printing:

```
>>> print(1 + 1)
2
>>> print("The Latin 'Oryctolagus cuniculus' means 'domestic rabbit'.")
The Latin 'Oryctolagus cuniculus' means 'domestic rabbit'.
```

Function print doesn't allow any styling of the output: no colors, no italics, no boldface. All output is plain text.

The first function call does what you would expect from the numeric examples we have seen previously, but the second does something slightly different from previous string examples: it strips off the quotes around the string and shows us the string's contents rather than its representation. This example makes the difference between the two even clearer:

```
>>> print('In 1859, Charles Darwin revolutionized biology')
In 1859, Charles Darwin revolutionized biology
>>> print('and our understanding of ourselves')
and our understanding of ourselves
>>> print('by publishing "On the Origin of Species".')
by publishing "On the Origin of Species".
```

And the following example shows that when Python prints a string, it prints the values of any escape sequences in the string rather than their backslashed representations:

```
>>> print('one\ttwo\nthree\tfour')
one     two
three   four
```

The example above shows how the tab character \t can be used to lay values out in columns.

In Section 4.3, *Creating a Multiline String*, on page 70, we saw that \n indicates a new line in multiline strings. When a multiline string is printed, those \n sequences are displayed as new lines:

```
>>> numbers = '''one
... two
... three'''
>>> numbers
'one\ntwo\nthree'
>>> print(numbers)
one
two
three
```

Function print takes a comma-separated list of values to print and prints the values with a single space between them and a newline after the last value:

```
>>> print(1, 2, 3)
1 2 3
>>>
```

When called with no arguments, print ends the current line, advancing to the next one:

```
>>> print()

>>>
```

Function print can print values of any type, and it can even print values of different types in the same function call:

```
>>> print(1, 'two', 'three', 4.0)
1 two three 4.0
```

It is also possible to call print with an expression as an argument. It will print the value of that expression:

```
>>> radius = 5
>>> print("The diameter of the circle is", radius * 2, "cm.")
The diameter of the circle is 10 cm.
```

Function print has a few extra helpful features; here is the help documentation for it:

```
>>> help(print)
Help on built-in function print in module builtins:

print(...)
    print(value, ..., sep=' ', end='\n', file=sys.stdout, flush=False)

    Prints the values to a stream, or to sys.stdout by default.
    Optional keyword arguments:
    file:  a file-like object (stream); defaults to the current sys.stdout.
    sep:   string inserted between values, default a space.
    end:   string appended after the last value, default a newline.
    flush: whether to forcibly flush the stream.
```

The parameters sep, end, file, and flush have assignment statements in the function header! These are called *default parameter values*: by default, if we call function print with a comma-separated list of values, the separator is a space; similarly, a newline character appears at the end of every printed string. (We won't discuss file and flush; they are beyond the scope of this text.)

We can supply different values by using *keyword arguments*. (In the Python documentation, these are often referred to explicitly as kwargs.) That's a fancy term for assigning a value to a parameter name in the function call. Here, we separate each value with a comma and a space instead of just a space by including sep=', ' as an argument:

```
>>> print('a', 'b', 'c')  # The separator is a space by default
a b c
>>> print('a', 'b', 'c', sep=', ')
a, b, c
```

Often you'll want to print information but not start a new line. To do this, use the keyword argument end='' to tell Python to end with an empty string instead of a new line:

```
>>> print('a', 'b', 'c', sep=', ', end='')
a, b, c>>>
```

Notice how the last prompt appeared right after the 'c'. Typically, end='' is used only in programs, not in the shell. Here is a program that converts three temperatures from Fahrenheit to Celsius and prints using keyword arguments:

```
def convert_to_celsius(fahrenheit):
    """ (number) -> float

    Return the number of Celsius degrees equivalent to fahrenheit degrees.

    >>> convert_to_celsius(75)
    23.88888888888889
    """

    return (fahrenheit - 32.0) * 5.0 / 9.0

print('80, 78.8, and 10.4 degrees Fahrenheit are equal to ', end='')
print(convert_to_celsius(80), end=', \n')
print(convert_to_celsius(78.8), end=', and ')
print(convert_to_celsius(10.4), end=' Celsius.\n')
```

Here's the output of running this program:

```
80, 78.8, and 10.4 degrees Fahrenheit are equal to 26.666666666666668,
26.0, and -12.0 Celsius.
```

4.5 Getting Information from the Keyboard

In Chapter 3, *Designing and Using Functions*, on page 31, we explored some built-in functions. Another built-in function that you will find useful is input, which reads a single line of text from the keyboard. It returns whatever the user enters as a string, even if it looks like a number:

```
>>> species = input()
Homo sapiens
>>> species
'Homo sapiens'
>>> population = input()
6973738433
>>> population
'6973738433'
>>> type(population)
<class 'str'>
```

The second and sixth lines of that example, Homo sapiens and 6973738433, were typed by us in response to the calls on function input.

If you are expecting the user to enter a number, you must use int or float to get an integer or a floating-point representation of the string:

```
>>> population = input()
6973738433
>>> population
'6973738433'
>>> population = int(population)
>>> population
6973738433
>>> population = population + 1
>>> population
6973738434
```

We don't actually need to stash the value that the call to input produces before converting it. This time function int is called on the result of the call to input and is equivalent to the code above:

```
>>> population = int(input())
6973738433
>>> population = population + 1
6973738434
```

Finally, input can be given a string argument, which is used to prompt the user for input (notice the space at the end of our prompt):

```
>>> species = input("Please enter a species: ")
Please enter a species: Python curtus
>>> print(species)
Python curtus
```

4.6 Quotes About Strings in This Text

In this chapter, you learned the following:

- Python uses type str to represent text as sequences of characters.

- Strings are created by placing pairs of single or double quotes around the text. Multiline strings can be created using matching pairs of triple quotes.

- Special characters like newline and tab are represented using escape sequences that begin with a backslash.

- Values can be printed using built-in function print, and input can be provided by the user using built-in function input.

4.7 Exercises

Here are some exercises for you to try on your own. Solutions are available at http://pragprog.com/titles/gwpy2/practical-programming.

1. What value does each of the following expressions evaluate to? Verify your answers by typing the expressions into the Python shell.

   a. 'Computer' + ' Science'
   b. 'Darwin\'s'
   c. 'H2O' * 3
   d. 'CO2' * 0

2. Express each of the following phrases as Python strings using the appropriate type of quotation marks (single, double, or triple) and, if necessary, escape sequences. There is more than one correct answer for each of these phrases.

   a. They'll hibernate during the winter.
   b. "Absolutely not," he said.
   c. "He said, 'Absolutely not,'" recalled Mel.
   d. hydrogen sulfide
   e. left\right

3. Rewrite the following string using single or double quotes instead of triple quotes:

   '''A
   B
   C'''

4. Use built-in function len to find the length of the empty string.

5. Given variables x and y, which refer to values 3 and 12.5, respectively, use function print to print the following messages. When numbers appear in the messages, variables x and y should be used.

a. The rabbit is 3.
b. The rabbit is 3 years old.
c. 12.5 is average.
d. 12.5 * 3
e. 12.5 * 3 is 37.5.

6. Consider this code:

```
>>> first = 'John'
>>> last = 'Doe'
>>> print(last + ', ' + first)
```

What is printed by the code above?

7. Use input to prompt the user for a number, store the number entered as a float in a variable named num, and then print the contents of num.

8. Complete the examples in the docstring and then write the body of the following function:

```
def repeat(s, n):
    """ (str, int) -> str

    Return s repeated n times; if n is negative, return the empty string.

    >>> repeat('yes', 4)
    'yesyesyesyes'
    >>> repeat('no', 0)

    >>> repeat('no', -2)

    >>> repeat('yesnomaybe', 3)

    """
```

9. Complete the examples in the docstring and then write the body of the following function:

```
def total_length(s1, s2):
    """ (str, str) -> int

    Return the sum of the lengths of s1 and s2.

    >>> total_length('yes', 'no')
    5
    >>> total_length('yes', '')

    >>> total_length('YES!!!!', 'Noooooo')

    """
```

## CHAPTER 5

Making Choices

This chapter introduces another fundamental concept of programming: making choices. We do this whenever we want our program to behave differently depending on the data it's working with. For example, we might want to do different things depending on whether a solution is acidic or basic, or depending on whether a user types yes or no in response to a call on built-in function input.

We'll introduce statements for making choices in this chapter called *control flow* statements (because they control the way the computer executes programs). These statements involve a Python type that is used to represent truth and falsehood. Unlike the integers, floating-point numbers, and strings we have already seen, this type has only two values and three operators.

5.1 A Boolean Type

In Python, there is a type called bool (without an "e"). Unlike int and float, which have billions of possible values, bool has only two: True and False. True and False are values, just as much as the numbers 0 and -43.7.

> ### George Boole
>
> In the 1840s, the mathematician George Boole showed that the classical rules of logic could be expressed in purely mathematical form using only the two values *true* and *false*. A century later, Claude Shannon (the inventor of information theory) realized that Boole's work could be used to optimize the design of electromechanical telephone switches. His work led directly to the use of *Boolean logic* to design computer circuits.
>
> In honor of Boole's work, most modern programming languages use a type named after him to keep track of what's true and what isn't.

Boolean Operators

There are only three basic Boolean operators: and, or, and not. not has the highest precedence, followed by and, followed by or.

not is a unary operator: it is applied to just one value, like the negation in the expression -(3 + 2). An expression involving not produces True if the original value is False, and it produces False if the original value is True:

```
>>> not True
False
>>> not False
True
```

In the previous example, instead of not True, we could simply use False, and instead of not False, we could use True. Rather than apply not directly to a Boolean value, we would typically apply not to a Boolean variable or a more complex Boolean expression. The same goes for the following examples of the Boolean operators and and or, so although we apply them to Boolean constants in the following examples, we'll give an example of how they are typically used at the end of this section.

and is a binary operator; the expression left and right produces True if both left and right are True, and it produces False otherwise:

```
>>> True and True
True
>>> False and False
False
>>> True and False
False
>>> False and True
False
```

or is also a binary operator. It produces True if *either* operand is True, and it produces False only if both are False:

```
>>> True or True
True
>>> False or False
False
>>> True or False
True
>>> False or True
True
```

This definition is called *inclusive or*, since it allows both possibilities as well as either. In English, the word *or* is also sometimes an *exclusive or*. For example, if someone says, "You can have pizza or tandoori chicken," they probably don't mean that you can have both. Unlike English (but like most programming languages), Python always interprets or as inclusive.

Building an Exclusive Or Expression

If you want an exclusive or, you need to build a Boolean expression for it. We'll walk through the development of this expression.

Let's say you have two Boolean variables, b1 and b2, and you want an expression that evaluates to True if and only if exactly one of them is True. Evaluation of b1 and not b2 will produce True if b1 is True and b2 is False. Similarly, evaluation of b2 and not b1 will produce True if b2 is True and b1 is False.

It isn't possible for both of these expressions to produce True. Also, if b1 and b2 are both True or both False, both expressions will evaluate to False. We can, therefore, combine the two expressions with an or:

```
>>> b1 = False
>>> b2 = False
>>> (b1 and not b2) or (b2 and not b1)
False
>>> b1 = False
>>> b2 = True
>>> (b1 and not b2) or (b2 and not b1)
True
>>> b1 = True
>>> b2 = False
>>> (b1 and not b2) or (b2 and not b1)
True
>>> b1 = True
>>> b2 = True
>>> (b1 and not b2) or (b2 and not b1)
False
```

In a few pages, we'll see a much simpler version.

We mentioned earlier that Boolean operators are usually applied to Boolean expressions rather than Boolean constants. If we want to express "It is not cold and windy" using two variables, cold and windy, that refer to Boolean values, we first have to decide what the ambiguous English expression means: is it not cold but at the same time windy, or is it both not cold and not windy? A *truth table* for each alternative is shown in Table 5, *Boolean Operators*, on page 80, and the following code snippet shows what they look like translated into Python:

```
>>> cold = True
>>> windy = False
>>> (not cold) and windy
False
>>> not (cold and windy)
True
```

cold	windy	cold and windy	cold or windy	(not cold) and windy	not (cold and windy)
True	**True**	True	True	False	False
True	**False**	False	True	False	True
False	**True**	False	True	True	True
False	**False**	False	False	False	True

Table 5—Boolean Operators

Boolean Operators in Other Languages

If you already know another language such as C or Java, you might be used to && for and, || for or, and ! for not. These won't work in Python, but the idea is the same.

Relational Operators

We said earlier that True and False are values. Typically those values are not written down directly in expressions but rather created in expressions. The most common way to do that is by doing a comparison using a *relational operator*. For example, 3 < 5 is a comparison using the relational operator < that produces the value True, while 13 > 77 uses > and produces the value False.

As shown in Table 6, *Relational and Equality Operators*, Python has all the operators you're used to using. Some of them are represented using two characters instead of one, like <= instead of ≤.

Symbol	Operation
>	Greater than
<	Less than
>=	Greater than or equal to
<=	Less than or equal to
==	Equal to
!=	Not equal to

Table 6—Relational and Equality Operators

The most important representation rule is that Python uses == for equality instead of just =, because = is used for assignment. Avoid typing x = 3 when you mean to check whether variable x is equal to three.

All relational operators are binary operators: they compare two values and produce True or False as appropriate. The greater-than (>) and less-than (<) operators work as follows:

```
>>> 45 > 34
True
>>> 45 > 79
False
>>> 45 < 79
True
>>> 45 < 34
False
```

We can compare integers to floating-point numbers with any of the relational operators. Integers are automatically converted to floating point when we do this, just as they are when we add 14 to 23.3:

```
>>> 23.1 >= 23
True
>>> 23.1 >= 23.1
True
>>> 23.1 <= 23.1
True
>>> 23.1 <= 23
False
```

The same holds for "equal to" and "not equal to":

```
>>> 67.3 == 87
False
>>> 67.3 == 67
False
>>> 67.0 == 67
True
>>> 67.0 != 67
False
>>> 67.0 != 23
True
```

Of course, it doesn't make much sense to compare two numbers that you know in advance, since you would also know the result of the comparison. Relational operators therefore almost always involve variables, like this:

```
>>> def is_positive(x):
...     """ (number) -> bool
...
...     Return True iff x is positive.
...
...     >>> is_positive(3)
...     True
```

```
...        >>> is_positive(-4.6)
...        False
...        """
...        return x > 0
...
>>> is_positive(3)
True
>>> is_positive(-4.6)
False
>>> is_positive(0)
False
```

In the docstring above, we use the acronym "iff," which stands for "if and only if." An equivalent phrase is "exactly when." The type contract states that the function will return a bool. The docstring describes the conditions under which True will be returned. It is implied that when those conditions aren't met the function will return False.

We can now write our *exclusive or* expression from *Building an Exclusive Or Expression*, on page 79, much more simply:

```
b1 != b2
```

Exclusive or means that exactly one of b1 and b2 has to be True. If b1 is True, b2 can't be, and vice versa.

Combining Comparisons

We have now seen three types of operators: arithmetic (+, -, and so on), Boolean (and, or, and not), and relational (<, ==, and so on).

Here are the rules for combining them:

- Arithmetic operators have higher precedence than relational operators. For example, + and / are evaluated before < or >.

- Relational operators have higher precedence than Boolean operators. For example, comparisons are evaluated before and, or, and not.

- All relational operators have the same precedence.

These rules mean that the expression 1 + 3 > 7 is evaluated as (1 + 3) > 7, not as 1 + (3 > 7). These rules also mean that you can often skip the parentheses in complicated expressions:

```
>>> x = 2
>>> y = 5
>>> z = 7
>>> x < y and y < z
True
```

It's usually a good idea to put the parentheses in, though, since it helps the eye find the subexpressions and clearly communicates the order to anyone reading your code:

```
>>> x = 5
>>> y = 10
>>> z = 20
>>> (x < y) and (y < z)
True
```

It's very common in mathematics to check whether a value lies in a certain range—in other words, that it is between two other values. You can do this in Python by combining the comparisons with and:

```
>>> x = 3
>>> (1 < x) and (x <= 5)
True
>>> x = 7
>>> (1 < x) and (x <= 5)
False
```

This comes up so often, however, that Python lets you *chain* the comparisons:

```
>>> x = 3
>>> 1 < x <= 5
True
```

Most combinations work as you would expect, but there are cases that may startle you:

```
>>> 3 < 5 != True
True
>>> 3 < 5 != False
True
```

It seems impossible for both of these expressions to be True. However, the first one is equivalent to this:

```
(3 < 5) and (5 != True)
```

while the second is equivalent to this:

```
(3 < 5) and (5 != False)
```

Since 5 is neither True nor False, the second half of each expression is True, so the expression as a whole is True as well.

This kind of expression is an example of something that is a bad idea even though it is legal. We strongly recommend that you only chain comparisons in ways that would seem natural to a mathematician—in other words, that you use < and <= together, or > and >= together, and nothing else. If you feel the impulse to do something else, resist. Use simple comparisons and combine them with and in order to keep your code readable. It's also a good idea to use parentheses whenever you think the expression you are writing may not be entirely clear.

Using Numbers and Strings with Boolean Operators

We have already seen that Python will convert an int to a float when the integer is used in an expression involving a floating-point number. Along the same lines, numbers and strings can be used with Boolean operators. Python treats 0 and 0.0 as False and treats all other numbers as True:

```
>>> not 0
True
>>> not 1
False
>>> not 34.2
False
>>> not -87
False
```

Similarly, the empty string is treated as False and all other strings are treated as True:

```
>>> not ''
True
>>> not 'bad'
False
```

None is also treated as False. In general, you should only use Boolean operators on Boolean values.

Short-Circuit Evaluation

When Python evaluates an expression containing and or or, it does so from left to right. As soon as it knows enough to stop evaluating, it stops, even if some operands haven't been looked at yet. This is called *short-circuit evaluation*.

In an or expression, if the first operand is True, we know that the expression is True. Python knows this as well, so it doesn't even evaluate the second operand. Similarly, in an and expression, if the first operand is False, we know that the expression is False. Python knows this as well, and the second operand isn't evaluated.

To demonstrate this, we use an expression that results in an error:

```
>>> 1 / 0
Traceback (most recent call last):
  File "<stdin>", line 1, in <module>
ZeroDivisionError: division by zero
```

We now use that expression as the second operand to or:

```
>>> (2 < 3) or (1 / 0)
True
```

Since the first operand produces True, the second operand isn't evaluated, so the computer never actually tries to divide anything by zero.

Of course, if the first operand to an or is False, the second operand must be evaluated. The second operand also needs to be evaluated when the first operand to an and is True.

Comparing Strings

It's possible to compare strings just as you would compare numbers. The characters in strings are represented by integers: a capital *A*, for example, is represented by 65, while a space is 32, and a lowercase *z* is 122. This encoding is called *ASCII*, which stands for "American Standard Code for Information Interchange." One of its quirks is that all the uppercase letters come before all the lowercase letters, so a capital *Z* is less than a small *a*.

One of the most common reasons to compare two strings is to decide which one comes first alphabetically. This is often referred to as or Python decides which string is greater than which by comparing corresponding characters from left to right. If the character from one string is greater than the character from the other, the first string is greater than the second. If all the characters are the same, the two strings are equal; if one string runs out of characters while the comparison is being done (in other words, is shorter than the other), then it is less. The following code fragment shows a few comparisons in action:

```
>>> 'A' < 'a'
True
>>> 'A' > 'z'
False
>>> 'abc' < 'abd'
True
>>> 'abc' < 'abcd'
True
```

In addition to operators that compare strings lexicographically, Python provides an operator that checks whether one string appears inside another one:

```
>>> 'Jan' in '01 Jan 1838'
True
>>> 'Feb' in '01 Jan 1838'
False
```

Using this idea, we can prompt the user for a date in this format and report whether that date is in January:

```
>>> date = input('Enter a date in the format DD MTH YYYY: ')
Enter a date in the format DD MTH YYYY: 24 Feb 2013
>>> 'Jan' in date
False
>>> date = input('Enter a date in the format DD MTH YYYY: ')
Enter a date in the format DD MTH YYYY: 03 Jan 2002
>>> 'Jan' in date
True
```

The in operator produces True exactly when the first string appears in the second string. This is case sensitive:

```
>>> 'a' in 'abc'
True
>>> 'A' in 'abc'
False
```

The empty string is always a substring of every string:

```
>>> '' in 'abc'
True
>>> '' in ''
True
```

The in operator also applies to other types; you'll see examples of this in Chapter 8, *Storing Collections of Data Using Lists*, on page 129, and in Chapter 11, *Storing Data Using Other Collection Types*, on page 199.

5.2 Choosing Which Statements to Execute

An if statement lets you change how your program behaves based on a condition. The general form of an if statement is as follows:

```
if «condition»:
    «block»
```

The *condition* is an expression, such as color != "neon green" or x < y. (Note that this doesn't have to be a Boolean expression. As we discussed in *Using Numbers and Strings with Boolean Operators*, on page 84, non-Boolean values are treated as True or False when required.)

As with function bodies, the block of statements inside an if must be indented. As a reminder, the standard indentation for Python is four spaces.

If the condition is true, the statements in the block are executed; otherwise, they are not. As with functions, the block of statements must be indented to show that it belongs to the if statement. If you don't indent properly, Python might raise an error, or worse, might happily execute the code that you wrote but do something you didn't intend because some statements were not indented properly. We'll briefly explore both problems in this chapter.

Here is a table of solution categories based on pH level:

pH Level	Solution Category
0–4	Strong acid
5–6	Weak acid
7	Neutral
8–9	Weak base
10–14	Strong base

We can use an if statement to print a message only when the pH level given by the program's user is acidic:

```
>>> ph = float(input('Enter the pH level: '))
Enter the pH level: 6.0
>>> if ph < 7.0:
...     print(ph, "is acidic.")
...
6.0 is acidic.
```

Recall from Section 4.5, *Getting Information from the Keyboard*, on page 73, that we have to convert user input from a string to a floating-point number before doing the comparison. Also, here we are providing a *prompt* for the user by passing a string into function input: Python prints this string to let the user know what information to type.

If the condition is false, the statements in the block aren't executed:

```
>>> ph = float(input('Enter the pH level: '))
Enter the pH level: 8.0
>>> if ph < 7.0:
...     print(ph, "is acidic.")
...
>>>
```

If we don't indent the block, Python lets us know:

```
>>> ph = float(input('Enter the pH level: '))
Enter the pH level: 6
>>> if ph < 7.0:
... print(ph, "is acidic.")
  File "<stdin>", line 2
    print(ph, "is acidic.")
        ^
IndentationError: expected an indented block
```

Since we're using a block, we can have multiple statements that are executed only if the condition is true:

```
>>> ph = float(input('Enter the pH level: '))
Enter the pH level: 6.0
>>> if ph < 7.0:
...       print(ph, "is acidic.")
...       print("You should be careful with that!")
...
6.0 is acidic.
You should be careful with that!
```

When we indent the first line of the block, the Python interpreter changes its prompt to ... until the end of the block, which is signaled by a blank line:

```
>>> ph = float(input('Enter the pH level: '))
Enter the pH level: 8.0
>>> if ph < 7.0:
...       print(ph, "is acidic.")
...
>>> print("You should be careful with that!")
You should be careful with that!
```

If we don't indent the code that's in the block, the interpreter complains:

```
>>> ph = float(input('Enter the pH level: '))
Enter the pH level: 8.0
>>> if ph < 7.0:
...       print(ph, "is acidic.")
... print("You should be careful with that!")
  File "<stdin>", line 3
    print("You should be careful with that!")
        ^
SyntaxError: invalid syntax
```

If the program is in a file, then no blank line is needed. As soon as the indentation ends, Python assumes that the block has ended as well. This is therefore legal:

```
ph = 8.0
if ph < 7.0:
    print(ph, "is acidic.")
print("You should be careful with that!")
```

In practice, this slight inconsistency is never a problem, and most people won't even notice it.

Of course, sometimes there are situations where a single decision isn't sufficient. If there are multiple criteria to examine, there are a couple of ways to handle it. One way is to use multiple if statements. For example, we might print different messages depending on whether a pH level is acidic or basic (if it's exactly 7, then it's neutral and our code won't print anything):

```
>>> ph = float(input('Enter the pH level: '))
Enter the pH level: 8.5
>>> if ph < 7.0:
...     print(ph, "is acidic.")
...
>>> if ph > 7.0:
...     print(ph, "is basic.")
...
8.5 is basic.
>>>
```

Here's a flow chart that shows how Python executes the if statements. The diamonds are conditions, and the arrows indicate what path to take depending on the results of evaluating those conditions:

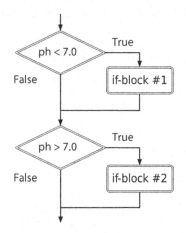

Notice that both conditions are always evaluated, even though we know that only one of the blocks can be executed.

We can merge both cases by adding another condition/block pair using the elif keyword (which stands for "else if"); each condition/block pair is called a *clause*:

```
>>> ph = float(input('Enter the pH level: '))
Enter the pH level: 8.5
>>> if ph < 7.0:
...     print(ph, "is acidic.")
... elif ph > 7.0:
...     print(ph, "is basic.")
...
8.5 is basic.
>>>
```

The difference between the two is that elif is checked only when the if condition above it evaluated to False. Here's a flow chart for this code:

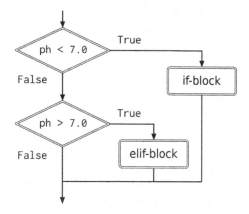

This flow chart shows that if the first condition evaluates to True, the second condition is skipped.

If the pH is exactly 7.0, neither clause matches, so nothing is printed:

```
>>> ph = float(input('Enter the pH level: '))
Enter the pH level: 7.0
>>> if ph < 7.0:
...     print(ph, "is acidic.")
... elif ph > 7.0:
...     print(ph, "is basic.")
...
>>>
```

With the ph example, we accomplished the same thing with two if statements as we did with an if/elif.

This is not always the case; for example, if the body of the first if changes the value of a variable used in the second condition, they are not equivalent. Here is the version with two ifs:

```
>>> ph = float(input('Enter the pH level: '))
Enter the pH level: 6.0
>>> if ph < 7.0:
...     ph = 8.0
...
>>> if ph > 7.0:
...     print(ph, "is acidic.")
...
8.0 is acidic.
```

And here is the version with an if/elif:

```
>>> ph = float(input('Enter the pH level: '))
Enter the pH level: 6.0
>>> if ph < 7.0:
...     ph = 8.0
>>> elif ph > 7.0:
...     print(ph, "is acidic.")
...
>>>
```

As a rule of thumb, if two conditions are related, use if/elif instead of two ifs.

An if statement can be followed by multiple elif clauses. This longer example translates a chemical formula into English:

```
>>> compound = input('Enter the compound: ')
Enter the compound: CH4
>>> if compound == "H2O":
...     print("Water")
... elif compound == "NH3":
...     print("Ammonia")
... elif compound == "CH4":
...     print("Methane")
...
Methane
>>>
```

As we saw in the code on page 90, if none of the conditions in a chain of if/elif statements are satisfied, Python does not execute any of the associated blocks. This isn't always what we'd like, though. In our translation example, we probably want our program to print something even if it doesn't recognize the compound.

To do this, we add an else clause at the end of the chain:

```
>>> compound = input('Enter the compound: ')
Enter the compound: H2SO4
>>> if compound == "H2O":
...     print("Water")
... elif compound == "NH3":
...     print("Ammonia")
... elif compound == "CH4":
...     print("Methane")
... else:
...     print("Unknown compound")
...
Unknown compound
>>>
```

An if statement can have at most one else clause, and it has to be the final clause in the statement. Notice there is no condition associated with else:

```
if «condition»:
    «if_block»
else:
    «else_block»
```

Logically, that code is the same as this code (except that the condition is evaluated only once in the first form but twice in the second form):

```
if «condition»:
    «if_block»
if not «condition»:
    «else_block»
```

5.3 Nested If Statements

An if statement's block can contain any type of Python statement, which implies that it can include other if statements. An if statement inside another is called a *nested* if statement.

```
value = input('Enter the pH level: ')
if len(value) > 0:
    ph = float(value)
    if ph < 7.0:
        print(ph, "is acidic.")
    elif ph > 7.0:
        print(ph, "is basic.")
    else:
        print(ph, "is neutral.")
else:
    print("No pH value was given!")
```

In this case, we ask the user to provide a pH value, which we'll initially receive as a string. The first, or *outer*, if statement checks whether the user typed something, which determines whether we examine the value of pH with the *inner* if statement. (If the user didn't enter a number, then function call float(value) will produce a ValueError.)

Nested if statements are sometimes necessary, but they can get complicated and difficult to understand. To describe when a statement is executed, we have to mentally combine conditions; for example, the statement print(ph, "is acidic.") is executed only if the length of the string that value refers to is greater than 0 *and* pH < 7.0 also evaluates to True (assuming the user entered a number).

5.4 Remembering the Results of a Boolean Expression Evaluation

Take a look at the following line of code and guess what value is stored in x:

```
>>> x = 15 > 5
```

If you said True, you were right: 15 is greater than 5, so the comparison produces True, and since that's a value like any other, it can be assigned to a variable.

The most common situation in which you would want to do this comes up when translating decision tables into software. For example, suppose you want to calculate someone's risk of heart disease using the following rules based on age and body mass index (BMI):

		Age	
		<45	≥45
BMI	<22.0	Low	Medium
	≥22.0	Medium	High

One way to implement this would be to use nested if statements:

```
if age < 45:
    if bmi < 22.0:
        risk = 'low'
    else:
        risk = 'medium'
else:
    if bmi < 22.0:
        risk = 'medium'
    else:
        risk = 'high'
```

The expression bmi < 22.0 is used multiple times. To simplify this code, we can evaluate each of the Boolean expressions once, create variables that refer to the values produced by those expressions, and use those variables multiple times:

```
young = age < 45
slim = bmi < 22.0
if young:
    if slim:
        risk = 'low'
    else:
        risk = 'medium'
else:
    if slim:
        risk = 'medium'
    else:
        risk = 'high'
```

We could also write this without nesting as follows:

```
young = age < 45
slim = bmi < 22.0
if young and slim:
    risk = 'low'
elif young and not slim:
    risk = 'medium'
elif not young and slim:
    risk = 'medium'
elif not young and not slim:
    risk = 'high'
```

5.5 You Learned About Booleans: True or False?

In this chapter, you learned the following:

- Python uses Boolean values, True and False, to represent what is true and what isn't. Programs can combine these values using three operators: not, and, and or.

- Boolean operators can also be applied to numeric values. 0, 0.0, the empty string, and None are treated as False; all other numeric values and strings are treated as True. It is best to avoid applying Boolean operators to non-Boolean values.

- Relational operators such as "equals" and "less than" compare values and produce a Boolean result.

- When different operators are combined in an expression, the order of precedence from highest to lowest is arithmetic, relational, and then Boolean.

- if statements control the flow of execution. As with function definitions, the bodies of if statements are indented, as are the bodies of elif and else clauses.

5.6 Exercises

Here are some exercises for you to try on your own. Solutions are available at http://pragprog.com/titles/gwpy2/practical-programming.

1. What value does each expression produce? Verify your answers by typing the expressions into Python.

    a. True and not False
    b. True and not false (Notice the capitalization.)
    c. True or True and False
    d. not True or not False
    e. True and not 0

    f.   52 < 52.3

    g. 1 + 52 < 52.3

    h. 4 != 4.0

2. Variables x and y refer to Boolean values.

    a. Write an expression that produces True iff both variables are True.

    b. Write an expression that produces True iff x is False.

    c. Write an expression that produces True iff at least one of the variables is True.

3. Variables full and empty refer to Boolean values. Write an expression that produces True iff at most one of the variables is True.

4. You want an automatic wildlife camera to switch on if the light level is less than 0.01 lux or if the temperature is above freezing, but not if both conditions are true. (You should assume that function turn_camera_on has already been defined.)

Your first attempt to write this is as follows:

```
if (light < 0.01) or (temperature > 0.0):
    if not ((light < 0.01) and (temperature > 0.0)):
        turn_camera_on()
```

A friend says that this is an exclusive or and that you could write it more simply as follows:

```
if (light < 0.01) != (temperature > 0.0):
    turn_camera_on()
```

Is your friend right? If so, explain why. If not, give values for light and temperature that will produce different results for the two fragments of code.

5. In Section 3.1, *Functions That Python Provides*, on page 31, we saw built-in function abs. Variable x refers to a number. Write an expression that evaluates to True if x and its absolute value are equal and evaluates to False otherwise. Assign the resulting value to a variable named result.

6. Write a function named different that has two parameters, a and b. The function should return True if a and b refer to different values and should return False otherwise.

7. Variables population and land_area refer to floats.

    a. Write an if statement that will print the population if it is less than 10,000,000.

b. Write an if statement that will print the population if it is between 10,000,000 and 35,000,000.

c. Write an if statement that will print "Densely populated" if the land density (number of people per unit of area) is greater than 100.

d. Write an if statement that will print "Densely populated" if the land density (number of people per unit of area) is greater than 100, and "Sparsely populated" otherwise.

8. Function convert_to_celsius from Section 3.3, *Defining Our Own Functions*, on page 35, converts from Fahrenheit to Celsius. Wikipedia, however, discusses eight temperature scales: Kelvin, Celsius, Fahrenheit, Rankine, Delisle, Newton, Rèaumur, and Rømer. Visit http://en.wikipedia.org/wiki/Comparison_of_temperature_scales to read about them.

a. Write a convert_temperatures(t, source, target) function to convert temperature t from source units to target units, where source and target are each one of "Kelvin", "Celsius", "Fahrenheit", "Rankine", "Delisle", "Newton", "Reaumur", and "Romer" units.

Hint: On the Wikipedia page there are eight tables, each with two columns and seven rows. That translates to an awful lot of if statements—at least 8 * 7—because each of the eight units can be converted to the seven other units. Possibly even worse, if you decided to add another temperature scale, you would need to add at least sixteen more if statements: eight to convert from your new scale to each of the current ones and eight to convert from the current ones to your new scale.

A better way is to choose one canonical scale, such as Celsius. Your conversion function could work in two steps: convert from the source scale to Celsius and then from Celsius to the target scale.

b. Now if you added a new temperature scale, how many if statements would you need to add?

9. Assume we want to print a strong warning message if a pH value is below 3.0 and otherwise simply report on the acidity. We try this if statement:

```
>>> ph = 2
>>> if ph < 7.0:
...     print(ph, "is acidic.")
... elif ph < 3.0:
...     print(ph, "is VERY acidic! Be careful.")
...
2 is acidic.
```

This prints the wrong message when a pH of 2 is entered. What is the problem, and how can you fix it?

10. The following code displays a message(s) about the acidity of a solution:

```
ph = float(input("Enter the ph level: "))
if ph < 7.0:
    print("It's acidic!")
elif ph < 4.0:
    print("It's a strong acid!")
```

   a. What message(s) are displayed when the user enters 6.4?

   b. What message(s) are displayed when the user enters 3.6?

   c. Make a small change to one line of the code so that both messages are displayed when a value less than 4 is entered.

11. Why does the last example in Section 5.4, *Remembering the Results of a Boolean Expression Evaluation*, on page 92, check to see whether someone is light (that is, that person's BMI is less than the threshold) rather than heavy? If you wanted to write the second assignment statement as heavy = bmi >= 22.0, what change(s) would you have to make to the code?

## CHAPTER 6

A Modular Approach
to Program Organization

Mathematicians don't prove every theorem from scratch. Instead, they build their proofs on the truths their predecessors have already established. In the same way, it's vanishingly rare for someone to write all of a program alone; it's much more common—and productive—to make use of the millions of lines of code that other programmers have written before.

What Happens When You Import This?

```
>>> import this
The Zen of Python, by Tim Peters

Beautiful is better than ugly.
Explicit is better than implicit.
Simple is better than complex.
Complex is better than complicated.
Flat is better than nested.
Sparse is better than dense.
Readability counts.
Special cases aren't special enough to break the rules.
Although practicality beats purity.
Errors should never pass silently.
Unless explicitly silenced.
In the face of ambiguity, refuse the temptation to guess.
There should be one-- and preferably only one --obvious way to do it.
Although that way may not be obvious at first unless you're Dutch.
Now is better than never.
Although never is often better than *right* now.
If the implementation is hard to explain, it's a bad idea.
If the implementation is easy to explain, it may be a good idea.
Namespaces are one honking great idea -- let's do more of those!
```

A *module* is a collection of variables and functions that are grouped together in a single file. The variables and functions in a module are usually related to one another in some way; for example, module math contains the variable pi and mathematical functions such as cos (cosine) and sqrt (square root). This chapter shows you how to use some of the hundreds of modules that come with Python, as well as how to create your own modules.

6.1 Importing Modules

To gain access to the variables and functions from a module, you have to *import* it. To tell Python that you want to use functions in module math, for example, you use this import statement:

```
>>> import math
```

Importing a module creates a new variable with that name. That variable refers to an object whose type is module:

```
>>> type(math)
<class 'module'>
```

Once you have imported a module, you can use built-in function help to see what it contains. Here is the first part of the help output:

```
>>> help(math)

Help on module math:

NAME
    math

MODULE REFERENCE
    http://docs.python.org/3.3/library/math

    The following documentation is automatically generated from the Python
    source files.  It may be incomplete, incorrect or include features that
    are considered implementation detail and may vary between Python
    implementations.  When in doubt, consult the module reference at the
    location listed above.

DESCRIPTION
    This module is always available.  It provides access to the
    mathematical functions defined by the C standard.

FUNCTIONS
    acos(...)
        acos(x)

        Return the arc cosine (measured in radians) of x.
```

```
acosh(...)
    acosh(x)

    Return the hyperbolic arc cosine (measured in radians) of x.
```

```
[Lots of other functions not shown here.]
```

The statement import math creates a variable called math that refers to a module object. In that object are all the names defined in that module. Each of them refers to a function object:

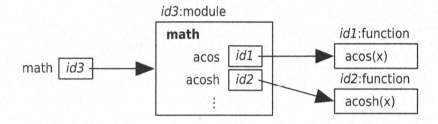

Great—our program can now use all the standard mathematical functions. When we try to calculate a square root, though, we get an error telling us that Python is still unable to find function sqrt:

```
>>> sqrt(9)
Traceback (most recent call last):
  File "<stdin>", line 1, in <module>
NameError: name 'sqrt' is not defined
```

The solution is to tell Python explicitly to look for the function in module math by combining the module's name with the function's name using a dot:

```
>>> math.sqrt(9)
3.0
```

The dot is an operator, just like + and ** are operators. Its meaning is "look up the object that the variable to the left of the dot refers to and, in that object, find the name that occurs to the right of the dot." In math.sqrt(9), Python finds math in the current namespace, looks up the module object that math refers to, finds function sqrt inside that module, and then executes the function call following the standard rules described in Section 3.5, *Tracing Function Calls in the Memory Model*, on page 40.

Modules can contain more than just functions. Module math, for example, also defines some variables like pi. Once the module has been imported, you can use these variables like any others:

```
>>> import math
>>> math.pi
3.141592653589793
>>> radius = 5
>>> print('area is', math.pi * radius ** 2)
area is 78.53981633974483
```

You can even assign to variables imported from modules:

```
>>> import math
>>> math.pi = 3
>>> radius = 5
>>> print('area is', math.pi * radius ** 2)
area is 75
```

Don't do this! Changing the value of π isn't a good idea. In fact, it's such a bad idea that many languages allow programmers to define unchangeable *constants* as well as variables. As the name suggests, the value of a constant cannot be changed after it has been defined: π is always 3.14159 and a little bit, while SECONDS_PER_DAY is always 86,400. The fact that Python doesn't allow programmers to "freeze" values like this is one of the language's few significant flaws.

Combining the module's name with the names of the things it contains is safe, but it isn't always convenient. For this reason, Python lets you specify exactly what you want to import from a module, like this:

```
>>> from math import sqrt, pi
>>> sqrt(9)
3.0
>>> radius = 5
>>> print('circumference is', 2 * pi * radius)
circumference is 31.41592653589793
```

This doesn't introduce a variable called math. Instead, it creates function sqrt and variable pi in the current namespace, as if you had typed the function definition and variable assignment yourself. Restart your shell and try this:

```
>>> from math import sqrt, pi
>>> math.sqrt(9)
Traceback (most recent call last):
  File "<pyshell#12>", line 1, in <module>
    math.sqrt(9)
NameError: name 'math' is not defined
>>> sqrt(9)
3.0
```

Here, we don't have a variable called math. Instead, we imported variables sqrt and pi directly into the current namespace, as shown in this diagram:

Restoring a Module

If you change the value of a variable or function from an imported module, you can restart the shell and reimport the module to restore it to its original value. In IDLE, you can restart the shell by choosing Shell→Restart Shell.

Without having to restart the shell, you can restore the module to its original state using function reload from module imp:

```
>>> import math
>>> math.pi = 3
>>> math.pi
3
>>> import imp
>>> math = imp.reload(math)
>>> math.pi
3.141592653589793
>>>
```

Function imp.reload returns the module.

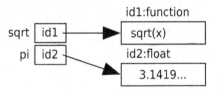

This can lead to problems when different modules provide functions that have the same name. If you import a function called spell from a module called magic and then you import another function called spell from the grammar module, the second replaces the first. It's exactly like assigning one value to a variable and then assigning another value: the most recent assignment or import wins.

This is why it's usually *not* a good idea to use import *, which brings in everything from the module at once:

```
>>> from math import *
>>> print(sqrt(8))
2.8284271247461903
```

Although import * saves some typing, you run the risk of your program accessing the incorrect function and not working properly.

The standard Python library contains several hundred modules to do everything from figuring out what day of the week it is to fetching data from a website. The full list is online at http://docs.python.org/release/3.3.0/py-modindex.html; although it's far too much to absorb in one sitting (or even one course), knowing how to use the library well is one of the things that distinguishes good programmers from poor ones.

Module __builtins__

Python's built-in functions are actually in a module named __builtins__ (with two underscores before and after 'builtins'). The double underscores before and after the name signal that it's part of Python; we'll see this convention used again later for other things. You can see what's in the module using help(__builtins__), or if you just want to see what functions and variables are available, you can use dir instead (which works on other modules as well):

```
>>> dir(__builtins__)
['ArithmeticError', 'AssertionError', 'AttributeError', 'BaseException',
'BlockingIOError', 'BrokenPipeError', 'BufferError', 'BytesWarning',
'ChildProcessError', 'ConnectionAbortedError', 'ConnectionError',
'ConnectionRefusedError', 'ConnectionResetError', 'DeprecationWarning',
'EOFError', 'Ellipsis', 'EnvironmentError','Exception', 'False',
'FileExistsError', 'FileNotFoundError','FloatingPointError', 'FutureWarning',
'GeneratorExit', 'IOError', 'ImportError', 'ImportWarning', 'IndentationError',
'IndexError', 'InterruptedError', 'IsADirectoryError', 'KeyError',
'KeyboardInterrupt', 'LookupError', 'MemoryError', 'NameError', 'None',
'NotADirectoryError', 'NotImplemented', 'NotImplementedError', 'OSError',
'OverflowError', 'PendingDeprecationWarning', 'PermissionError',
'ProcessLookupError', 'ReferenceError', 'ResourceWarning', 'RuntimeError',
'RuntimeWarning', 'StopIteration', 'SyntaxError', 'SyntaxWarning',
'SystemError', 'SystemExit', 'TabError', 'TimeoutError', 'True', 'TypeError',
'UnboundLocalError', 'UnicodeDecodeError', 'UnicodeEncodeError', 'UnicodeError',
'UnicodeTranslateError', 'UnicodeWarning', 'UserWarning', 'ValueError',
'Warning', 'ZeroDivisionError', '_', '__build_class__', '__debug__',
'__doc__', '__import__', '__name__', '__package__', 'abs', 'all', 'any',
'ascii', 'bin', 'bool', 'bytearray', 'bytes', 'callable', 'chr', 'classmethod',
'compile', 'complex', 'copyright', 'credits', 'delattr', 'dict', 'dir',
'divmod', 'enumerate', 'eval', 'exec', 'exit', 'filter', 'float', 'format',
'frozenset', 'getattr', 'globals', 'hasattr', 'hash', 'help', 'hex', 'id',
'input', 'int', 'isinstance', 'issubclass', 'iter', 'len', 'license', 'list',
'locals', 'map', 'max', 'memoryview', 'min', 'next', 'object', 'oct', 'open',
'ord', 'pow', 'print', 'property', 'quit', 'range', 'repr', 'reversed',
'round', 'set', 'setattr', 'slice', 'sorted', 'staticmethod', 'str', 'sum',
'super', 'tuple', 'type', 'vars', 'zip']
```

As of Python 3.3.0, 46 of the 147 items in __builtins__ are used to signal errors of particular kinds, such as SyntaxError and ZeroDivisionError. All errors, warnings, and exceptions are types like int, float, and function. Their names follow a naming convention in which the first letter of each word is uppercase.

We'll introduce some of this module's other members in later chapters.

6.2 Defining Your Own Modules

Section 3.7, *Writing and Running a Program*, on page 59, explained that in order to save code for later use, you can put it in a file with a .py extension, and it demonstrated how to run that code. Chapter 3, *Designing and Using Functions*, on page 31, also included this function definition:

```
>>> def convert_to_celsius(fahrenheit):
...     """ (number) -> float
...
...     Return the number of Celsius degrees equivalent to fahrenheit degrees.
...
...     >>> convert_to_celsius(75)
...     23.88888888888889
...     """
...     return (fahrenheit - 32.0) * 5.0 / 9.0
...
```

Put the function definition for convert_to_celsius from Section 3.3, *Defining Our Own Functions*, on page 35, in a file called temperature.py. (You can save this file anywhere you like, although most programmers create a separate directory for each set of related files that they write.)

Now add another function to temperature.py called above_freezing that returns True if and only if its parameter celsius is above freezing:

```
⬤ ⬤ ⬤               temperature.py - /Users/user/temperature.py
def convert_to_celsius(fahrenheit):
    """ (number) -> float

    Return the number of Celsius degrees equivalent to fahrenheit degrees.

    >>> convert_to_celsius(75)
    23.88888888888889
    """

    return (fahrenheit - 32.0) * 5.0 / 9.0

def above_freezing(celsius):
    """ (number) -> bool

    Return True iff temperature     celsius degrees is above freezing.

    >>> above_freezing(5.2)
    True
    >>> above_freezing(-2)
    False
    """

    return celsius > 0
                                                              Ln: 1 Col: 0
```

Congratulations—you have created a module called temperature. Now that you've created this file, you can run it and import it like any other module:

```
>>> import temperature
>>> celsius = temperature.convert_to_celsius(33.3)
>>> temperature.above_freezing(celsius)
True
```

What Happens During Import

Let's try another experiment. Create a file called experiment.py with this one statement inside it:

```
print("The panda's scientific name is 'Ailuropoda melanoleuca'")
```

Run experiment.py and then import it:

```
>>> import experiment
The panda's scientific name is 'Ailuropoda melanoleuca'
```

What this shows is that *Python executes modules as it imports them*. You can do anything in a module you would do in any other program, because as far as Python is concerned, it's just another bunch of statements to be run.

Let's try another experiment. Start a fresh Python session, run experiment.py, and try importing module experiment twice in a row:

```
>>> import experiment
The panda's scientific name is 'Ailuropoda melanoleuca'
>>> import experiment
>>>
```

Notice that the message wasn't printed the second time. That's because Python loads modules only the first time they're imported. Internally, Python keeps track of the modules it has already seen; when it is asked to load one that's already in that list, it just skips over it. This saves time and will be particularly important when you start writing modules that import other modules, which in turn import other modules—if Python didn't keep track of what was already in memory, it could wind up loading commonly used modules like math dozens of times.

Even if you import a module, edit that module's file, and then reimport, the module won't be reloaded. Your edits won't have any effect until you restart the shell or call imp.reload. For example, after we've imported experiment, we'll change the file contents to this:

```
print("The koala's scientific name is 'Phascolarctos cinereus'")
```

We'll now call imp.reload to reload module experiment:

```
>>> import experiment
The panda's scientific name is 'Ailuropoda melanoleuca'
>>> import experiment
>>> import imp
>>> imp.reload(experiment)
The koala's scientific name is 'Phascolarctos cinereus'
<module 'experiment' from '/Users/campbell/Documents/experiment.py'>
```

In the example above, the call on imp.reload returns the module that was imported.

Selecting Which Code Gets Run on Import: __main__

As we saw in Section 3.7, *Writing and Running a Program*, on page 59, every Python module can be run directly (from the command line or by running it from an IDE like IDLE), or, as we saw earlier in this section, it can be run indirectly (imported by another program). If a module is to be imported by another module, then the files containing the two modules should be saved in the same directory (an alternative approach would be to use absolute file paths, which are explained in Section 10.2, *Opening a File*, on page 173).

Sometimes we want to write code that should only be run when the module is run directly and not when the module is imported. Python defines a special string variable called _name_ in every module to help us figure this out. Suppose we put the following into echo.py:

```
print("__name__ is", __name__)
```

If we run this file, its output is as follows:

```
__name__ is __main__
```

As promised, Python has created variable _name_. Its value is "_main_", meaning this module is the main program. But look at what happens when we import echo (instead of running it directly):

```
>>> import echo
__name__ is echo
```

The same thing happens if we write a program that does nothing but import our echoing module. Create a file import_echo.py with this code inside it:

```
import echo

print("After import, __name__ is", __name__,
      "and echo.__name__ is", echo.__name__)
```

When run from the command line, this code produces this:

```
__name__ is echo
After import, __name__ is __main__ and echo.__name__ is echo
```

When Python imports a module, it sets that module's _name_ variable to be the name of the module rather than the special string "_main_". This means that a module can tell whether it is the main program. Now create a file named main_example.py with this code inside it:

```
if __name__ == "__main__":
    print("I am the main program.")
else:
    print("Another module is importing me.")
```

Try it. See what happens when you run main_example.py directly and when you import it.

Some of our modules contain not only function definitions but also programs. For example, create a new module temperature_program that contains the functions from temperature and a little program:

```
○ ○ ○        temperature_program.py – /Users/user/temperature_program.py
def convert_to_celsius(fahrenheit):
    """ (number) -> float

    Return the number of Celsius degrees equivalent to fahrenheit degrees.

    >>> convert_to_celsius(75)
    23.88888888888889
    """

    return (fahrenheit - 32.0) * 5.0 / 9.0

def above_freezing(celsius):
    """ (number) -> bool

    Return True iff temperature celsius degrees is above freezing.

    >>> above_freezing(5.2)
    True
    >>> above_freezing(-2)
    False
    """

    return celsius > 0

fahrenheit = float(input('Enter the temperature in degrees Fahrenheit: '))
celsius = convert_to_celsius(fahrenheit)
if above_freezing(celsius):
    print('It is above freezing.')
else:
    print('It is below freezing.')
                                                                  Ln: 19 Col: 1
```

When that module is run, it prompts the user to enter a value and, depending on the value entered, prints one of two messages:

```
○ ○ ○                        Python 3.3.2 Shell
Python 3.3.2 (v3.3.2:d047928ae3f6, May 13 2013, 13:52:24)
[GCC 4.2.1 (Apple Inc. build 5666) (dot 3)] on darwin
Type "copyright", "credits" or "license()" for more information.
>>> ================================ RESTART ================================
>>>
Enter the temperature in degrees Fahrenheit: 35
It is above freezing.
>>>
                                                                  Ln: 4 Col: 0
```

Let's create another module, baking.py, that uses the conversion function from module temperature_program. (See the following figure.)

```
● ○ ○                    baking.py – /Users/user/baking.py
import temperature_program

def get_preheating_instructions(fahrenheit):
    """ (number) -> string

    Return instructions for preheating the oven in fahreneheit degrees and
    Celsius degrees.

    >>> get_preheating_instructions(500)
    'Preheat oven to 500 degrees F (260.0 degrees C).'
    """

    cels = str(temperature_program.convert_to_celsius(fahrenheit))
    fahr = str(fahrenheit)
    return 'Preheat oven to ' + fahr + ' degrees F ('+ cels +' degrees C).'


fahr = float(input('Enter the baking temperature in degrees Fahrenheit: '))
print(get_preheating_instructions(fahr))



                                                              Ln: 3 Col: 0
```

When baking.py is run, it imports temperature_program, so the program at the
bottom of temperature_program.py is executed:

```
● ○ ○                         Python 3.3.2 Shell
Python 3.3.2 (v3.3.2:d047928ae3f6, May 13 2013, 13:52:24)
[GCC 4.2.1 (Apple Inc. build 5666) (dot 3)] on darwin
Type "copyright", "credits" or "license()" for more information.
>>> ============================ RESTART ============================
>>>
Enter the temperature in degrees Fahrenheit: 15
It is below freezing.
Enter the baking temperature in degrees Fahrenheit: 500
Preheat oven to 500.0 degrees F (260.0 degrees C).
>>>


                                                              Ln: 10 Col: 4
```

Since we don't care whether a temperature is above freezing when preheating
our oven, when importing temperature_program.py we can prevent that part of the
code from executing by putting it in an if __name__ == '__main__': block (Figure 2,
The Main Temperature Program, on page 110).

Now when baking.py is run, only the code from temperature_program that is outside
of the if __name__ == '__main__': block is executed (Figure 3, *Output for Execution
of baking.py*, on page 110).

We will see other uses of __name__ in the following sections and in later chapters.

```
● ○ ○        temperature_program.py – /Users/user/temperature_program.py
def convert_to_celsius(fahrenheit):
    """ (number) -> float

    Return the number of Celsius degrees equivalent to fahrenheit degrees.

    >>> convert_to_celsius(75)
    23.88888888888889
    """

    return (fahrenheit - 32.0) * 5.0 / 9.0


def above_freezing(celsius):
    """ (number) -> bool

    Return True iff temperature celsius degrees is above freezing.

    >>> above_freezing(5.2)
    True
    >>> above_freezing(-2)
    False
    """

    return celsius > 0


if __name__ == '__main__':
    fahrenheit = float(input('Enter the temperature in degrees Fahrenheit: '))
    celsius = convert_to_celsius(fahrenheit)
    if above_freezing(celsius):
        print('It is above freezing.')
    else:
        print('It is below freezing.')
                                                                    Ln: 10 Col: 30
```

Figure 2—The Main Temperature Program

```
● ○ ○                        Python 3.3.2 Shell
Python 3.3.2 (v3.3.2:d047928ae3f6, May 13 2013, 13:52:24)
[GCC 4.2.1 (Apple Inc. build 5666) (dot 3)] on darwin
Type "copyright", "credits" or "license()" for more information.
>>> ================================ RESTART ================================
>>>
Enter the baking temperature in degrees Fahrenheit: 500
Preheat oven to 500.0 degrees F (260.0 degrees C).
>>>
                                                                    Ln: 8 Col: 4
```

Figure 3—Output for Execution of baking.py

6.3 Testing Your Code Semiautomatically

In Section 3.6, *Designing New Functions: A Recipe*, on page 47, we introduced the function design recipe (FDR). Following the FDR, the docstrings that we write include example function calls.

The last step of the FDR involves testing the function. Up until now, we have been typing the function calls from the docstrings to the shell (or copying and pasting them) to run them and then have been comparing the results with what we expect to make sure they match.

Python has a module called *doctest* that allows us to run the tests that we include in docstrings all at once. It reports on whether the function calls return what we expect. (See Figure 4, *The doctest Module Running the Tests from Module temperature_program*.) We will use doctest to run the tests from module temperature_program from *Selecting Which Code Gets Run on Import: __main__*, on page 107:

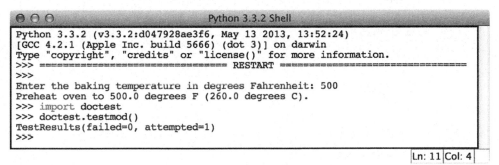

```
Python 3.3.2 (v3.3.2:d047928ae3f6, May 13 2013, 13:52:24)
[GCC 4.2.1 (Apple Inc. build 5666) (dot 3)] on darwin
Type "copyright", "credits" or "license()" for more information.
>>> ================================ RESTART ================================
>>>
Enter the baking temperature in degrees Fahrenheit: 500
Preheat oven to 500.0 degrees F (260.0 degrees C).
>>> import doctest
>>> doctest.testmod()
TestResults(failed=0, attempted=1)
>>>
```

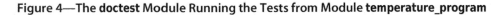

Figure 4—The doctest Module Running the Tests from Module temperature_program

That message tells us that three tests were run and none of them failed. That is, the three function calls in the docstrings were run, and they returned the same value that we expected and stated in the docstring.

Now let's see what happens when there is an error in our calculation. Instead of the calculation we've been using, (fahrenheit - 32.0) * 5.0/9.0, let's remove the parentheses: fahrenheit - 32.0 * 5.0 / 9.0. (See Figure 5, *Results of Removing the Parentheses*, on page 112.)

Figure 6, *Failure Message for doctest*, on page 113 shows the result of running doctest on that module.

The failure message above indicates that function call convert_to_celsius(75) was expected to return 23.88888888888889 but it actually returned 57.22222222222222. The other two tests ran and passed.

When a failure occurs, we need to review our code to identify the problem. We should also check the expected return value listed in the docstring to make sure that the expected value matches both the type contract and the description of the function.

```
● ○ ○          temperature_program.py – /Users/user/temperature_program.py
def convert_to_celsius(fahrenheit):
    """ (number) -> float

    Return the number of Celsius degrees equivalent to fahrenheit degrees.

    >>> convert_to_celsius(75)
    23.88888888888889
    """

    return fahrenheit - 32.0 * 5.0 / 9.0

def above_freezing(celsius):
    """ (number) -> bool

    Return True iff temperature celsius degrees is above freezing.

    >>> above_freezing(5.2)
    True
    >>> above_freezing(-2)
    False
    """

    return celsius > 0

if __name__ == '__main__':
    fahrenheit = float(input('Enter the temperature in degrees Fahrenheit: '))
    celsius = convert_to_celsius(fahrenheit)
    if above_freezing(celsius):
        print('It is above freezing.')
    else:
        print('It is below freezing.')
                                                                    Ln: 10 Col: 28
```

Figure 5—Results of Removing the Parentheses

6.4   Tips for Grouping Your Functions

Put functions and variables that logically belong together in the same module. If there isn't some logical connection—for example, if one of the functions calculates how much carbon monoxide different kinds of cars produce, while another figures out bone strength given the bone's diameter and density—then you shouldn't put them in one module just because you happen to be the author of both.

Of course, people often have different opinions about what is logical and what isn't. Take Python's math module, for example; should functions to multiply matrices go in there too, or should they go in a separate linear algebra module? What about basic statistical functions? Going back to the previous paragraph, should a function that calculates gas mileage go in the same module as one that calculates carbon monoxide emissions? You can always find a reason why two functions should *not* be in the same module, but a thousand modules with one function each are going to be hard for people (including you) to work with.

```
Python 3.3.2 Shell
Python 3.3.2 (v3.3.2:d047928ae3f6, May 13 2013, 13:52:24)
[GCC 4.2.1 (Apple Inc. build 5666) (dot 3)] on darwin
Type "copyright", "credits" or "license()" for more information.
>>> ============================== RESTART ==============================
>>>
Enter the baking temperature in degrees Fahrenheit: 500
Preheat oven to 500.0 degrees F (482.22222222222223 degrees C).
>>> import doctest
>>> doctest.testmod()
**********************************************************************
File "/Users/user/baking.py", line 9, in __main__.get_preheating_instructions
Failed example:
    get_preheating_instructions(500)
Expected:
    'Preheat oven to 500 degrees F (260.0 degrees C).'
Got:
    'Preheat oven to 500 degrees F (482.22222222222223 degrees C).'
**********************************************************************
1 items had failures:
   1 of    1 in __main__.get_preheating_instructions
***Test Failed*** 1 failures.
TestResults(failed=1, attempted=1)
>>>
                                                              Ln: 23 Col: 4
```

Figure 6—Failure Message for doctest

As a rule of thumb, if a module has less than a handful of things in it, it's probably too small, and if you can't sum up the contents and purpose of a module in a one- or two-sentence docstring, it's probably too large. These are just guidelines, though; in the end, you'll have to decide based on how more experienced programmers have organized modules, like the ones in the Python standard library, and eventually on your own sense of style.

6.5 Organizing Our Thoughts

In this chapter, you learned the following:

- A module is a collection of functions and variables grouped together in a file. To use a module, you must first import it using import «modulename». After it has been imported, you refer to its contents using «modulename».«functionname» or «modulename».«variable».

- Variable _name_ is created by Python and can be used to specify that some code should only run when the module is run directly and not when the module is imported.

- Programs have to do more than just run to be useful; they have to run correctly. One way to ensure that they do is to test them, which you can do in Python using module doctest.

6.6 Exercises

Here are some exercises for you to try on your own. Solutions are available at http://pragprog.com/titles/gwpy2/practical-programming.

1. Import module math, and use its functions to complete the following exercises. (You can call dir(math) to get a listing of the items in math.)

   a. Write an expression that produces the floor of -2.8.
   b. Write an expression that rounds the value of -4.3 and then produces the absolute value of that result.
   c. Write an expression that produces the ceiling of the sine of 34.5.

2. In the following exercises, you will work with Python's calendar module:

   a. Visit the Python documentation website at http://docs.python.org/release/3.3.0/py-modindex.html, and look at the documentation on module calendar.
   b. Import module calendar.
   c. Using function help, read the description of function isleap.
   d. Use isleap to determine the next leap year.
   e. Use dir to get a list of what calendar contains.
   f. Find and use a function in module calendar to determine how many leap years there will be between the years 2000 and 2050, inclusive.
   g. Find and use a function in module calendar to determine which day of the week July 29, 2016, will be.

3. Create a file named exercise.py with this code inside it:

```
def average(num1, num2):
    """ (number, number) -> number

    Return the average of num1 and num2.

    >>> average(10,20)
    15.0
    >>> average(2.5, 3.0)
    2.75
    """

    return num1 + num2 / 2
```

   a. Run exercise.py. Import doctest and run doctest.testmod().

   b. Both of the tests in function average's docstring fail. Fix the code and rerun the tests. Repeat this procedure until the tests pass.

## CHAPTER 7

Using Methods

So far we've seen lots of functions: built-in functions, functions inside modules, and functions that we've defined. A *method* is another kind of function that is attached to a particular type. There are str methods, int methods, bool methods, and more—every type has its own set of methods. In this chapter, we'll explore how to use methods and also how they differ from the rest of the functions that we've seen.

7.1 Modules, Classes, and Methods

In Section 6.1, *Importing Modules*, on page 100, we saw that a module is a kind of object, one that can contain functions and other variables. There is another kind of object that is similar to a module: a *class*. You've been using classes all along, probably without realizing it: a class is how Python represents a type.

You may have called built-in function help on int, float, bool, or str. We'll do that now with str (notice that the first line says that it's a class):

```
>>> help(str)
Help on class str in module builtins:

class str(object)
 |  str(object[, encoding[, errors]]) -> str
 |
 |  Create a new string object from the given object. If encoding or
 |  errors is specified, then the object must expose a data buffer
 |  that will be decoded using the given encoding and error handler.
 |  Otherwise, returns the result of object.__str__() (if defined)
 |  or repr(object).
 |  encoding defaults to sys.getdefaultencoding().
 |  errors defaults to 'strict'.
 |
 |  Methods defined here:
```

```
  |
  |  __add__(...)
  |      x.__add__(y) <==> x+y
  |
  |  __contains__(...)
  |      x.__contains__(y) <==> y in x
```

[Lots of other names with leading and trailing underscores not shown here.]

```
  |  capitalize(...)
  |      S.capitalize() -> str
  |
  |      Return a capitalized version of S, i.e. make the first character
  |      have upper case and the rest lower case.
  |
  |  center(...)
  |      S.center(width[, fillchar]) -> str
  |
  |      Return S centered in a string of length width. Padding is
  |      done using the specified fill character (default is a space)
  |
  |  count(...)
  |      S.count(sub[, start[, end]]) -> int
  |
  |      Return the number of non-overlapping occurrences of substring sub in
  |      string S[start:end].  Optional arguments start and end are
  |      interpreted as in slice notation.
```

[There are many more of these as well.]

Near the top of this documentation is this:

```
  |  str(object[, encoding[, errors]]) -> str
  |
  |  Create a new string object from the given object.
```

That describes how to use str as a function: we can call it to create a string. For example, str(17) creates the string '17'.

We can also use str to call a method in class str, much like we call a function in module math. The main difference is that every method in class str requires a string as its first argument:

```
>>> str.capitalize('browning')
'Browning'
```

This is how methods are different from functions: the first argument to every string method must be a string, and the parameter is *not* described in the documentation for the method. This is because *all* string methods require a string as the first argument, and more generally, all methods in a class require an object of that class as the first argument. Here are two more examples, this time using the other two string methods from the code on page 115. Both of these also require a string as the first argument.

```
>>> str.center('Sonnet 43', 26)
'        Sonnet 43         '
>>> str.count('How do I love thee?  Let me count the ways.', 'the')
2
```

The first method call produces a new string that centers 'Sonnet 43' in a string of length 26, padding to the left and right with spaces.

The second method call counts how many times 'the' occurs in 'How do I love thee? Let me count the ways.' (once in the word thee and once as the penultimate word in the string).

7.2 Calling Methods the Object-Oriented Way

Because every method in class str requires a string as the first argument (and, more generally, because every method in any class requires an object of that class as the first argument), Python provides a shorthand form for calling a method where the object appears first and then the method call:

```
>>> 'browning'.capitalize()
'Browning'
>>> 'Sonnet 43'.center(26)
'        Sonnet 43         '
>>> 'How do I love thee?  Let me count the ways.'.count('the')
2
```

When Python encounters one of these method calls, it translates it to the more long-winded form. We will use this shorthand form throughout the rest of the book.

The help documentation for methods uses this form. Here is the help for method lower in class str. (Notice that we can get help for a single method by prefixing it with the class it belongs to.)

```
>>> help(str.lower)
Help on method_descriptor:

lower(...)
    S.lower() -> str

    Return a copy of the string S converted to lowercase.
```

Contrast that documentation with the help for function sqrt in module math:

```
>>> import math
>>> help(math.sqrt)
Help on built-in function sqrt in module math:

sqrt(...)
    sqrt(x)

    Return the square root of x.
```

The help for str.lower shows that you need to prefix the call with the string value S; the help for math.sqrt doesn't show any such prefix.

The general form of a method call is as follows:

«expression».«method_name»(«arguments»)

So far every example we've seen has a single object as the expression, but any expression can be used as long as it evaluates to the correct type. Here's an example:

```
>>> ('TTA' + 'G' * 3).count('T')
2
```

The expression ('TTA' + 'G' * 3) evaluates to the DNA sequence 'TTAGGG', and that is the object that is used in the call on string method count.

Here are the steps for executing a method call. These steps are quite similar to those for executing a function call in Section 3.5, *Tracing Function Calls in the Memory Model*, on page 40.

1. Evaluate «expression»; this may be something simple, like 'Elizabeth Barrett Browning' (a poet from the 1800s), or it may be more complicated, like ('TTA' + 'G' * 3). Either way, a single object is produced, and that will be the object we are interacting with during the method call.

2. Now that we have an object, evaluate the method arguments left to right. In our DNA example, the argument is 'T'.

3. Pass the result of evaluating the initial expression as the first argument, and also pass the argument values from the previous step, into the method. In our DNA example, our code is equivalent to str.count('TTAGGG', 'T').

4. Execute the method.

When the method call finishes, it produces a value. In our DNA example, str.count('TTAGGG', 'T') returns the number of times 'T' occurs in 'TTAGGG', which is 2.

> ### Why Programming Languages Are Called *Object Oriented*
>
> The phrase *object oriented* was introduced to describe the style of programming where the objects are the main focus: we tell objects to do things (by calling their methods), as opposed to *imperative* programming, where functions are the primary focus and we pass them objects to work with. Python allows a mixture of both styles.

7.3 Exploring String Methods

Strings are central to programming; almost every program uses strings in some way. We'll explore some of the ways in which we can manipulate strings and, at the same time, firm up our understanding of methods.

The most commonly used string methods are listed in Table 7, *Common String Methods*. (You can find the complete list in Python's online documentation, or type help(str) into the shell.)

Method	Description
str.capitalize()	Returns a copy of the string with the first letter capitalized and the rest lowercase
str.count(s)	Returns the number of nonoverlapping occurrences of s in the string
str.endswith(end)	Returns True iff the string ends with the characters in the end string—this is case sensitive.
str.find(s)	Returns the index of the first occurrence of s in the string, or -1 if s doesn't occur in the string—the first character is at index 0. This is case sensitive.
str.find(s, beg)	Returns the index of the first occurrence of s at or after index beg in the string, or -1 if s doesn't occur in the string at or after index beg—the first character is at index 0. This is case sensitive.
str.find(s, beg, end)	Returns the index of the first occurrence of s between indices beg (inclusive) and end (exclusive) in the string, or -1 if s does not occur in the string between indices beg and end—the first character is at index 0. This is case sensitive.
str.format(«expressions»)	Returns a string made by substituting for placeholder fields in the string—each field is a pair of braces ('{' and '}') with an integer in between; the expression arguments are numbered from left to right starting

Method	Description
	at 0. Each field is replaced by the value produced by evaluating the expression whose index corresponds with the integer in between the braces of the field. If an expression produces a value that isn't a string, that value is converted into a string.
str.islower()	Returns True iff all characters in the string are lowercase
str.isupper()	Returns True iff all characters in the string are uppercase
str.lower()	Returns a copy of the string with all letters converted to lowercase
str.lstrip()	Returns a copy of the string with leading whitespace removed
str.lstrip(s)	Returns a copy of the string with leading occurrences of the characters in s removed
str.replace(old, new)	Returns a copy of the string with all occurrences of substring old replaced with string new
str.rstrip()	Returns a copy of the string with trailing whitespace removed
str.rstrip(s)	Returns a copy of the string with trailing occurrences of the characters in s removed
str.split()	Returns the whitespace-separated words in the string as a list (We'll introduce the list type in Section 8.1, *Storing and Accessing Data in Lists*, on page 129.)
str.startswith(beginning)	Returns True iff the string starts with the letters in the string beginning—this is case sensitive.
str.strip()	Returns a copy of the string with leading and trailing whitespace removed
str.strip(s)	Returns a copy of the string with leading and trailing occurrences of the characters in s removed
str.swapcase()	Returns a copy of the string with all lowercase letters capitalized and all uppercase letters made lowercase
str.upper()	Returns a copy of the string with all letters converted to uppercase

Table 7—Common String Methods

Method calls look almost the same as function calls, except that in order to call a method we need an object of the type associated with that method. For example, let's call the method startswith on the string 'species':

```
>>> 'species'.startswith('a')
False
>>> 'species'.startswith('spe')
True
```

String method startswith takes a string argument and returns a bool indicating whether the string whose method was called—the one to the left of the dot—starts with the string that is given as an argument. There is also an endswith method:

```
>>> 'species'.endswith('a')
False
>>> 'species'.endswith('es')
True
```

Sometimes strings have extra whitespace at the beginning and the end. The string methods lstrip, rstrip, and strip remove this whitespace from the front, from the end, and from both, respectively. This example shows the result of applying these three methods to a string with leading and trailing whitespace:

```
>>> compound = '    \n  Methyl \n butanol   \n'
>>> compound.lstrip()
'Methyl \n butanol   \n'
>>> compound.rstrip()
'    \n  Methyl \n butanol'
>>> compound.strip()
'Methyl \n butanol'
```

Note that the other whitespace inside the string is unaffected; these methods only work from the front and end. Here is another example that uses string method swapcase to change lowercase letters to uppercase and uppercase to lowercase:

```
>>> 'Computer Science'.swapcase()
'cOMPUTER sCIENCE'
```

String method format has a complex description, but a couple of examples should clear up the confusion. Here we show that we can substitute a series of strings into a format string:

```
>>> '"{0}" is derived from "{1}"'.format('none', 'no one')
'"none" is derived from "no one"'
>>> '"{0}" is derived from the {1} "{2}"'.format('Etymology', 'Greek',
...                                              'ethos')
'"Etymology" is derived from the Greek "ethos"'
>>> '"{0}" is derived from the {2} "{1}"'.format('December', 'decem', 'Latin')
'"December" is derived from the Latin "decem"'
```

We can have any number of fields. The last example shows that we don't have to use the numbers in order.

Next, using string method format, we'll specify the number of decimal places to round a number to. We indicate this by following the field number with a colon and then using .2f to state that the number should be formatted as a floating-point number with two digits to the right of the decimal point:

```
>>> my_pi = 3.14159
>>> 'Pi rounded to {0} decimal places is {1:.2f}.'.format(2, my_pi)
'Pi rounded to 2 decimal places is 3.14.'
>>> 'Pi rounded to {0} decimal places is {1:.3f}.'.format(3, my_pi)
'Pi rounded to 3 decimal places is 3.142.'
```

It's possible to omit the position numbers. If that's done, then the arguments passed to format replace each placeholder field in order from left to right:

```
>>> 'Pi rounded to {} decimal places is {:.3f}.'.format(3, my_pi)
'Pi rounded to 3 decimal places is 3.142.'
```

Remember how a method call starts with an expression? Because 'Computer Science'.swapcase() is an expression, we can immediately call method endswith on the result of that expression to check whether that result has 'ENCE' as its last four characters:

```
>>> 'Computer Science'.swapcase().endswith('ENCE')
True
```

Figure 7, *Chaining Method Calls*, gives a picture of what happens when we do this:

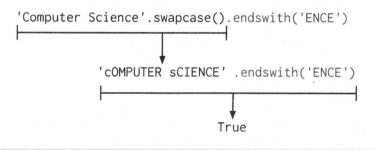

Figure 7—Chaining Method Calls

The call on method swapcase produces a new string, and that new string is used for the call on method endswith.

Both int and float are classes. It is possible to access the documentation for these either by calling help(int) or by calling help on an object of the class:

```
>>> help(0)
Help on int object:

class int(object)
 |  int(x[, base]) -> integer
 |
 |  Convert a string or number to an integer, if possible.  A floating
 |  point argument will be truncated towards zero (this does not include a
 |  string representation of a floating point number!)  When converting a
 |  string, use the optional base.  It is an error to supply a base when
 |  converting a non-string.
 |
 |  Methods defined here:
 |
 |  __abs__(...)
 |      x.__abs__() <==> abs(x)
 |
 |  __add__(...)
 |      x.__add__(y) <==> x+y
 ...
```

Most modern programming languages are structured this way: the "things" in the program are objects, and most of the code in the program consists of methods that use the data stored in those objects. Chapter 14, *Object-Oriented Programming*, on page 269, will show you how to create new kinds of objects; until then, we'll work with objects of types that are built into Python.

7.4 What Are Those Underscores?

Any method (or other name) beginning and ending with two underscores is considered special by Python. The help documentation for strings shows these methods, among many others:

```
 |  Methods defined here:
 |
 |  __add__(...)
 |      x.__add__(y) <==> x+y
```

These methods are typically connected with some other syntax in Python: use of that syntax will trigger a method call. For example, string method _add_ is called when anything is added to a string:

```
>>> 'TTA' + 'GGG'
'TTAGGG'
>>> 'TTA'.__add__('GGG')
'TTAGGG'
```

Programmers almost *never* call these special methods directly, but is eye-opening to see this and may help you to understand how Python works.

Integers and floating-point numbers have similar features. Here is part of the help documentation for int:

```
Help on class int in module builtins:

class int(object)
...
 |  Methods defined here:
 |
 |  __abs__(...)
 |      x.__abs__() <==> abs(x)
 |
 |  __add__(...)
 |      x.__add__(y) <==> x+y
 |
 |  __gt__(...)
 |      x.__gt__(y) <==> x>y
```

The documentation describes when these are called. Here we show both versions of getting the absolute value of a number:

```
>>> abs(-3)
3
>>> -3 .__abs__()
3
```

We need to put a space after -3 in the second instance (with the underscores) so that Python doesn't think we're making a floating-point number -3. (remember that we can leave off the trailing 0).

Let's add two integers using this trick:

```
>>> 3 + 5
8
>>> 3 .__add__(5)
8
```

And here we compare two numbers to see whether one is bigger than the other:

```
>>> 3 > 5
False
>>> 3 .__gt__(5)
False
>>> 5 > 3
True
>>> 5 .__gt__(3)
True
```

Again, programmers don't typically do this, but it is worth knowing that Python uses methods to handle all of these operators.

Function objects, like other objects, contain double-underscore variables. For example, the documentation for each function is stored in a variable called __doc__:

```
>>> abs.__doc__
'abs(number) -> number\n\nReturn the absolute value of the argument.'
```

When we use built-in function print to print that _doc_ string, look what comes out! It looks just like the output from calling built-in function help on abs:

```
>>> print(abs.__doc__)
abs(number) -> number

Return the absolute value of the argument.
>>> help(abs)
Help on built-in function abs in module builtins:

abs(...)
    abs(number) -> number

    Return the absolute value of the argument.
```

Every function object keeps track of its docstring in a special variable called __doc__.

7.5 A Methodical Review

- Classes are like modules, except that classes contain methods and modules contain functions.

- Methods are like functions, except that the first argument must be an object of the class in which the method is defined.

- Method calls in this form—'browning'.capitalize()—are shorthand for this: str.capitalize('browning').

- Methods beginning and ending with two underscores are considered special by Python, and they are triggered by particular syntax.

7.6 Exercises

Here are some exercises for you to try on your own. Solutions are available at http://pragprog.com/titles/gwpy2/practical-programming.

1. In the Python shell, execute the following method calls:

    a. 'hello'.upper()
    b. 'Happy Birthday!'.lower()
    c. 'WeeeEEEEeeeEEEEeee'.swapcase()

    d.   'ABC123'.isupper()

    e.   'aeiouAEIOU'.count('a')

    f.   'hello'.endswith('o')

    g.   'hello'.startswith('H')

    h.   'Hello {0}'.format('Python')

    i.   'Hello {0}! Hello {1}!'.format('Python', 'World')

2. Using string method count, write an expression that produces the number of o's in 'tomato'.

3. Using string method find, write an expression that produces the index of the first occurrence of o in 'tomato'.

4. Using string method find, write a *single* expression that produces the index of the *second* occurrence of o in 'tomato'. Hint: Call find twice.

5. Using your expression from the previous exercise, find the second o in 'avocado'. If you don't get the result you expect, revise the expression and try again.

6. Using string method replace, write an expression that produces a string based on 'runner' with the n's replaced by b's.

7. Variable s refers to ' yes   '. When a string method is called with s as its argument, the string 'yes' is produced. Which string method was called?

8. Variable fruit refers to 'pineapple'. For the following function calls, in what order are the subexpressions evaluated?

    a.   fruit.find('p', fruit.count('p'))

    b.   fruit.count(fruit.upper().swapcase())

    c.   fruit.replace(fruit.swapcase(), fruit.lower())

9. Variable season refers to 'summer'. Using string method format and variable season, write an expression that produces 'I love summer!'

10. Variables side1, side2, and side3 refer to 3, 4, and 5, respectively. Using string method format and those three variables, write an expression that produces 'The sides have lengths 3, 4, and 5.'

11. Using string methods, write expressions that produce the following:

    a.   A copy of 'boolean' capitalized

    b.   The first occurrence of '2' in 'CO2 H2O'

    c.   The second occurrence of '2' in 'CO2 H2O'

    d.   True if and only if 'Boolean' begins lowercase

    e.   A copy of "MoNDaY" converted to lowercase and then capitalized

    f.   A copy of " Monday" with the leading whitespace removed

12. Complete the examples in the docstring and then write the body of the following function:

```python
def total_occurrences(s1, s2, ch):
    """ (str, str, str) -> int

    Precondition: len(ch) == 1

    Return the total number of times that ch occurs in s1 and s2.

    >>> total_occurrences('color', 'yellow', 'l')
    3
    >>> total_occurrences('red', 'blue', 'l')

    >>> total_occurrences('green', 'purple', 'b')

    """
```

CHAPTER 8

Storing Collections of Data Using Lists

Up to this point, we have seen numbers, Boolean values, strings, functions, and a few other types. Once one of these objects has been created, it can't be modified. In this chapter, you will learn how to use a Python type named list. Lists contain zero or more objects and are used to keep track of collections of data. Unlike the other types you've learned about, lists can be modified.

8.1 Storing and Accessing Data in Lists

Table 8, *Gray Whale Census*, shows the number of gray whales counted near the Coal Oil Point Natural Reserve in a two-week period starting on February 24, 2008.[1]

Day	Number of Whales	Day	Number of Whales
1	5	8	6
2	4	9	4
3	7	10	2
4	3	11	1
5	2	12	7
6	3	13	1
7	2	14	3

Table 8—Gray Whale Census

Using what we have seen so far, we would have to create fourteen variables to keep track of the number of whales counted each day:

1. Gray Whales Count nonprofit 501(c)(3) corporation for research and education: http://www.graywhalescount.org/GWC/Do_Whales_Count_files/2008CountDaily.pdf.

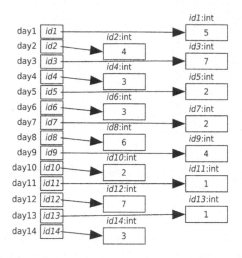

To track an entire year's worth of observations, we would need 365 variables (366 for a leap year).

Rather than dealing with this programming nightmare, we can use a *list* to keep track of the 14 days of whale counts. That is, we can use a list to keep track of the 14 int objects that contain the counts:

```
>>> whales = [5, 4, 7, 3, 2, 3, 2, 6, 4, 2, 1, 7, 1, 3]
>>> whales
[5, 4, 7, 3, 2, 3, 2, 6, 4, 2, 1, 7, 1, 3]
```

A list is an object; like any other object, it can be assigned to a variable. Here is what happens in the memory model:

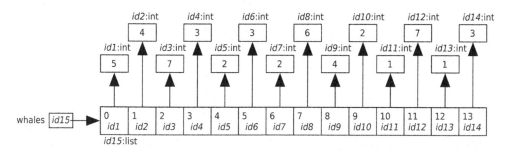

The general form of a list expression is as follows:

```
[«expression1», «expression2», ... , «expressionN»]
```

The empty list is expressed as [].

In our whale count example, variable whales refers to a list with fourteen items, also known as *elements*. The list itself is an object, but it also contains the memory addresses of fourteen other objects. The memory model above shows whales after this assignment statement has been executed.

The items in a list are ordered, and each item has an *index* indicating its position in the list. The first item in a list is at index 0, the second at index 1, and so on. It would be more natural to use 1 as the first index, as human languages do. Python, however, uses the same convention as languages like C and Java and starts counting at zero. To refer to a particular list item, we put the index in brackets after a reference to the list (such as the name of a variable):

```
>>> whales = [5, 4, 7, 3, 2, 3, 2, 6, 4, 2, 1, 7, 1, 3]
>>> whales[0]
5
>>> whales[1]
4
>>> whales[12]
1
>>> whales[13]
3
```

We can use only those indices that are in the range from zero up to one less than the length of the list, because the list index starts at 0, not at 1. In a fourteen-item list, the legal indices are 0, 1, 2, and so on, up to 13. Trying to use an out-of-range index results in an error:

```
>>> whales = [5, 4, 7, 3, 2, 3, 2, 6, 4, 2, 1, 7, 1, 3]
>>> whales[1001]
Traceback (most recent call last):
  File "<stdin>", line 1, in ?
IndexError: list index out of range
```

Unlike most programming languages, Python also lets us index backward from the end of a list. The last item is at index -1, the one before it at index -2, and so on. Negative indices provide a way to access the last item, second-to-last item and so on, without having to figure out the size of the list:

```
>>> whales = [5, 4, 7, 3, 2, 3, 2, 6, 4, 2, 1, 7, 1, 3]
>>> whales[-1]
3
>>> whales[-2]
1
>>> whales[-14]
5
>>> whales[-15]
Traceback (most recent call last):
  File "<stdin>", line 1, in <module>
IndexError: list index out of range
```

Since each item in a list is an object, the items can be assigned to other variables:

```
>>> whales = [5, 4, 7, 3, 2, 3, 2, 6, 4, 2, 1, 7, 1, 3]
>>> third = whales[2]
>>> print('Third day:', third)
Third day: 7
```

In Section 8.5, *Aliasing: What's in a Name?*, on page 138, you will learn that an entire list, such as the one that whales refers to, can be assigned to other variables and discover the effect that that has.

The Empty List

In Chapter 4, *Working with Text*, on page 65, we saw the empty string, which doesn't contain any characters. There is also an *empty list*. An empty list is a list with no items in it. As with all lists, an empty list is represented using brackets:

```
>>> whales = []
```

Since an empty list has no items, trying to index an empty list results in an error:

```
>>> whales[0]
Traceback (most recent call last):
  File "<stdin>", line 1, in <module>
IndexError: list index out of range
>>> whales[-1]
Traceback (most recent call last):
  File "<stdin>", line 1, in <module>
IndexError: list index out of range
```

Lists Are Heterogeneous

Lists can contain any type of data, including integers, strings, and even other lists. Here is a list of information about the element krypton, including its name, symbol, melting point (in degrees Celsius), and boiling point (also in degrees Celsius):

```
>>> krypton = ['Krypton', 'Kr', -157.2, -153.4]
>>> krypton[1]
'Kr'
>>> krypton[2]
-157.2
```

A list is usually used to contain items of the same kind, like temperatures or dates or grades in a course. A list can be used to aggregate related information of different kinds, as we did with krypton, but this is prone to error. Here, we need to remember which temperature comes first and whether the name or the symbol starts the list. Another common source of bugs is when you forget to include a piece of data in your list (or perhaps it was missing in your source of information). How, for example, would you keep track of similar information for iridium if you don't know the melting point? What information would you put at index 2? A better, but more advanced, way to do this is described in Chapter 14, *Object-Oriented Programming*, on page 269.

8.2 Modifying Lists

Suppose you're typing in a list of the noble gases and your fingers slip:

```
>>> nobles = ['helium', 'none', 'argon', 'krypton', 'xenon', 'radon']
```

The error here is that you typed 'none' instead of 'neon'. Here's the memory model that was created by that assignment statement:

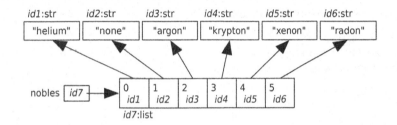

Rather than retyping the whole list, you can assign a new value to a specific element of the list:

```
>>> nobles[1] = 'neon'
>>> nobles
['helium', 'neon', 'argon', 'krypton', 'xenon', 'radon']
```

Here is the result after the assignment to nobles[1]:

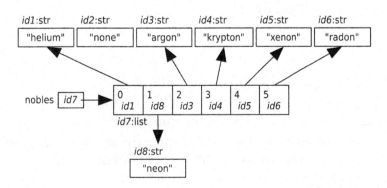

That memory model also shows that list objects are *mutable*. That is, the contents of a list can be *mutated*.

In the code above, nobles[1] was used on the left side of the assignment operator. It can also be used on the right side. In general, an expression of the form L[i] (list L at index i) behaves just like a simple variable (see Section 2.4, *Variables and Computer Memory: Remembering Values*, on page 15).

If L[i] is used in an expression (such as on the right of an assignment statement), it means "Get the value referred to by the memory address at index i of list L."

On the other hand, if L[i] is on the left of an assignment statement (as in nobles[1] = 'neon'), it means "Look up the memory address at index i of list L so it can be overwritten."

In contrast to lists, numbers and strings are *immutable*. You cannot, for example, change a letter in a string. Methods that appear to do that, like upper, actually create new strings:

```
>>> name = 'Darwin'
>>> capitalized = name.upper()
>>> print(capitalized)
DARWIN
>>> print(name)
Darwin
```

Because strings are immutable, it is only possible to use an expression of the form s[i] (string s at index i) on the right side of the assignment operator.

8.3 Operations on Lists

Section 3.1, *Functions That Python Provides*, on page 31, and *Operations on Strings*, on page 66, introduced a few of Python's built-in functions. Some of these, such as len, can be applied to lists, as well as others we haven't seen before. (See the following table.)

Function	Description
len(L)	Returns the number of items in list L
max(L)	Returns the maximum value in list L
min(L)	Returns the minimum value in list L
sum(L)	Returns the sum of the values in list L
sorted(L)	Returns a copy of list L where the items are in order from smallest to largest (This does not mutate L.)

Table 9—List Functions

Here are some examples. The half-life of a radioactive substance is the time taken for half of it to decay. After twice this time has gone by, three quarters of the material will have decayed; after three times, seven eighths, and so on.

An *isotope* is a form of a chemical element. Plutonium has several isotopes, and each has a different half-life. Here are some of the built-in functions in action working on a list of the half-lives of plutonium isotopes Pu-238, Pu-239, Pu-240, Pu-241, and Pu-242:

```
>>> half_lives = [887.7, 24100.0, 6563.0, 14, 373300.0]
>>> len(half_lives)
5
>>> max(half_lives)
373300.0
>>> min(half_lives)
14
>>> sum(half_lives)
404864.7
>>> sorted(half_lives)
[14, 887.7, 6563.0, 24100.0, 373300.0]
>>> half_lives
[887.7, 24100.0, 6563.0, 14, 373300.0]
```

In addition to built-in functions, some of the operators that we have seen can also be applied to lists. Like strings, lists can be combined using the concatenation (+) operator:

```
>>> original = ['H', 'He', 'Li']
>>> final = original + ['Be']
>>> final
['H', 'He', 'Li', 'Be']
```

This code doesn't mutate either of the original list objects. Instead, it creates a new list whose entries refer to the items in the original lists.

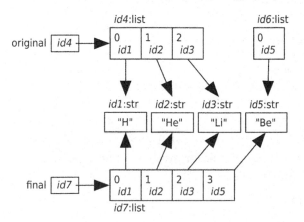

A list has a type, and Python complains if you use a value of some type in an inappropriate way. For example, an error occurs when the concatenation operator is applied to a list and a string:

```
>>> ['H', 'He', 'Li'] + 'Be'
Traceback (most recent call last):
  File "<stdin>", line 1, in <module>
TypeError: can only concatenate list (not "str") to list
```

You can also multiply a list by an integer to get a new list containing the elements from the original list repeated that number of times:

```
>>> metals = ['Fe', 'Ni']
>>> metals * 3
['Fe', 'Ni', 'Fe', 'Ni', 'Fe', 'Ni']
```

As with concatenation, the original list isn't modified; instead, a new list is created.

One operator that does modify a list is del, which stands for delete. It can be used to remove an item from a list, as follows:

```
>>> metals = ['Fe', 'Ni']
>>> del metals[0]
>>> metals
['Ni']
```

The In Operator on Lists

The in operator can be applied to lists to check whether an object is in a list:

```
>>> nobles = ['helium', 'neon', 'argon', 'krypton', 'xenon', 'radon']
>>> gas = input('Enter a gas: ')
Enter a gas: argon
>>> if gas in nobles:
...     print('{} is noble.'.format(gas))
...
argon is noble.
>>> gas = input('Enter a gas: ')
Enter a gas: nitrogen
>>> if gas in nobles:
...     print('{} is noble.'.format(gas))
...
>>>
```

Unlike with strings, when used with lists, the in operator checks only for a single item; it does not check for sublists. This code checks whether the list [1, 2] is an item in the list [0, 1, 2, 3]:

```
>>> [1, 2] in [0, 1, 2, 3]
False
```

8.4 Slicing Lists

Geneticists describe *C. elegans* phenotypes (nematodes, a type of microscopic worms) using three-letter short-form markers. Examples include *Emb* (embryonic lethality), *Him* (high incidence of males), *Unc* (uncoordinated), *Dpy* (dumpy: short and fat), *Sma* (small), and *Lon* (long). We can keep a list:

```
>>> celegans_phenotypes = ['Emb', 'Him', 'Unc', 'Lon', 'Dpy', 'Sma']
>>> celegans_phenotypes
['Emb', 'Him', 'Unc', 'Lon', 'Dpy', 'Sma']
```

It turns out that *Dpy* worms and *Sma* worms are difficult to distinguish from each other, so they aren't as easily differentiated in complex strains. We can produce a new list based on celegans_phenotypes but without *Dpy* or *Sma* by taking a *slice* of the list:

```
>>> celegans_phenotypes = ['Emb', 'Him', 'Unc', 'Lon', 'Dpy', 'Sma']
>>> useful_markers = celegans_phenotypes[0:4]
```

This creates a new list consisting of only the four distinguishable markers, which are the first four items from the list that celegans_phenotypes refers to:

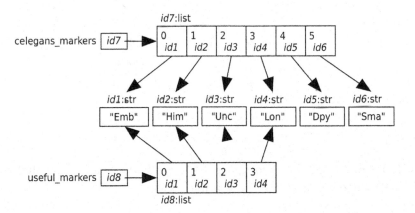

The first index in the slice is the starting point. The second index is *one more than* the index of the last item we want to include. For example, the last item we wanted to include, Lon, had an index of 3, so we use 4 for the second index. More rigorously, list[i:j] is a slice of the original list from index i (inclusive) up to, but not including, index j (exclusive). Python uses this convention to be consistent with the rule that the legal indices for a list go from 0 up to one less than the list's length.

The first index can be omitted if we want to slice from the beginning of the list, and the last index can be omitted if we want to slice to the end:

```
>>> celegans_phenotypes = ['Emb', 'Him', 'Unc', 'Lon', 'Dpy', 'Sma']
>>> celegans_phenotypes[:4]
['Emb', 'Him', 'Unc', 'Lon']
>>> celegans_phenotypes[4:]
['Dpy', 'Sma']
```

To create a copy of the entire list, omit both indices so that the "slice" runs from the start of the list to its end:

```
>>> celegans_phenotypes = ['Emb', 'Him', 'Unc', 'Lon', 'Dpy', 'Sma']
>>> celegans_copy = celegans_phenotypes[:]
>>> celegans_phenotypes[5] = 'Lvl'
>>> celegans_phenotypes
['Emb', 'Him', 'Unc', 'Lon', 'Dpy', 'Lvl']
>>> celegans_copy
['Emb', 'Him', 'Unc', 'Lon', 'Dpy', 'Sma']
```

The list referred to by celegans_copy is a *clone* of the list referred to by celegans_phenotypes. The lists have the same items, but the lists themselves are different objects at different memory addresses:

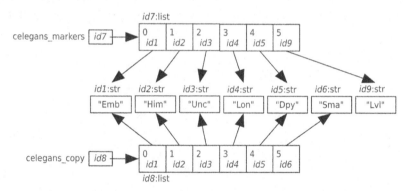

In Section 8.6, *List Methods*, on page 140, you will learn about a list method that can be used to make a copy of a list.

8.5 Aliasing: What's in a Name?

An *alias* is an alternative name for something. In Python, two variables are said to be aliases when they contain the same memory address. For example, the following code creates two variables, both of which refer to a single list:

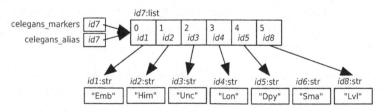

When we modify the list using one of the variables, references through the other variable show the change as well:

```
>>> celegans_phenotypes = ['Emb', 'Him', 'Unc', 'Lon', 'Dpy', 'Sma']
>>> celegans_alias = celegans_phenotypes
>>> celegans_phenotypes[5] = 'Lvl'
>>> celegans_phenotypes
['Emb', 'Him', 'Unc', 'Lon', 'Dpy', 'Lvl']
>>> celegans_alias
['Emb', 'Him', 'Unc', 'Lon', 'Dpy', 'Lvl']
```

Aliasing is one of the reasons why the notion of mutability is important. For example, if x and y refer to the same list, then any changes you make to the list through x will be "seen" by y, and vice versa. This can lead to all sorts of hard-to-find errors in which a list's value changes as if by magic, even though your program doesn't appear to assign anything to it. This can't happen with immutable values like strings. Since a string can't be changed after it has been created, it's safe to have aliases for it.

Mutable Parameters

Aliasing occurs when you use list parameters as well, since parameters are variables. Here is a simple function that takes a list, removes its last item, and returns the list:

```
>>> def remove_last_item(L):
...     """ (list) -> list
...
...     Return list L with the last item removed.
...
...     Precondition: len(L) >= 0
...
...     >>> remove_last_item([1, 3, 2, 4])
...     [1, 3, 2]
...     """
...     del L[-1]
...     return L
...
>>>
```

In the code that follows, a list is created and stored in a variable; then that variable is passed as an argument to remove_last_item:

```
>>> celegans_markers = ['Emb', 'Him', 'Unc', 'Lon', 'Dpy', 'Lvl']
>>> remove_last_item(celegans_markers)
['Emb', 'Him', 'Unc', 'Lon', 'Dpy']
>>> celegans_markers
['Emb', 'Him', 'Unc', 'Lon', 'Dpy']
```

When the call on function remove_last_item is executed, parameter L is assigned the memory address that celegans_markers contains. That makes celegans_markers and L aliases. When the last item of the list that L refers to is removed, that change is "seen" by celegan_markers as well.

Since remove_last_item modifies the list parameter, the modified list doesn't actually need to be returned. You can remove the return statement:

```
>>> def remove_last_item(L):
...     """ (list) -> NoneType
...
...     Remove the last item from L.
...
...     Precondition: len(L) >= 0
...
...     >>> remove_last_item([1, 3, 2, 4])
...     """
...     del L[-1]
...
>>> celegans_markers = ['Emb', 'Him', 'Unc', 'Lon', 'Dpy', 'Lvl']
>>> remove_last_item(celegans_markers)
>>> celegans_markers
['Emb', 'Him', 'Unc', 'Lon', 'Dpy']
```

As we'll see in Section 8.6, *List Methods*, on page 140, several methods modify a list and return None, like the second version of remove_last_item.

8.6 List Methods

Lists are objects and thus have methods. Table 10, *List Methods*, on page 141 gives some of the most commonly used list methods.

Here is a sample interaction showing how we can use list methods to construct a list of many colors:

```
>>> colors = ['red', 'orange', 'green']
>>> colors.extend(['black', 'blue'])
>>> colors
['red', 'orange', 'green', 'black', 'blue']
>>> colors.append('purple')
>>> colors
['red', 'orange', 'green', 'black', 'blue', 'purple']
>>> colors.insert(2, 'yellow')
>>> colors
['red', 'orange', 'yellow', 'green', 'black', 'blue', 'purple']
>>> colors.remove('black')
>>> colors
['red', 'orange', 'yellow', 'green', 'blue', 'purple']
```

Method	Description
L.append(v)	Appends value v to list L
L.clear()	Removes all items from list L
L.count(v)	Returns the number of occurrences of v in list L
L.extend(v)	Appends the items in v to L
L.index(v)	Returns the index of the first occurrence of v in L—an error is raised if v doesn't occur in L.
L.index(v, beg)	Returns the index of the first occurrence of v at or after index beg in L—an error is raised if v doesn't occur in that part of L.
L.index(v, beg, end)	Returns the index of the first occurrence of v between indices beg (inclusive) and end (exclusive) in L; an error is raised if v doesn't occur in that part of L.
L.insert(i, v)	Inserts value v at index i in list L, shifting subsequent items to make room
L.pop()	Removes and returns the last item of L (which must be nonempty)
L.remove(v)	Removes the first occurrence of value v from list L
L.reverse()	Reverses the order of the values in list L
L.sort()	Sorts the values in list L in ascending order (for strings with the same letter case, it sorts in alphabetical order)
L.sort(reverse=True)	Sorts the values in list L in descending order (for strings with the same letter case, it sorts in reverse alphabetical order)

Table 10—List Methods

All the methods shown above modify the list instead of creating a new list. The same is true for the methods clear, reverse, sort, and pop. Of those methods, only pop returns a value other than None. (pop returns the item that was removed from the list.) In fact, the only method that returns a list is copy, which is equivalent to L[:].

Finally, a call to append isn't the same as using +. First, append appends a single value, while + expects two lists as operands. Second, append modifies the list rather than creating a new one.

Where Did My List Go?

Programmers occasionally forget that many list methods return None rather than creating and returning a new list. As a result, lists sometimes seem to disappear:

```
>>> colors = 'red orange yellow green blue purple'.split()
>>> colors
['red', 'orange', 'yellow', 'green', 'blue', 'purple']
>>> sorted_colors = colors.sort()
>>> print(sorted_colors)
None
```

In this example, colors.sort() did two things: it sorted the items in the list, and it returned the value None. That's why variable sorted_colors refers to None. Variable colors, on the other hand, refers to the sorted list:

```
>>> colors
['blue', 'green', 'orange', 'purple', 'red', 'yellow']
```

Methods that mutate a collection, such as append and sort, return None; it's a common error to expect that they'll return the resulting list. As we discussed in Section 6.3, *Testing Your Code Semiautomatically*, on page 110, mistakes like these can be caught by writing and running a few tests.

8.7 Working with a List of Lists

We said in *Lists Are Heterogeneous*, on page 132, that lists can contain any type of data. That means that they can contain other lists. A list whose items are lists is called a *nested list*. For example, the following nested list describes life expectancies in different countries:

```
>>> life = [['Canada', 76.5], ['United States', 75.5], ['Mexico', 72.0]]
```

Here is the memory model that results from execution of that assignment statement:

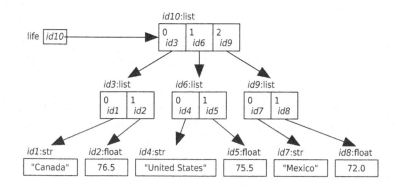

Notice that each item in the outer list is itself a list of two items. We use the standard indexing notation to access the items in the outer list:

```
>>> life = [['Canada', 76.5], ['United States', 75.5], ['Mexico', 72.0]]
>>> life[0]
['Canada', 76.5]
>>> life[1]
['United States', 75.5]
>>> life[2]
['Mexico', 72.0]
```

Since each of these items is also a list, we can index it again, just as we can chain together method calls or nest function calls:

```
>>> life = [['Canada', 76.5], ['United States', 75.5], ['Mexico', 72.0]]
>>> life[1]
['United States', 75.5]
>>> life[1][0]
'United States'
>>> life[1][1]
75.5
```

We can also assign sublists to variables:

```
>>> life = [['Canada', 76.5], ['United States', 75.5], ['Mexico', 72.0]]
>>> canada = life[0]
>>> canada
['Canada', 76.5]
>>> canada[0]
'Canada'
>>> canada[1]
76.5
```

Assigning a sublist to a variable creates an alias for that sublist:

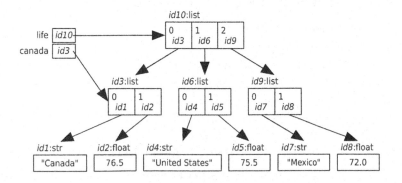

As before, any change we make through the sublist reference will be seen when we access the main list, and vice versa:

```
>>> life = [['Canada', 76.5], ['United States', 75.5], ['Mexico', 72.0]]
>>> canada = life[0]
>>> canada[1] = 80.0
>>> canada
['Canada', 80.0]
>>> life
[['Canada', 80.0], ['United States', 75.5], ['Mexico', 72.0]]
```

8.8 A Summary List

In this chapter, you learned the following:

- Lists are used to keep track of zero or more objects. The objects in a list are called items or elements. Each item has a position in the list called an index and that position ranges from zero to one less than the length of the list.

- Lists can contain any type of data, including other lists.

- Lists are mutable, which means that their contents can be modified.

- Slicing is used to create new lists that have the same values or a subset of the values of the originals.

- When two variables refer to the same object, they are called aliases.

8.9 Exercises

Here are some exercises for you to try on your own. Solutions are available at http://pragprog.com/titles/gwpy2/practical-programming.

1. Variable kingdoms refers to the list ['Bacteria', 'Protozoa', 'Chromista', 'Plantae', 'Fungi', 'Animalia']. Using kingdoms and either slicing or indexing with positive indices, write expressions that produce the following:

   a. The first item of kingdoms
   b. The last item of kingdoms
   c. The list ['Bacteria', 'Protozoa', 'Chromista']
   d. The list ['Chromista', 'Plantae', 'Fungi']
   e. The list ['Fungi', 'Animalia']
   f. The empty list

2. Repeat the previous exercise using negative indices.

3. Variable appointments refers to the list ['9:00', '10:30', '14:00', '15:00', '15:30']. An appointment is scheduled for 16:30, so '16:30' needs to be added to the list.

a. Using list method append, add '16:30' to the end of the list that appoint-
    ments refers to.

b. Instead of using append, use the + operator to add '16:30' to the end of
    the list that appointments refers to.

c. You used two approaches to add '16:30' to the list. Which approach
    modified the list and which approach created a new list?

4. Variable ids refers to the list [4353, 2314, 2956, 3382, 9362, 3900]. Using list
    methods, do the following:

    a. Remove 3382 from the list.
    b. Get the index of 9362.
    c. Insert 4499 in the list after 9362.
    d. Extend the list by adding [5566, 1830] to it.
    e. Reverse the list.
    f. Sort the list.

5. In this exercise, you'll create a list and then answer questions about that
    list.

    a. Assign a list that contains the atomic numbers of the six alkaline earth
        metals—beryllium (4), magnesium (12), calcium (20), strontium (38),
        barium (56), and radium (88)—to a variable called alkaline_earth_metals.
    b. Which index contains radium's atomic number? Write the answer in two
        ways, one using a positive index and one using a negative index.
    c. Which function tells you how many items there are in alkaline_earth_metals?
    d. Write code that returns the highest atomic number in alkaline_earth_metals.
        (Hint: Use one of the functions from Table 9, *List Functions*, on page 134.)

6. In this exercise, you'll create a list and then answer questions about that
    list.

    a. Create a list of temperatures in degrees Celsius with the values 25.2,
        16.8, 31.4, 23.9, 28, 22.5, and 19.6, and assign it to a variable called
        temps.
    b. Using one of the list methods, sort temps in ascending order.
    c. Using slicing, create two new lists, cool_temps and warm_temps, which contain
        the temperatures below and above 20 degrees Celsius, respectively.
    d. Using list arithmetic, recombine cool_temps and warm_temps into a new
        list called temps_in_celsius.

7. Complete the examples in the docstring and then write the body of the
    following function:

```
def same_first_last(L):
    """ (list) -> bool
    Precondition: len(L) >= 2

    Return True if and only if first item of the list is the same as the
    last.

    >>> same_first_last([3, 4, 2, 8, 3])
    True
    >>> same_first_last(['apple', 'banana', 'pear'])

    >>> same_first_last([4.0, 4.5])

    """
```

8. Complete the examples in the docstring and then write the body of the following function:

```
def is_longer(L1, L2):
    """ (list, list) -> bool
    Return True if and only if the length of L1 is longer than the length
    of L2.

    >>> is_longer([1, 2, 3], [4, 5])
    True
    >>> is_longer(['abcdef'], ['ab', 'cd', 'ef'])

    >>> is_longer(['a', 'b', 'c'], [1, 2, 3]

    """
```

9. Draw a memory model showing the effect of the following statements:

```
values = [0, 1, 2]
values[1] = values
```

10. Variable units refers to the nested list [['km', 'miles', 'league'], ['kg', 'pound', 'stone']]. Using units and either slicing or indexing with positive indices, write expressions that produce the following:

   a. The first item of units (the first inner list)
   b. The last item of units (the last inner list)
   c. The string 'km'
   d. The string 'kg'
   e. The list ['miles', 'league']
   f. The list ['kg', 'pound']

11. Repeat the previous exercise using negative indices.

## CHAPTER 9

Repeating Code Using Loops

This chapter introduces another fundamental kind of control flow: repetition. Up to now, to execute an instruction two hundred times, you would need to write that instruction two hundred times. Now you'll see how to write the instruction once and use loops to repeat that code the desired number of times.

9.1 Processing Items in a List

With what you've learned so far, to print the items from a list of velocities of falling objects in metric and Imperial units, you would need to write a call on function print for each velocity in the list:

```
>>> velocities = [0.0, 9.81, 19.62, 29.43]
>>> print('Metric:', velocities[0], 'm/sec;',
... 'Imperial:', velocities[0] * 3.28, 'ft/sec')
Metric: 0.0 m/sec; Imperial: 0.0 ft/sec
>>> print('Metric:', velocities[1], 'm/sec;',
... 'Imperial:', velocities[1] * 3.28, 'ft/sec')
Metric: 9.81 m/sec; Imperial: 32.1768 ft/sec
>>> print('Metric:', velocities[2], 'm/sec; ',
... 'Imperial:', velocities[2] * 3.28, 'ft/sec')
Metric: 19.62 m/sec; Imperial: 64.3536 ft/sec
>>> print('Metric:', velocities[3], 'm/sec; ',
... 'Imperial:', velocities[3] * 3.28, 'ft/sec')
Metric: 29.43 m/sec; Imperial: 96.5304 ft/sec
```

The code above is used to process a list with just four values. Imagine processing a list with a thousand values. Lists were invented so that you wouldn't have to create a thousand variables to store a thousand values. For the same reason, Python has a *for loop* that lets you process each element in a list in turn without having to write one statement per element. You can use a for loop to print the velocities:

```
>>> velocities = [0.0, 9.81, 19.62, 29.43]
>>> for velocity in velocities:
...     print('Metric:', velocity, 'm/sec;',
...     'Imperial:', velocity * 3.28, 'ft/sec')
...
Metric: 0.0 m/sec; Imperial: 0.0 ft/sec
Metric: 9.81 m/sec; Imperial: 32.1768 ft/sec
Metric: 19.62 m/sec; Imperial: 64.3536 ft/sec
Metric: 29.43 m/sec; Imperial: 96.5304 ft/sec
```

The general form of a for loop over a list is as follows:

```
for «variable» in «list»:
    «block»
```

A for loop is executed as follows:

- The loop variable is assigned the first item in the list, and the loop block—the *body* of the for loop—is executed.

- The loop variable is then assigned the second item in the list and the loop body is executed again.

  ...

- Finally, the loop variable is assigned the last item of the list and the loop body is executed one last time.

As we saw in Section 3.3, *Defining Our Own Functions*, on page 35, a block is just a sequence of one or more statements. Each pass through the block is called an *iteration*; and at the start of each iteration, Python assigns the next item in the list to the loop variable. As with function definitions and if statements, the statements in the loop block are indented.

In the code above, before the first iteration, variable velocity is assigned velocities[0] and then the loop body is executed; before the second iteration it is assigned velocities[1] and then the loop body is executed; and so on. In this way, the program can do something with each item in turn. Table 11, *Looping Over List Velocities*, on page 149, contains the value of velocity at the start of each iteration, as well as what is printed during that iteration.

In the previous example, we created a new variable, velocity, to refer to the current item of the list inside the loop. We could equally well have used an existing variable.

If we use an existing variable, the loop still starts with the variable referring to the first element of the list. The content of the variable before the loop is lost, exactly as if we had used an assignment statement to give a new value to that variable:

Iteration	List Item Referred to at Start of Iteration	What Is Printed During This Iteration
1st	velocities[0]	Metric: 0.0 m/sec; Imperial: 0.0 ft/sec
2nd	velocities[1]	Metric: 9.81 m/sec; Imperial: 32.1768 ft/sec
3rd	velocities[2]	Metric: 19.62 m/sec; Imperial: 64.3536 ft/sec
4th	velocities[3]	Metric: 29.43 m/sec; Imperial: 96.5304 ft/sec

Table 11—Looping Over List Velocities

```
>>> speed = 2
>>> velocities = [0.0, 9.81, 19.62, 29.43]
>>> for speed in velocities:
...     print('Metric:', speed, 'm/sec')
...
Metric: 0.0 m/sec
Metric: 9.81 m/sec
Metric: 19.62 m/sec
Metric: 29.43 m/sec
>>> print('Final:', speed)
Final: 29.43
```

The variable is left holding its last value when the loop finishes. Notice that the last print statement isn't indented, so it is not part of the for loop. It is executed, only once, after the for loop execution has finished.

9.2 Processing Characters in Strings

It is also possible to loop over the characters of a string. The general form of a for loop over a string is as follows:

```
for «variable» in «str»:
    «block»
```

As with a for loop over a list, the loop variable gets assigned a new value at the beginning of each iteration. In the case of a loop over a string, the variable is assigned a single character.

For example, we can loop over each character in a string, printing the uppercase letters:

```
>>> country = 'United States of America'
>>> for ch in country:
...     if ch.isupper():
...         print(ch)
...
U
S
A
```

In the code above, variable ch is assigned country[0] before the first iteration, country[1] before the second, and so on. The loop iterates twenty-four times (once per character) and the if statement block is executed three times (once per uppercase letter).

9.3 Looping Over a Range of Numbers

We can also loop over a range of values. This allows us to perform tasks a certain number of times and to do more sophisticated processing of lists and strings. To begin, we need to generate the range of numbers over which to iterate.

Generating Ranges of Numbers

Python's built-in function range produces an object that will generate a sequence of integers. When passed a single argument, as in range(stop), the sequence starts at 0 and continues to the integer before stop:

```
>>> range(10)
range(0, 10)
```

This is the first time that you've seen Python's range type. You can use a loop to access each number in the sequence one at a time:

```
>>> for num in range(10):
...         print(num)
...
0
1
2
3
4
5
6
7
8
9
```

To get the numbers from the sequence all at once, we can use built-in function list to create a list of those numbers:

```
>>> list(range(10))
[0, 1, 2, 3, 4, 5, 6, 7, 8, 9]
```

Here are some more examples:

```
>>> list(range(3))
[0, 1, 2]
>>> list(range(1))
[0]
>>> list(range(0))
[]
```

The sequence produced includes the start value and excludes the stop value, which is (deliberately) consistent with how sequence indexing works: the expression seq[0:5] takes a slice of seq up to, but not including, the value at index 5.

Notice that in the code above, we call list on the value produced by the call on range. Function range returns a range object, and we create a list based on its values in order to work with it using the set of list operations and methods we are already familiar with.

Function range can also be passed two arguments, where the first is the start value and the second is the stop value:

```
>>> list(range(1, 5))
[1, 2, 3, 4]
>>> list(range(1, 10))
[1, 2, 3, 4, 5, 6, 7, 8, 9]
>>> list(range(5, 10))
[5, 6, 7, 8, 9]
```

By default, function range generates numbers that successively increase by one—this is called its *step size*. We can specify a different step size for range with an optional third parameter.

Here we produce a list of leap years in the first half of this century:

```
>>> list(range(2000, 2050, 4))
[2000, 2004, 2008, 2012, 2016, 2020, 2024, 2028, 2032, 2036, 2040, 2044, 2048]
```

The step size can also be negative, which produces a descending sequence. When the step size is negative, the starting index should be *larger* than the stopping index:

```
>>> list(range(2050, 2000, -4))
[2050, 2046, 2042, 2038, 2034, 2030, 2026, 2022, 2018, 2014, 2010, 2006, 2002]
```

Otherwise, range's result will be empty:

```
>>> list(range(2000, 2050, -4))
[]
>>> list(range(2050, 2000, 4))
[]
```

It's possible to loop over the sequence produced by a call on range. For example, the following program calculates the sum of the integers from 1 to 100:

```
>>> total = 0
>>> for i in range(1, 101):
...     total = total + i
...
>>> total
5050
```

Notice that the upper bound passed to range is 101. It's one more than the greatest integer we actually want.

9.4 Processing Lists Using Indices

The loops over lists that we have written so far have been used to access list items. But what if we want to change the items in a list? For example, suppose we want to double all of the values in a list. The following doesn't work:

```
>>> values = [4, 10, 3, 8, -6]
>>> for num in values:
...     num = num * 2
...
>>> values
[4, 10, 3, 8, -6]
```

Each loop iteration assigned an item in the list values to variable num. Doubling that value inside the loop changes what num refers to, but it *doesn't* mutate the list object:

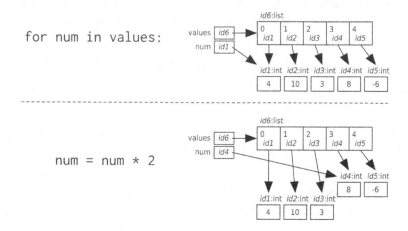

Let's add a call on function print to show how the value that num refers to changes during each iteration:

```
>>> values = [4, 10, 3, 8, -6]
>>> for num in values:
...     num = num * 2
...     print(num)
...
8
20
6
16
-12
>>> print(values)
[4, 10, 3, 8, -6]
```

The correct approach is to loop over the indices of the list. If variable values refers to a list, then len(values) is the number of items it contains, and the expression range(len(values)) produces a sequence containing exactly the indices for values:

```
>>> values = [4, 10, 3, 8, -6]
>>> len(values)
5
>>> list(range(5))
[0, 1, 2, 3, 4]
>>> list(range(len(values)))
[0, 1, 2, 3, 4]
```

The list that values refers to has five items, so its indices are 0, 1, 2, 3, and 4. Rather than looping over values, you can iterate over its indices, which are produced by range(len(values)):

```
>>> values = [4, 10, 3, 8, -6]
>>> for i in range(len(values)):
...      print(i)
...
0
1
2
3
4
```

Notice that we called the variable i, which stands for *index*. You can use each index to access the items in the list:

```
>>> values = [4, 10, 3, 8, -6]
>>> for i in range(len(values)):
...      print(i, values[i])
...
0 4
1 10
2 3
3 8
4 -6
```

You can also use them to modify list items:

```
>>> values = [4, 10, 3, 8, -6]
>>> for i in range(len(values)):
...      values[i] = values[i] * 2
...
>>> values
[8, 20, 6, 16, -12]
```

Evaluation of the expression on the right side of the assignment looks up the value at index i and multiplies it by two. Python then assigns that value to the item at index i in the list. When i refers to 1, for example, values[i] refers to 10, which is multiplied by 2 to produce 20. The list item values[1] is then assigned 20.

Processing Parallel Lists Using Indices

Sometimes the data from one list corresponds to data from another. For example, consider these two lists:

```
>>> metals = ['Li', 'Na', 'K']
>>> weights = [6.941, 22.98976928, 39.0983]
```

The item at index 0 of metals has its atomic weight at index 0 of weights. The same is true for the items at index 1 in the two lists, and so on. These lists are *parallel lists*, because the item at index i of one list corresponds to the item at index i of the other list.

We would like to print each metal and its weight. To do so, we can loop over each index of the lists, accessing the items in each:

```
>>> metals = ['Li', 'Na', 'K']
>>> weights = [6.941, 22.98976928, 39.0983]
>>> for i in range(len(metals)):
...     print(metals[i], weights[i])
...
Li 6.941
Na 22.98976928
K 39.0983
```

The code above only works when the length of weights is at least as long as the length of metals. If the length of weights is less than the length of metals, then an error would occur when trying to access an index of weights that doesn't exist. For example, if metals has three items and weights only has two, the first two print function calls would be executed, but during the third function call, an error would occur when evaluating the second argument.

9.5   Nesting Loops in Loops

The block of statements inside a loop can contain another loop. In this code, the inner loop is executed once for each item of list outer:

```
>>> outer = ['Li', 'Na', 'K']
>>> inner = ['F', 'Cl', 'Br']
>>> for metal in outer:
...     for halogen in inner:
...         print(metal + halogen)
...
...
```

```
LiF
LiCl
LiBr
NaF
NaCl
NaBr
KF
KCl
KBr
```

The number of times that function print is called is len(outer) * len(inner). In Table 12, *Nested Loops Over Inner and Outer Lists*, we show that for each iteration of the outer loop (that is, for each item in outer), the inner loop executes three times (once per item in inner).

Iteration of Outer Loop	What metal Refers To	Iteration of Inner Loop	What halogen Refers To	What Is Printed
1st	outer[0]	1st	inner[0]	LiF
		2nd	inner[1]	LiCl
		3rd	inner[2]	LiBr
2nd	outer[1]	1st	inner[0]	NaF
		2nd	inner[1]	NaCl
		3rd	Inner[2]	NaBr
3rd	outer[2]	1st	inner[0]	KF
		2nd	inner[1]	KCl
		3rd	inner[2]	KBr

Table 12—Nested Loops Over Inner and Outer Lists

Sometimes an inner loop uses the same list as the outer loop. An example of this is shown in a function used to generate a multiplication table. After printing the header row, we use a nested loop to print each row of the table in turn, using tabs (see Table 4, *Escape Sequences*, on page 69) to make the columns line up:

```
def print_table(n):
    """ (int) -> NoneType

    Print the multiplication table for numbers 1 through n inclusive.

    >>> print_table(5)
            1       2       3       4       5
    1       1       2       3       4       5
    2       2       4       6       8       10
    3       3       6       9       12      15
    4       4       8       12      16      20
    5       5       10      15      20      25
    """
```

```
    # The numbers to include in the table.
    numbers = list(range(1, n + 1))

    # Print the header row.
    for i in numbers:
        print('\t' + str(i), end='')

    # End the header row.
    print()

    # Print each row number and the contents of each row.
❶  for i in numbers:

❷      print (i, end='')
❸      for j in numbers:
❹          print('\t' + str(i * j), end='')

        # End the current row.
❺      print()
```

Each iteration of the outer loop prints a row. Each row consists of a row number, n tab-number pairs, and a newline. It's the inner loop's job to print the tabs and numbers' part of the row. For print_table(5), let's take a closer look at what happens during the third iteration of the outer loop:

❶ i is assigned 3, the third item of numbers.

❷ The row number, 3, is printed.

❸ This line of code is the inner loop header, and it will be executed five times. Before the first iteration of the inner loop, j is assigned 1; before the second iteration, it is assigned 2; and so on; until it is assigned 5 before the last iteration.

❹ Five times this line is executed right after the previous line using whatever value j was just assigned. The first time it prints a tab followed by 3, then a tab followed by 6, and so on until it prints a tab followed by 15.

❺ Now that a row has been printed, the program prints a newline. This line of code occurs outside of the inner loop so that it is only executed once per row.

Looping Over Nested Lists

In addition to looping over lists of numbers, strings, and Booleans, we can also loop over lists of lists. Here is an example of a loop over an outer list. The loop variable, which we've named inner_list, is assigned an item of nested list elements at the beginning of each iteration:

```
>>> elements = [['Li', 'Na', 'K'], ['F', 'Cl', 'Br']]
>>> for inner_list in elements:
...     print(inner_list)
...
['Li', 'Na', 'K']
['F', 'Cl', 'Br']
```

To access each string in the inner lists, you can loop over the outer list and then over each inner list using a nested loop. Here, we print every string in every inner list:

```
>>> elements = [['Li', 'Na', 'K'], ['F', 'Cl', 'Br']]
>>> for inner_list in elements:
...     for item in inner_list:
...         print(item)
...
Li
Na
K
F
Cl
Br
```

In the code above, the outer loop variable, inner_list, refers to a list of strings, and the inner loop variable, item, refers to a string from that list.

When you have a nested list and you want to do something with every item in the inner lists, you need to use a nested loop.

Looping Over Ragged Lists

Nothing says that nested lists have to be the same length:

```
>>> info = [['Isaac Newton', 1643, 1727],
...         ['Charles Darwin', 1809, 1882],
...         ['Alan Turing', 1912, 1954, 'alan@bletchley.uk']]
>>> for item in info:
...     print(len(item))
...
3
3
4
```

Nested lists with inner lists of varying lengths are called *ragged lists*. Ragged lists can be tricky to process if the data isn't uniform; for example, trying to assemble a list of email addresses for data where some addresses are missing requires careful thought.

Ragged data does arise normally. For example, if a record is made each day of the time at which a person has a drink of water, each day will have a different number of entries:

```
>>> drinking_times_by_day = [["9:02", "10:17", "13:52", "18:23", "21:31"],
...                          ["8:45", "12:44", "14:52", "22:17"],
...                          ["8:55", "11:11", "12:34", "13:46",
...                           "15:52", "17:08", "21:15"],
...                          ["9:15", "11:44", "16:28"],
...                          ["10:01", "13:33", "16:45", "19:00"],
...                          ["9:34", "11:16", "15:52", "20:37"],
...                          ["9:01", "12:24", "18:51", "23:13"]]
>>> for day in drinking_times_by_day:
...     for drinking_time in day:
...         print(drinking_time, end=' ')
...     print()
...
9:02 10:17 13:52 18:23 21:31
8:45 12:44 14:52 22:17
8:55 11:11 12:34 13:46 15:52 17:08 21:15
9:15 11:44 16:28
10:01 13:33 16:45 19:00
9:34 11:16 15:52 20:37
9:01 12:24 18:51 23:13
```

The inner loop iterates over the items of day, and the length of that list varies.

9.6 Looping Until a Condition Is Reached

for loops are useful only if you know how many iterations of the loop you need. In some situations, it is not known in advance how many loop iterations to execute. In a game program, for example, you can't know whether a player is going to want to play again or quit. In these situations, we use a while loop. The general form of a while loop is as follows:

```
while «expression»:
    «block»
```

The while loop expression is sometimes called the *loop condition,* just like the condition of an if statement. When Python executes a while loop, it evaluates the expression. If that expression evaluates to False, that is the end of the execution of the loop. If the expression evaluates to True, on the other hand, Python executes the loop body once and then goes back to the top of the loop and reevaluates the expression. If it still evaluates to True, the loop body is executed again. This is repeated—expression, body, expression, body—until the expression evaluates to False, at which point Python stops executing the loop.

Here's an example:

```
>>> rabbits = 3
>>> while rabbits > 0:
...     print(rabbits)
...     rabbits = rabbits - 1
...
3
2
1
```

Notice that this loop did *not* print 0. When the number of rabbits reaches zero, the loop expression evaluates to False, so the body isn't executed. Here's a flow chart for this code:

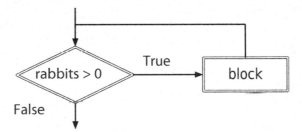

As a more useful example, we can calculate the growth of a bacterial colony using a simple exponential growth model, which is essentially a calculation of compound interest:

$P(t + 1) = P(t) + rP(t)$

In this formula, $P(t)$ is the population size at time t, and r is the growth rate. Using this program, let's see how long it takes the bacteria to double their numbers:

```
time = 0
population = 1000    # 1000 bacteria to start with
growth_rate = 0.21 # 21% growth per minute
while population < 2000:
    population = population + growth_rate * population
    print(round(population))
    time = time + 1

print("It took", time, "minutes for the bacteria to double.")
print("The final population was", round(population), "bacteria.")
```

Because variable time was updated in the loop body, its value after the loop was the time of the last iteration, which is exactly what we want. Running this program gives us the answer we were looking for:

```
1210
1464
1772
2144
It took 4 minutes for the bacteria to double.
The final population was 2144 bacteria.
```

Infinite Loops

The preceding example used population < 2000 as a loop condition so that the loop stopped when the population reached double its initial size *or more*. What would happen if we stopped only when the population was *exactly* double its initial size?

```
# Use multivalued assignment to set up controls
time, population, growth_rate = 0, 1000, 0.21

# Don't stop until we're exactly double the original size
while population != 2000:
    population = population + growth_rate * population
    print(round(population))
    time = time + 1

print("It took", time, "minutes for the bacteria to double.")
```

Here is this program's output:

```
1210
1464
1772
2144
...3,680 lines or so later...
inf
inf
inf
...and so on forever...
```

Whoops—since the population is never exactly two thousand bacteria, the loop never stops. The first set of dots represents more than three thousand values, each 21 percent larger than the one before. Eventually, these values are too large for the computer to represent, so it displays inf (or on some computers 1.#INF), which is its way of saying "effectively infinity."

A loop like this one is called an *infinite loop*, because the computer will execute it forever (or until you kill your program, whichever comes first). In IDLE, you kill your program by selecting Restart Shell from the Shell menu; from the command-line shell, you can kill it by pressing Ctrl-C. Infinite loops are a common kind of bug; the usual symptoms include printing the same value over and over again or *hanging* (doing nothing at all).

9.7   Repetition Based on User Input

We can use function input in a loop to make the chemical formula translation example from Section 5.2, *Choosing Which Statements to Execute*, on page 86, interactive. We will ask the user to enter a chemical formula, and our program, which is saved in a file named formulas.py, will print its name. This should continue until the user types quit:

```
text = ""
while text != "quit":
    text = input("Please enter a chemical formula (or 'quit' to exit): ")
    if text == "quit":
        print("…exiting program")
    elif text == "H2O":
        print("Water")
    elif text == "NH3":
        print("Ammonia")
    elif text == "CH4":
        print("Methane")
    else:
        print("Unknown compound")
```

Since the loop condition checks the value of text, we have to assign it a value before the loop begins. Now we can run the program in formulas.py and it will exit whenever the user types quit:

```
Please enter a chemical formula (or 'quit' to exit): CH4
Methane
Please enter a chemical formula (or 'quit' to exit): H2O
Water
Please enter a chemical formula (or 'quit' to exit): quit
…exiting program
```

The number of times that this loop executes will vary depending on user input, but it will execute at least once.

9.8   Controlling Loops Using Break and Continue

As a rule, for and while loops execute all the statements in their body on each iteration. However, sometimes it is handy to be able to break that rule. Python provides two ways of controlling the iteration of a loop: break, which terminates execution of the loop immediately, and continue, which skips ahead to the next iteration.

The Break Statement

In Section 9.7, *Repetition Based on User Input*, on page 161, we showed a program that continually read input from a user until the user typed quit. Here is a program that accomplishes the same task, but this one uses break to terminate execution of the loop when the user types quit:

```
while True:
    text = input("Please enter a chemical formula (or 'quit' to exit): ")
    if text == "quit":
        print("…exiting program")
        break
    elif text == "H2O":
        print("Water")
    elif text == "NH3":
        print("Ammonia")
    elif text == "CH4":
        print("Methane")
    else:
        print("Unknown compound")
```

The loop condition is strange: it evaluates to True, so this looks like an infinite loop. However, when the user types quit, the first condition, text == "quit", evaluates to True. The print("…exiting program") statement is executed, and then the break statement, which causes the loop to terminate.

As a style point, we are somewhat allergic to loops that are written like this. We find that a loop with an explicit condition is easier to understand.

Sometimes a loop's task is finished before its final iteration. Using what you have seen so far, though, the loop still has to finish iterating. For example, let's write some code to find the index of the first digit in string 'C3H7'. The digit 3 is at index 1 in this string. Using a for loop, we would have to write something like this:

```
>>> s = 'C3H7'
>>> digit_index = -1 # This will be -1 until we find a digit.
>>> for i in range(len(s)):
...     # If we haven't found a digit, and s[i] is a digit
...     if digit_index == -1 and s[i].isdigit():
...         digit_index = i
...
>>> digit_index
1
```

Here we use variable digit_index to represent the index of the first digit in the string. It initially refers to -1, but when a digit is found, the digit's index, i, is assigned to digit_index. If the string doesn't contain any digits, then digit_index remains -1 throughout execution of the loop.

Once digit_index has been assigned a value, it is never again equal to -1, so the if condition will not evaluate to True. Even though the job of the loop is done, the loop continues to iterate until the end of the string is reached.

To fix this, you can terminate the loop early using a break statement, which jumps out of the loop body immediately:

```
>>> s = 'C3H7'
>>> digit_index = -1 # This will be -1 until we find a digit.
>>> for i in range(len(s)):
...     # If we find a digit
...     if s[i].isdigit():
...         digit_index = i
...         break  # This exits the loop.
...
>>> digit_index
1
```

Notice that because the loop terminates early, we were able to simplify the if statement condition. As soon as digit_index is assigned a new value, the loop terminates, so it isn't necessary to check whether digit_index refers to -1. That check only existed to prevent digit_index from being assigned the index of a subsequent digit in the string.

Here's a flow chart for this code:

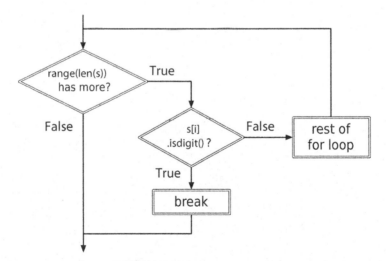

One more thing about break: it terminates only the *innermost* loop in which it's contained. This means that in a nested loop, a break statement inside the inner loop will terminate only the inner loop, not both loops.

The Continue Statement

Another way to bend the rules for iteration is to use the continue statement, which causes Python to skip immediately ahead to the next iteration of a loop. Here, we add up all the digits in a string, and we also count how many digits there are. Whenever a nondigit is encountered, we use continue to skip the rest of the loop body and go back to the top of the loop in order to start the next iteration.

```
>>> s = 'C3H7'
>>> total = 0 # The sum of the digits seen so far.
>>> count = 0 # The number of digits seen so far.
>>> for i in range(len(s)):
...     if s[i].isalpha():
...         continue
...     total = total + int(s[i])
...     count = count + 1
...
>>> total
10
>>> count
2
```

When continue is executed, it *immediately* begins the next iteration of the loop. All statements in the loop body that appear after it are skipped, so we only execute the assignments to total and count when s[i] isn't a letter. Here's a flow chart for this code:

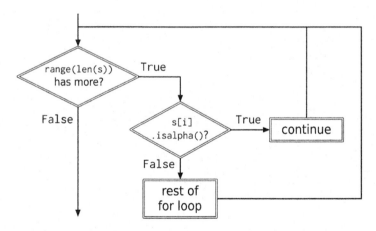

Using continue is one way to skip alphabetic characters, but this can also be accomplished by using if statements. In the previous code, continue prevents the variables from being modified; in other words, if the character isn't alphabetic, it should be processed.

The form of the previous sentence matches that of an if statement, and the updated code is as follows:

```
>>> s = 'C3H7'
>>> total = 0
```

```
>>> count = 0
>>> for i in range(len(s)):
...     if not s[i].isalpha():
...         total = total + int(s[i])
...         count = count + 1
...
>>> total
10
>>> count
2
```

This new version is easier to read than the first one. Most of the time, it is better to rewrite the code to avoid continue; almost always, the code ends up being more readable.

A Warning About Break and Continue

break and continue have their place, but they should be used sparingly since they can make programs harder to understand. When people see while and for loops in programs, their first assumption is that the whole body will be executed every time—in other words, that the body can be treated as a single "super statement" when trying to understand the program. If the loop contains break or continue, though, that assumption is false. Sometimes only part of the statement body will be executed, which means the reader has to keep two scenarios in mind.

There are always alternatives: well-chosen loop conditions (as in Section 9.7, *Repetition Based on User Input*, on page 161) can replace break, and if statements can be used to skip statements instead of continue. It is up to the programmer to decide which option makes the program clearer and which makes it more complicated. As we said in Section 2.7, *Describing Code*, on page 25, programs are written for human beings; taking a few moments to make your code as clear as possible, or to make clarity a habit, will pay dividends for the lifetime of the program.

Now that code is getting pretty complicated, it's even more important to write comments describing the purpose of each tricky block of statements.

9.9 Repeating What You've Learned

In this chapter, you learned the following:

- Repeating a block is a fundamental way to control a program's behavior. A for loop can be used to iterate over the items of a list, over the characters of a string, and over a sequence of integers generated by built-in function range.

- The most general kind of repetition is the while loop, which continues executing as long as some specified Boolean condition is true. However, the condition is tested only at the beginning of each iteration. If that condition is never false, the loop will be executed forever.

- The break and continue statements can be used to change the way loops execute.

- Control structures like loops and conditionals can be nested inside one another to any desired depth.

9.10 Exercises

Here are some exercises for you to try on your own. Solutions are available at http://pragprog.com/titles/gwpy2/practical-programming.

1. Write a for loop to print all the values in the celegans_phenotypes list from Section 8.4, *Slicing Lists*, on page 137, one per line. celegans_phenotypes refers to ['Emb', 'Him', 'Unc', 'Lon', 'Dpy', 'Sma'].

2. Write a for loop to print all the values in the half_lives list from Section 8.3, *Operations on Lists*, on page 134, all on a single line. half_lives refers to [87.74, 24110.0, 6537.0, 14.4, 376000.0].

3. Write a for loop to add 1 to all the values from whales from Section 8.1, *Storing and Accessing Data in Lists*, on page 129, and store the converted values in a new list called more_whales. The whales list shouldn't be modified. whales refers to [5, 4, 7, 3, 2, 3, 2, 6, 4, 2, 1, 7, 1, 3].

4. In this exercise, you'll create a nested list and then write code that performs operations on that list.

   a. Create a nested list where each element of the outer list contains the atomic number and atomic weight for an alkaline earth metal. The values are beryllium (4 and 9.012), magnesium (12 and 24.305), calcium (20 and 40.078), strontium (38 and 87.62), barium (56 and 137.327), and radium (88 and 226). Assign the list to variable alkaline_earth_metals.

   b. Write a for loop to print all the values in alkaline_earth_metals, with the atomic number and atomic weight for each alkaline earth metal on a different line.

   c. Write a for loop to create a new list called number_and_weight that contains the elements of alkaline_earth_metals in the same order but not nested.

5. The following function doesn't have a docstring or comments. Write enough of both to make it easy for another programmer to understand what the function does and how, and then compare your solution with those of at least two other people. How similar are they? Why do they differ?

```
def mystery_function(values):
    result = []
    for sublist in values:
        result.append([sublist[0]])
        for i in sublist[1:]:
            result[-1].insert(0, i)

    return result
```

6. In Section 9.7, *Repetition Based on User Input*, on page 161, you saw a loop that prompted users until they typed quit. This code won't work if users type Quit, or QUIT, or any other version that isn't exactly quit. Modify that loop so that it terminates if a user types that word with any capitalization.

7. Consider the following statement, which creates a list of populations of countries in eastern Asia (China, DPR Korea, Hong Kong, Mongolia, Republic of Korea, and Taiwan) in millions: country_populations = [1295, 23, 7, 3, 47, 21]. Write a for loop that adds up all the values and stores them in variable total. (Hint: Give total an initial value of zero, and, inside the loop body, add the population of the current country to total.)

8. You are given two lists, rat_1 and rat_2, that contain the daily weights of two rats over a period of ten days. Assume the rats never have exactly the same weight. Write statements to do the following:

    a. If the weight of rat 1 is greater than that of rat 2 on day 1, print "Rat 1 weighed more than rat 2 on day 1."; otherwise, print "Rat 1 weighed less than rat 2 on day 1.".

    b. If rat 1 weighed more than rat 2 on day 1 and if rat 1 weighs more than rat 2 on the last day, print "Rat 1 remained heavier than Rat 2."; otherwise, print "Rat 2 became heavier than Rat 1."

    c. If your solution to the previous exercise used nested if statements, then do it without nesting, or vice versa.

9. Print the numbers in the range 33 to 49 (inclusive).

10. Print the numbers from 1 to 10 (inclusive) in descending order, all on one line.

11. Using a loop, sum the numbers in the range 2 to 22 (inclusive), and then calculate the average.

12. Consider this code:

```
def remove_neg(num_list):
    """ (list of number) -> NoneType

    Remove the negative numbers from the list num_list.

    >>> numbers = [-5, 1, -3, 2]
    >>> remove_neg(numbers)
    >>> numbers
    [1, 2]
    """

    for item in num_list:
        if item < 0:
            num_list.remove(item)
```

When remove_neg([1, 2, 3, -3, 6, -1, -3, 1]) is executed, it produces [1, 2, 3, 6, -3, 1]. The for loop traverses the elements of the list, and when a negative value (like -3 at position 3) is reached, it is removed, shifting the subsequent values one position earlier in the list (so 6 moves into position 3). The loop then continues on to process the next item, skipping over the value that moved into the removed item's position. If there are two negative numbers in a row (like -1 and -3), then the second one won't be removed.

Rewrite the code to avoid this problem.

13. Using nested for loops, print a right triangle of the character *T* on the screen where the triangle is one character wide at its narrowest point and seven characters wide at its widest point:

```
T
TT
TTT
TTTT
TTTTT
TTTTTT
TTTTTTT
```

14. Using nested for loops, print the triangle described in the previous exercise with its hypotenuse on the left side:

```
      T
     TT
    TTT
   TTTT
  TTTTT
 TTTTTT
TTTTTTT
```

15. Redo the previous two exercises using while loops instead of for loops.

16. Variables rat_1_weight and rat_2_weight contain the weights of two rats at the beginning of an experiment. Variables rat_1_rate and rat_2_rate are the rate that the rats' weights are expected to increase each week (for example, 4 percent per week).

   a. Using a while loop, calculate how many weeks it would take for the weight of the first rat to become 25 percent heavier than it was originally.

   b. Assume that the two rats have the same initial weight, but rat 1 is expected to gain weight at a faster rate than rat 2. Using a while loop, calculate how many weeks it would take for rat 1 to be 10 percent heavier than rat 2.

## CHAPTER 10

Reading and Writing Files

Data is often stored in plain-text files, which can be organized in several different ways. The most straightforward data organization is one piece of data per line; for example, the rainfall amount in Oregon for each separate day in a study period might be stored on a line of its own. Alternatively, each line might store the values for an entire week or month, with a *delimiter* such as a space, tab, or comma used to separate values to make the data easier for humans to read.

Often, data organization is more complex. For example, a study might keep track of the heights, weights, and ages of the participants. Each *record* can appear on a line by itself, with the pieces of data in each record separated by delimiters. Some records might even span multiple lines, in which case each record will usually have some kind of a separator (such as a blank line) or use special symbols to mark the start or end of each record.

In this chapter, you'll learn about different file formats, common ways to organize data, and how to read and write that data using Python. You'll first learn how to open and read information from files. After that, you'll learn about the different techniques for writing to files, and then you'll see several case studies that use the various techniques.

10.1 What Kinds of Files Are There?

There are many kinds of files. Text files, music files, videos, and various word processor and presentation documents are common. Text files only contain characters; all the other file formats include formatting information that is specific to that particular file format, and in order to use a file in a particular format you need a special program that understands that format.

Try opening a Microsoft Powerpoint (.pptx) file in a text editor such as Apple TextEdit, Microsoft Notepad, or one of the many Linux text editors such as vi, emacs, and gedit. Scroll through it; you'll see what looks like gobbledygook. This is because those files contain a lot of information: what's a title, what are the headings, which words are bold, which are italic, what the line height should be, what the margins are, what the links to embedded content are, and a lot more. Without a program such as Microsoft Powerpoint, .ppt files are unusable.

Text files, on the other hand, don't contain any style information. They contain only readable characters. You can open a text file in any text editor and read it. You can't include style information in text files, but you gain a lot in portability.

Plain-text files take up very little disk space. Compare the size of an empty text file to "empty" OpenOffice, Apple Pages, and Microsoft Word documents:

empty.docx	21 KB	Microsoft Word document
empty.odt	8 KB	OpenDocument Text (.odt) Document
empty.pages	29 KB	Pages document
empty.txt	Zero bytes	Plain Text File

The empty text file is truly empty: there is no styling information or *metadata* such as author information, number of pages, or anything else in the file. This makes text files much faster to process than other kinds of documents, and *any* editing program can read an empty text file.

They take up little disk space and are easy to process. The power comes from applications that can process text files that are written with a particular syntax. The Python programs we have been writing are text files, and by themselves they are only letters in a file. But combined with a Python interpreter, these Python text files are robust: you can express a powerful algorithm and the interpreter will follow your instructions.

Similarly, web browsers read and process HTML files, spreadsheets read and process comma-separated value files, calendar programs read and process calendar data files, and other programming language applications read and process files written with a particular programming language syntax. A database, which you'll learn about in Chapter 17, *Databases*, on page 339, is another way to store and manage data.

In the next section, you'll learn how to write programs that open and print the contents of a text file.

10.2 Opening a File

When you want to write a program that opens and reads a file, that program needs to tell Python where that file is. By default, Python assumes that the file you want to read is in the same directory as the program that is doing the reading. If you're working in IDLE as you read this book, there's a little setup you should do:

1. Make a directory, perhaps called file_examples.

2. In IDLE, select File→New Window and type (or copy and paste) the following:

    ```
    First line of text
    Second line of text
    Third line of text
    ```

3. Save this file in your file_examples directory under the name file_example.txt.

4. In IDLE, select File→New Window and type (or copy and paste) this program:

    ```
    file = open('file_example.txt', 'r')
    contents = file.read()
    print(contents)
    file.close()
    ```

5. Save this as file_reader.py in your file_examples directory.

When you run this program, this is what gets printed:

```
First line of text
Second line of text
Third line of text
```

It's important that you save the two files in the same directory, as you'll see in the next section. Also, this won't work if you try those same commands from the Python shell.

Built-in function open opens a file (much like you open a book when you want to read it) and returns an object that knows how to get information from the file, how much you've read, and which part of the file you're about to read next. The marker that keeps track of the current location in the file is called a *file cursor* and acts much like a bookmark. The file cursor is initially at the beginning of the file, but as we read or write data it moves to the end of what we just read or wrote.

The first argument in the example call on function open, 'file_example.txt', is the name of the file to open, and the second argument, 'r', tells Python that you want to read the file; this is called the file *mode*. Other options for the mode include 'w' for writing and 'a' for appending, which you'll see later in this chapter. If you call open with only the name of the file (omitting the mode), then the default is 'r'.

The second statement, contents = file.read(), tells Python that you want to read the contents of the entire file into a string, which we assign to a variable called contents. The third statement prints that string. When you run the program, you'll see that newline characters are treated just like every other character; a newline character is just another character in the file.

The last statement, file.close(), releases all resources associated with the open file object.

The with Statement

Because every call on function open should have a corresponding call on method close, Python provides a with statement that automatically closes a file when the end of the block is reached. Here is the same example using a with statement:

```
with open('file_example.txt', 'r') as file:
    contents = file.read()

print(contents)
```

The general form of a with statement is as follows:

```
with open(«filename», «mode») as «variable»:
    «block»
```

How Files Are Organized on Your Computer

A *file path* specifies a location in your computer's file system. A file path contains the sequence of directories to a file, starting at the *root directory* at the top of the file system, and optionally includes the name of a file.

Here is an example of the file path for file_example.txt:

```
/Users/pgries/Desktop/file_example.txt
```

This file path is on a computer running Apple OS X. A file path in Linux would look similar. Both operating systems use a forward slash as the directory separator.

In Microsoft Windows, the path usually begins with a *drive letter*, such as C:. There is one drive letter per disk partition. Also, Microsoft Windows uses a backslash as the directory separator. (When working with backslashes as directory separators, you might want to review Section 4.2, *Using Special Characters in Strings*, on page 68.)

Here is a path in Windows:

C:\Users\pgries\Desktop\file_example.txt

If you always use forward slashes, Python's file-handling operations will automatically translate them to work in Windows.

Specifying Which File You Want

Python keeps track of the *current working directory*; this is the directory in which it looks for files. When you run a Python program, the current working directory is the directory where that program is saved. For example, perhaps this is the path of the file that you have open in IDLE:

/home/pgries/Documents/py3book/Book/code/fileproc/program.py

Then this is the current working directory:

/home/pgries/Documents/py3book/Book/code/fileproc

When you call function open, it looks for the specified file in the current working directory.

The default current working directory for the Python shell is operating-system dependent. You can find out the current working directory using function getcwd from module os:

```
>>> import os
>>> os.getcwd()
'/home/pgries'
```

If you want to open a file in a different directory, you need to say where that file is. You can do that with either an *absolute path* or with a *relative path*. An absolute path (like all the examples above) is one that starts at the root of the file system, and a relative path is relative to the current working directory. Alternatively, you can change Python's current working directory to a different directory using function chdir (short for "change directory"):

```
>>> os.chdir('/home/pgries/Documents/py3book')
>>> os.getcwd()
'/home/pgries/Documents/py3book'
```

Let's say that you have a program called reader.py and a directory called data in the same directory as reader.py. Inside data you might have files called data1.txt and data2.txt. This is how you would open data1.txt:

```
open('data/data1.txt', 'r')
```

Here, data/data1.txt is a relative path.

To look in the directory *above* the current working directory, you can use two dots:

```
open('../data1.txt', 'r')
```

You can chain them to go up multiple directories. Here, Python looks for data1.txt three directories above the current working directory and then down into a data directory:[1]

```
open('../../../data/data1.txt', 'r')
```

10.3 Techniques for Reading Files

As we mentioned at the beginning of the chapter, Python provides several techniques for reading files. You'll learn about them in this section.

All of these techniques work starting at the current file cursor. That allows us to combine the techniques as we need to.

The Read Technique

Use this technique when you want to read the contents of a file into a single string, or when you want to specify exactly how many characters to read. This technique was introduced in Section 10.2, *Opening a File*, on page 173; here is the same example:

```
with open('file_example.txt', 'r') as file:
    contents = file.read()

print(contents)
```

When called with no arguments, it reads everything from the current file cursor all the way to the end of the file and moves the file cursor to the end of the file. When called with one integer argument, it reads that many characters and moves the file cursor after the characters that were just read. Here is a version of the same program in a file called file_reader_with_10.py; it reads ten characters and then the rest of the file:

```
with open('file_example.txt', 'r') as example_file:
    first_ten_chars = example_file.read(10)
    the_rest = example_file.read()

print("The first 10 characters:", first_ten_chars)
print("The rest of the file:", the_rest)
```

---

1. If you're still not clear on how directory paths work, try looking at this discussion on Wikipedia: http://en.wikipedia.org/wiki/Path_(computing).

Method call example_file.read(10) moves the file cursor, so the next call, example_file.read(), reads everything from character 11 to the end of the file.

Reading at the End of a File

When the file cursor is at the end of the file, functions read, readlines, and readline all return an empty string. In order to read the contents of a file a second time, you'll need to close and reopen the file.

The Readlines Technique

Use this technique when you want to get a Python list of strings containing the individual lines from a file. Function readlines works much like function read, except that it splits up the lines into a list of strings. As with read, the file cursor is moved to the end of the file.

This example reads the contents of a file into a list of strings and then prints that list:

```
with open('file_example.txt', 'r') as example_file:
    lines = example_file.readlines()

print(lines)
```

Here is the output:

```
['First line of text.\n', 'Second line of text.\n', 'Third line of text.\n']
```

Take a close look at that list; you'll see that each line ends in \n characters. Python does not remove any characters from what is read; it only splits them into separate strings.

The last line of a file may or may not end with a newline character, as you learned in Section 7.3, *Exploring String Methods*, on page 119.

Assume file planets.txt contains the following text:

```
Mercury
Venus
Earth
Mars
```

This example prints the lines in planets.txt backward, from the last line to the first (here, we use built-in function reversed, which returns the items in the list in reverse order):

```
>>> with open('planets.txt', 'r') as planets_file:
...     planets = planets_file.readlines()
...
>>> planets
['Mercury\n', 'Venus\n', 'Earth\n', 'Mars\n']
>>> for planet in reversed(planets):
...     print(planet.strip())
...
Mars
Earth
Venus
Mercury
```

We can use the Readlines technique to read the file, sort the lines, and print the planets alphabetically (here, we use built-in function sorted, which returns the items in the list in order from smallest to largest):

```
>>> with open('planets.txt', 'r') as planets_file:
...     planets = planets_file.readlines()
...
>>> planets
['Mercury\n', 'Venus\n', 'Earth\n', 'Mars\n']
>>> for planet in sorted(planets):
...     print(planet.strip())
...
Earth
Mars
Mercury
Venus
```

The "For Line in File" Technique

Use this technique when you want to do the same thing to every line from the file cursor to the end of a file. On each iteration, the file cursor is moved to the beginning of the next line.

This code opens file planets.txt and prints the length of each line in that file:

```
>>> with open('planets.txt', 'r') as data_file:
...     for line in data_file:
...         print(len(line))
...
8
6
6
5
```

Take a close look at the last line of output. There are only four characters in the word *Mars*, but our program is reporting that the line is five characters long. The reason for this is the same as for function readlines: each of the lines we read from the file has a newline character at the end. We can get rid of it using string method strip, which returns a copy of a string that has leading and trailing whitespace characters (spaces, tabs, and newlines) stripped away:

```
>>> with open('planets.txt', 'r') as data_file:
...     for line in data_file:
...         print(len(line.strip()))
...
7
5
5
4
```

The Readline Technique

This technique reads one line at a time, unlike the Readlines technique. Use this technique when you want to read only part of a file.

For example, you might want to treat lines differently depending on context; perhaps you want to process a file that has a *header* section followed by a series of records, either one record per line or with multiline records.

The following data, taken from the *Time Series Data Library [Hyn06]*, describes the number of colored fox fur pelts produced in Hopedale, Labrador, in the years 1834–1842. (The full data set has values for the years 1834–1925.)

```
Coloured fox fur production, HOPEDALE, Labrador, 1834-1842
#Source: C. Elton (1942) "Voles, Mice and Lemmings", Oxford Univ. Press
#Table 17, p.265--266
       22
       29
        2
       16
       12
       35
        8
       83
      166
```

The first line contains a description of the data. The next two lines contain comments about the data, each of which begins with a # character. Each piece of actual data appears on a single line.

We'll use the Readline technique to skip the header, and then we'll use the For Line in File technique to process the data in the file, counting how many fox fur pelts were produced.

```
with open('hopedale.txt', 'r') as hopedale_file:

    # Read the description line.
    hopedale_file.readline()

    # Keep reading comment lines until we read the first piece of data.
    data = hopedale_file.readline().strip()
    while data.startswith('#'):
        data = hopedale_file.readline().strip()

    # Now we have the first piece of data.  Accumulate the total number of
    # pelts.
    total_pelts = int(data)

    # Read the rest of the data.
    for data in hopedale_file:
        total_pelts = total_pelts + int(data.strip())

print("Total number of pelts:", total_pelts)
```

And here is the output:

```
Total number of pelts: 373
```

Each call on function readline moves the file cursor to the beginning of the next line.

Sometimes leading whitespace is important and you'll want to preserve it. In the Hopedale data, for example, the integers are right-justified to make them line up nicely. In order to preserve this, you can use rstrip instead of strip to remove the trailing newline; here is a program that prints the data from that file, preserving the whitespace:

```
with open('hopedale.txt', 'r') as hopedale_file:

    # Read the description line.
    hopedale_file.readline()

    # Keep reading comment lines until we read the first piece of data.
    data = hopedale_file.readline().rstrip()
    while data.startswith('#'):
        data = hopedale_file.readline().rstrip()

    # Now we have the first piece of data.
    print(data)

    # Read the rest of the data.
    for data in hopedale_file:
        print(data.rstrip())
```

And here is the output:

```
 22
 29
  2
 16
 12
 35
  8
 83
166
```

10.4 Files over the Internet

These days, of course, the file containing the data we want could be on a machine half a world away. Provided the file is accessible over the Internet, though, we can read it just as we do a local file. For example, the Hopedale data not only exists on our computers, but it's also on a web page. At the time of writing, the URL for the file is http://robjhyndman.com/tsdldata/ecology1/hopedale.dat (you can look at it online!).

(Note that the examples in this section will work only if your computer is actually connected to the Internet.)

Module urllib.request contains a function called urlopen that opens a web page for reading. urlopen returns a file-like object that you can use much as if you were reading a local file.

There's a hitch: because there are many kinds of files (images, music, videos, text, and more), the file-like object's read and readline methods both return a type you haven't yet encountered: bytes.

What's a Byte?

To a computer, information is nothing but *bits*, which we think of as ones and zeros. All data—for example, characters, sounds, and pixels—are represented as sequences of bits. Computers organize these bits into groups of eight. Each group of eight bits is called a *byte*. Programming languages interpret these bytes for us and let us think of them as integers, strings, functions, and documents.

When dealing with type bytes, such as a piece of information returned by a call on function urllib.urlrequest.read, we need to decode it. In order to decode it, we need to know how it was encoded.

Common encoding schemes are described in the online Python documentation here: http://docs.python.org/3/library/codecs.html#standard-encodings.

The Hopedale data on the Web is encoded using UTF-8. This program reads that web page and uses string method decode in order to decode the bytes object:

```
import urllib.request
url = 'http://robjhyndman.com/tsdldata/ecology1/hopedale.dat'
with urllib.request.urlopen(url) as webpage:
    for line in webpage:
        line = line.strip()
        line = line.decode('utf-8')
        print(line)
```

10.5 Writing Files

This program opens a file called topics.txt, writes the words Computer Science to the file, and then closes the file:

```
with open('topics.txt', 'w') as output_file:
    output_file.write('Computer Science')
```

In addition to writing characters to a file, method write returns the number of characters written. For example, output_file.write('Computer Science') returns 16.

To create a new file or to replace the contents of an existing file, we use write mode ('w'). If the filename doesn't exist already, then a new file is created; otherwise the file contents are erased and replaced. Once opened for writing, you can use method write to write a string to the file.

Rather than replacing the file contents, we can also add to a file using the append mode ('a'). When we write to a file that is opened in append mode, the data we write is added to the end of the file and the current file contents are not overwritten. For example, to add to our previous file topics.txt, we can append the words Software Engineering:

```
with open('topics.txt', 'a') as output_file:
    output_file.write('Software Engineering')
```

At this point, if we print the contents of topics.txt, we'd see the following:

```
Computer ScienceSoftware Engineering
```

Unlike function print, method write doesn't automatically start a new line; if you want a string to end in a newline, you have to include it manually using '\n'. In each of the previous examples, we called write only once, but you'll typically call it multiple times.

The next example, in a file called total.py, is more complex, and it involves both reading from and writing to a file. Our input file contains two numbers per line separated by a space. The output file will contain three numbers: the two from the input file and their sum (all separated by spaces):

```
def sum_number_pairs(input_file, output_filename):
    """ (file open for reading, str) -> NoneType

    Read the data from input_file, which contains two floats per line
    separated by a space.  Open file named output_file and, for each line in
    input_file, write a line to the output file that contains the two floats
    from the corresponding line of input_file plus a space and the sum of the
    two floats.
    """

    with open(output_filename, 'w') as output_file:
        for number_pair in input_file:
            number_pair = number_pair.strip()
            operands = number_pair.split()
            total = float(operands[0]) + float(operands[1])
            new_line = '{0} {1}\n'.format(number_pair, total)
            output_file.write(new_line)
```

Assume that a file called number_pairs.txt exists with these contents:

```
1.3 3.4
2 4.2
-1 1
```

Then total.sum_number_pairs(open('number_pairs.txt', 'r'), 'out.txt') creates this file:

```
1.3 3.4 4.7
2 4.2 6.2
-1 1 0.0
```

10.6 Writing Algorithms That Use the File-Reading Techniques

There are several common ways to organize information in files. The rest of this chapter will show how to apply the various file-reading techniques to these situations and how to develop some algorithms to help with this.

Skipping the Header

Many data files begin with a header. As described in *The Readline Technique*, on page 179, TSDL files begin with a one-line description followed by comments in lines beginning with a #, and the Readline technique can be used to skip that header. The technique ends when we read the first real piece of data, which will be the first line after the description that doesn't start with a #.

In English, we might try this algorithm to process this kind of a file:

```
Skip the first line in the file
Skip over the comment lines in the file
For each of the remaining lines in the file:
    Process the data on that line
```

The problem with this approach is that we can't tell whether a line is a comment line until we've read it, but we can read a line from a file only once—there's no simple way to "back up" in the file. An alternative approach is to read the line, skip it if it's a comment, and process it if it's not. Once we've processed the first line of data, we process the remaining lines:

```
Skip the first line in the file
Find and process the first line of data in the file
For each of the remaining lines:
    Process the data on that line
```

The thing to notice about this algorithm is that it processes lines in two places: once when it finds the first "interesting" line in the file and once when it handles all of the following lines:

```python
def skip_header(reader):
    """ (file open for reading) -> str
    Skip the header in reader and return the first real piece of data.
    """

    # Read the description line
    line = reader.readline()

    # Find the first non-comment line
    line = reader.readline()
    while line.startswith('#'):
        line = reader.readline()

    # Now line contains the first real piece of data
    return line

def process_file(reader):
    """ (file open for reading) -> NoneType
    Read and print the data from reader, which must start with a single
    description line, then a sequence of lines beginning with '#', then a
    sequence of data.
    """

    # Find and print the first piece of data
    line = skip_header(reader).strip()
    print(line)

    # Read the rest of the data
    for line in reader:
        line = line.strip()
        print(line)

if __name__ == '__main__':
    with open('hopedale.txt', 'r') as input_file:
        process_file(input_file)
```

In skip_header, we return the first line of read data, because once we've found it, we can't read it again (we can go forward but not backward). We'll want to use skip_header in all of the file-processing functions in this section. Rather than copying the code each time we want to use it, we can put the function in a file called time_series.py (for *Time Series Data Library*) and use it in other programs using import time_series, as shown in the next example. This allows us to reuse the skip_header code, and if it needs to be modified, then there is only one copy of the function to edit.

This program processes the Hopedale data set to find the smallest number of fox pelts produced in any year. As we progress through the file, we keep the smallest value seen so far in a variable called smallest. That variable is initially set to the value on the first line, since it's the smallest (and only) value seen so far:

```python
import time_series


def smallest_value(reader):
    """ (file open for reading) -> int

    Read and process reader and return the smallest value after the
    time_series header.
    """

    line = time_series.skip_header(reader).strip()

    # Now line contains the first data value; this is also the smallest value
    # found so far, because it is the only one we have seen.
    smallest = int(line)

    for line in reader:
        value = int(line.strip())

        # If we find a smaller value, remember it.
        if value < smallest:
            smallest = value

    return smallest

if __name__ == '__main__':
    with open('hopedale.txt', 'r') as input_file:
        print(smallest_value(input_file))
```

As with any algorithm, there are other ways to write this; for example, we can replace the if statement with this single line:

```python
smallest = min(smallest, value)
```

Dealing with Missing Values in Data

We also have data for colored fox production in Hebron, Labrador:

```
Coloured fox fur production, Hebron, Labrador, 1834-1839
#Source: C. Elton (1942) "Voles, Mice and Lemmings", Oxford Univ. Press
#Table 17, p.265--266
#remark: missing value for 1836
    55
   262
    -
   102
   178
   227
```

The hyphen indicates that data for the year 1836 is missing. Unfortunately, calling read_smallest on the Hebron data produces this error:

```
>>> import read_smallest
>>> read_smallest.smallest_value(open('hebron.txt', 'r'))
Traceback (most recent call last):
  File "<stdin>", line 1, in <module>
  File "./read_smallest.py", line 19, in smallest_value
    value = int(line.strip())
ValueError: invalid literal for int() with base 10: '-'
```

The problem is that '-' isn't an integer, so calling int('-') fails. This isn't an isolated problem. In general, we will often need to skip blank lines, comments, or lines containing other "nonvalues" in our data. Real data sets often contain omissions or contradictions; dealing with them is just a fact of scientific life.

To fix our code, we must add a check inside the loop that processes a line only if it contains a real value. In the TSDL data sets, missing entries are always marked with hyphens, so we just need to check for that before trying to convert the string we have read to an integer:

```
import time_series


def smallest_value_skip(reader):
    """ (file open for reading) -> int
    Read and process reader, which must start with a time_series header.
    Return the smallest value after the header.  Skip missing values, which
    are indicated with a hyphen.
    """

    line = time_series.skip_header(reader).strip()
    # Now line contains the first data value; this is also the smallest value
    # found so far, because it is the only one we have seen.
    smallest = int(line)
```

```
    for line in reader:
        line = line.strip()
        if line != '-':
            value = int(line)
            smallest = min(smallest, value)

    return smallest

if __name__ == '__main__':
    with open('hebron.txt', 'r') as input_file:
        print(smallest_value_skip(input_file))
```

Notice that the update to smallest is nested inside the check for hyphens.

Processing Whitespace-Delimited Data

The file at http://robjhyndman.com/tsdldata/ecology1/lynx.dat (*Time Series Data Library [Hyn06]*) contains information about lynx pelts in the years 1821–1934. All data values are integers, each line contains many values, the values are separated by whitespace, and for reasons best known to the file's author, each value ends with a period.

```
Annual Number of Lynx Trapped, MacKenzie River, 1821-1934
#Original Source: Elton, C. and Nicholson, M. (1942)
#"The ten year cycle in numbers of Canadian lynx",
#J. Animal Ecology, Vol. 11, 215--244.
#This is the famous data set which has been listed before in
#various publications:
#Cambell, M.J. and Walker, A.M. (1977) "A survey of statistical work on
#the MacKenzie River series of annual Canadian lynx trappings for the years
#1821-1934 with a new analysis", J.Roy.Statistical Soc. A 140, 432--436.
  269.  321.  585.  871. 1475. 2821. 3928. 5943. 4950. 2577.  523.   98.
  184.  279.  409. 2285. 2685. 3409. 1824.  409.  151.   45.   68.  213.
  546. 1033. 2129. 2536.  957.  361.  377.  225.  360.  731. 1638. 2725.
 2871. 2119.  684.  299.  236.  245.  552. 1623. 3311. 6721. 4245.  687.
  255.  473.  358.  784. 1594. 1676. 2251. 1426.  756.  299.  201.  229.
  469.  736. 2042. 2811. 4431. 2511.  389.   73.   39.   49.   59.  188.
  377. 1292. 4031. 3495.  587.  105.  153.  387.  758. 1307. 3465. 6991.
 6313. 3794. 1836.  345.  382.  808. 1388. 2713. 3800. 3091. 2985. 3790.
  674.   81.   80.  108.  229.  399. 1132. 2432. 3574. 2935. 1537.  529.
  485.  662. 1000. 1590. 2657. 3396.
```

To process this, we will break each line into pieces and strip off the periods. Our algorithm is the same as it was for the fox pelt data: find and process the first line of data in the file, and then process each of the subsequent lines. However, the notion of "processing a line" needs to be examined further because there are many values per line. Our refined algorithm, shown next, uses nested loops to handle the notion of "for each line and for each value on that line":

```
Find the first line containing real data after the header
For each piece of data in the current line:
    Process that piece

For each of the remaining lines of data:
    For each piece of data in the current line:
        Process that piece
```

Once again we are processing lines in two different places. That is a strong hint that we should write a helper function to avoid duplicate code. Rewriting our algorithm and making it specific to the problem of finding the largest value, makes this clearer:

```
Find the first line of real data after the header
Find the largest value in that line

For each of the remaining lines of data:
    Find the largest value in that line
    If that value is larger than the previous largest, remember it
```

The *helper function* required is one that finds the largest value in a line, and it must split up the line. String method split will split around the whitespace, but we still have to remove the periods at the ends of the values.

We can also simplify our code by initializing largest to -1, because that value is guaranteed to be smaller than any of the (positive) values in the file. That way, no matter what the first real value is, it will be larger than the "previous" value (our -1) and replace it.

```python
import time_series

def find_largest(line):
    """ (str) -> int

    Return the largest value in line, which is a whitespace-delimited string
    of integers that each end with a '.'.

    >>> find_largest('1. 3. 2. 5. 2.')
    5
    """
    # The largest value seen so far.
    largest = -1
    for value in line.split():
        # Remove the trailing period.
        v = int(value[:-1])
        # If we find a larger value, remember it.
        if v > largest:
            largest = v

    return largest
```

We now face the same choice as with skip_header: we can put find_largest in a module (possibly time_series), or we can include it in the same file as the rest of the code. We choose the latter this time because the code is specific to this particular data set and problem:

```python
import time_series

def find_largest(line):
    """ (str) -> int

    Return the largest value in line, which is a whitespace-delimited string
    of integers that each end with a '.'.

    >>> find_largest('1. 3. 2. 5. 2.')
    5
    """
    # The largest value seen so far.
    largest = -1
    for value in line.split():
        # Remove the trailing period.
        v = int(value[:-1])
        # If we find a larger value, remember it.
        if v > largest:
            largest = v

    return largest

def process_file(reader):
    """ (file open for reading) -> int

    Read and process reader, which must start with a time_series header.
    Return the largest value after the header.  There may be multiple pieces
    of data on each line.
    """

    line = time_series.skip_header(reader).strip()
    # The largest value so far is the largest on this first line of data.
    largest = find_largest(line)

    # Check the rest of the lines for larger values.
    for line in reader:
        large = find_largest(line)
        if large > largest:
            largest = large

    return largest

if __name__ == '__main__':
    with open('lynx.txt', 'r') as input_file:
        print(process_file(input_file))
```

Notice how simple the code in process_file looks! This happened only because we decided to write helper functions. To show you how much clearer this is, here is the same code without using time_series.skip_header and find_largest as helper methods:

```python
def process_file(reader):
    """ (file open for reading) -> int

    Read and process reader, which must start with a time_series header.
    Return the largest value after the header.  There may be multiple pieces
    of data on each line.
    """

    # Read the description line
    line = reader.readline()

    # Find the first non-comment line
    line = reader.readline()
    while line.startswith('#'):
        line = reader.readline()

    # Now line contains the first real piece of data

    # The largest value seen so far in the current line
    largest = -1

    for value in line.split():

        # Remove the trailing period
        v = int(value[:-1])

        # If we find a larger value, remember it
        if v > largest:
            largest = v

    # Check the rest of the lines for larger values
    for line in reader:

        # The largest value seen so far in the current line
        largest_in_line = -1

        for value in line.split():

            # Remove the trailing period
            v = int(value[:-1])

            # If we find a larger value, remember it
            if v > largest_in_line:
                largest_in_line = v
```

```
        if largest_in_line > largest:
            largest = largest_in_line

    return largest

if __name__ == '__main__':
    with open('lynx.txt', 'r') as input_file:
        print(process_file(input_file))
```

10.7 Multiline Records

Not every data record will fit onto a single line. Here is a file in simplified Protein Data Bank (PDB) format that describes the arrangements of atoms in ammonia:

```
COMPND      AMMONIA
ATOM     1  N  0.257  -0.363   0.000
ATOM     2  H  0.257   0.727   0.000
ATOM     3  H  0.771  -0.727   0.890
ATOM     4  H  0.771  -0.727  -0.890
END
```

The first line is the name of the molecule. All subsequent lines down to the one containing END specify the ID, type, and *XYZ* coordinates of one of the atoms in the molecule.

Reading this file is straightforward using the techniques we have built up in this chapter. But what if the file contained two or more molecules, like this:

```
COMPND      AMMONIA
ATOM     1  N  0.257  -0.363   0.000
ATOM     2  H  0.257   0.727   0.000
ATOM     3  H  0.771  -0.727   0.890
ATOM     4  H  0.771  -0.727  -0.890
END
COMPND      METHANOL
ATOM     1  C  -0.748  -0.015   0.024
ATOM     2  O  0.558   0.420  -0.278
ATOM     3  H  -1.293  -0.202  -0.901
ATOM     4  H  -1.263   0.754   0.600
ATOM     5  H  -0.699  -0.934   0.609
ATOM     6  H  0.716   1.404   0.137
END
```

As always, we tackle this problem by dividing into smaller ones and solving each of those in turn. Our first algorithm is as follows:

```
While there are more molecules in the file:
    Read a molecule from the file
    Append it to the list of molecules read so far
```

Simple, except the only way to tell whether there is another molecule left in the file is to try to read it. Our modified algorithm is as follows:

```
reading = True
while reading:
    Try to read a molecule from the file
    If there is one:
        Append it to the list of molecules read so far
    else:  # nothing left
        reading = False
```

In Python, this is as follows:

```python
def read_molecule(reader):
    """ (file open for reading) -> list or NoneType

    Read a single molecule from reader and return it, or return None to signal
    end of file.  The first item in the result is the name of the compound;
    each list contains an atom type and the X, Y, and Z coordinates of that
    atom.
    """

    # If there isn't another line, we're at the end of the file.
    line = reader.readline()
    if not line:
        return None

    # Name of the molecule: "COMPND    name"
    key, name = line.split()

    # Other lines are either "END" or "ATOM num atom_type x y z"
    molecule = [name]
    line = reader.readline()

    # Parse all the atoms in the molecule.
    while not line.startswith('END'):
        key, num, atom_type, x, y, z = line.split()
        molecule.append([atom_type, x, y, z])
        line = reader.readline()

    return molecule

def read_all_molecules(reader):
    """ (file open for reading) -> list
    Read zero or more molecules from reader, returning a list of the molecule
    information.
    """

    # The list of molecule information.
    result = []
```

```
        reading = True
        while reading:
            molecule = read_molecule(reader)
            if molecule:  # None is treated as False in an if statement
                result.append(molecule)
            else:
                reading = False
        return result

if __name__ == '__main__':
    molecule_file = open('multimol.pdb', 'r')
    molecules = read_all_molecules(molecule_file)
    molecule_file.close()
    print(molecules)
```

The work of actually reading a single molecule has been put in a function of its own that must return some false value (such as None) if it can't find another molecule in the file. This function checks the first line it tries to read to see whether there is actually any data left in the file. If not, it returns immediately to tell read_all_molecules that the end of the file has been reached. Otherwise, it pulls the name of the molecule out of the first line and then reads the molecule's atoms one at a time down to the END line:

```
def read_molecule(reader):
    """ (file open for reading) -> list or NoneType

    Read a single molecule from reader and return it, or return None to signal
    end of file.  The first item in the result is the name of the compound;
    each list contains an atom type and the X, Y, and Z coordinates of that
    atom.
    """
    # If there isn't another line, we're at the end of the file.
    line = reader.readline()
    if not line:
        return None

    # Name of the molecule: "COMPND    name"
    key, name = line.split()

    # Other lines are either "END" or "ATOM num atom_type x y z"
    molecule = [name]
    reading = True

    while reading:
        line = reader.readline()
        if line.startswith('END'):
            reading = False
        else:
            key, num, atom_type, x, y, z = line.split()
            molecule.append([atom_type, x, y, z])
```

```
return molecule
```

Notice that this function uses exactly the same trick to spot the END that marks the end of a single molecule as the first function used to spot the end of the file.

10.8 Looking Ahead

Let's add one final complication. Suppose that molecules didn't have END markers but instead just a COMPND line followed by one or more ATOM lines. How would we read multiple molecules from a single file in that case?

At first glance (Figure 8, *A PDB file Without END markers*), it doesn't seem much different from the problem we just solved: read_molecule could extract the molecule's name from the COMPND line and then read ATOM lines until it got either an empty string signaling the end of the file or another COMPND line signaling the start of the next molecule. But once it has read that COMPND line, the line isn't available for the next call to read_molecule, so how can we get the name of the second molecule (and all the ones following it)?

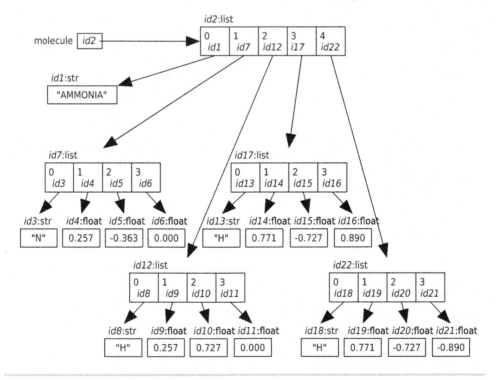

Figure 8—A PDB file Without END markers

To solve this problem, our functions must always "look ahead" one line. Let's start with the function that reads multiple molecules:

```python
def read_all_molecules(reader):
    """ (file open for reading) -> list

    Read zero or more molecules from reader,
    returning a list of the molecules read.
    """

    result = []
    line = reader.readline()
    while line:
        molecule, line = read_molecule(reader, line)
        result.append(molecule)

    return result
```

This function begins by reading the first line of the file. Provided that line is not the empty string (that is, the file being read is not empty), it passes both the opened file to read from and the line into read_molecule, which is supposed to return two things: the next molecule in the file and the first line immediately after the end of that molecule (or an empty string if the end of the file has been reached).

This simple description is enough to get us started writing the read_molecule function. The first thing it has to do is check that line is actually the start of a molecule. It then reads lines from reader one at a time, looking for one of three situations:

- The end of the file, which signals the end of both the current molecule and the file

- Another COMPND line, which signals the end of this molecule and the start of the next one

- An ATOM, which is to be added to the current molecule

The most important thing is that when this function returns, it returns both the molecule *and* the next line so that its caller can keep processing. The result is probably the most complicated function we have seen so far, but understanding the idea behind it will help you understand how it works. (Refer to the following code and Figure 9, *Looking ahead*, on page 196.)

```python
def read_molecule(reader, line):
    """ (file open for reading, str) -> list

    Read a molecule from reader, where line refers to the first line of
```

the molecule to be read. Return the molecule and the first line after
it (or the empty string if the end of file has been reached).
"""

```python
fields = line.split()
molecule = [fields[1]]

line = reader.readline()
while line and not line.startswith('COMPND'):
    fields = line.split()
    if fields[0] == 'ATOM':
        key, num, atom_type, x, y, z = fields
        molecule.append([atom_type, x, y, z])
    line = reader.readline()

return molecule, line
```

Figure 9—Looking ahead

10.9 Notes to File Away

In this chapter, you learned the following:

- When files are opened and read, their contents are commonly stored in lists of strings.

- Data stored in files is usually formatted in one of a small number of ways, from one value per line to multiline records with explicit end-of-record markers. Each format can be processed in a stereotypical way.

- Data processing programs should be broken into input, processing, and output stages so that each can be reused independently.

- Files can be read (content retrieved), written to (content replaced), and added to (new content appended). When a file is opened in writing mode and it doesn't exist, a new file is created.

- Data files come in many different formats, so custom code is often required, but we can reuse as much as possible by writing helper functions.

- To make the functions usable by different types of readers, the reader (for a file or web page) is opened outside the function, passed as an argument to the function, and then closed outside the function.

10.10 Exercises

Here are some exercises for you to try on your own. Solutions are available at http://pragprog.com/titles/gwpy2/practical-programming.

1. Write a program that makes a backup of a file. Your program should prompt the user for the name of the file to copy and then write a new file with the same contents but with .bak as the file extension.

2. Suppose the file alkaline_metals.txt contains the name, atomic number, and atomic weight of the alkaline earth metals:

```
beryllium 4 9.012
magnesium 12 24.305
calcium 20 20.078
strontium 38 87.62
barium 56 137.327
radium 88 226
```

    Write a for loop to read the contents of alkaline_metals.txt and store it in a list of lists, with each inner list containing the name, atomic number, and atomic weight for an element. (Hint: Use string.split.)

3. All of the file-reading functions we have seen in this chapter read forward through the file from the first character or line to the last. How could you write a function that would read backward through a file?

4. In *Processing Whitespace-Delimited Data*, on page 187, we used the "For Line in File" technique to process data line by line, breaking it into pieces using string method split. Rewrite function process_file to skip the header as normal but then use the Read technique to read all the data at once.

5. Modify the file reader in read_smallest_skip.py of *Skipping the Header*, on page 183, so that it can handle files with no data after the header.

6. Modify the file reader in read_smallest_skip.py of *Skipping the Header*, on page 183, so that it uses a continue inside the loop instead of an if. Which form do you find easier to read?

7. Modify the PDB file reader of Section 10.7, *Multiline Records*, on page 191, so that it ignores blank lines and comment lines in PDB files. A blank line is one

that contains only space and tab characters (that is, one that looks empty when viewed). A comment is any line beginning with the keyword CMNT.

8. Modify the PDB file reader to check that the serial numbers on atoms start at 1 and increase by 1. What should the modified function do if it finds a file that doesn't obey this rule?

## CHAPTER 11

Storing Data Using Other Collection Types

In Chapter 8, *Storing Collections of Data Using Lists*, on page 129, you learned how to store collections of data using lists. In this chapter, you will learn about three other kinds of collections: sets, tuples, and dictionaries. With four different options for storing your collections of data, you will be able to pick the one that best matches your problem in order to keep your code as simple and efficient as possible.

11.1 Storing Data Using Sets

A *set* is an unordered collection of distinct items. *Unordered* means that items aren't stored in any particular order. Something is either in the set or it's not, but there's no notion of it being the first, second, or last item. *Distinct* means that any item appears in a set at most once; in other words, there are no duplicates.

Python has a type called set that allows us to store mutable collections of unordered, distinct items. (Remember that a *mutable* object means one that you can modify.) Here we create a set containing these vowels:

```
>>> vowels = {'a', 'e', 'i', 'o', 'u'}
>>> vowels
{'a', 'u', 'o', 'i', 'e'}
```

It looks much like a list, except that sets use braces (that is, { and }) instead of brackets (that is, [and]). Notice that, when displayed in the shell, the set is unordered. Python does some mathematical tricks behind the scenes to make accessing the items very fast, and one of the side effects of this is that the items aren't in any particular order.

Here we show that each item is distinct; duplicates are ignored:

```
>>> vowels = {'a', 'e', 'a', 'a', 'i', 'o', 'u', 'u'}
>>> vowels
{'u', 'o', 'i', 'e', 'a'}
```

Even though there were three 'a's and two 'u's when we created the set, only one of each was kept. Python considers the two sets to be equal:

```
>>> {'a', 'e', 'i', 'o', 'u'} == {'a', 'e', 'a', 'a', 'i', 'o', 'u', 'u'}
True
```

The reason they are equal is that they contain the same items. Again, order doesn't matter, and only one of each element is kept.

Variable vowels refers to an object of type set:

```
>>> type(vowels)
<class 'set'>
>>> type({1, 2, 3})
<class 'set'>
```

In Section 11.3, *Storing Data Using Dictionaries*, on page 209, you'll learn about a type that uses the notation {}, which prevents us from using that notation to represent an empty set. Instead, to create an empty set, you need to call function set with no arguments:

```
>>> set()
set()
>>> type(set())
<class 'set'>
```

Function set expects either no arguments (to create an empty set) or a single argument that is a collection of values. We can, for example, create a set from a list:

```
>>> set([2, 3, 2, 5])
{2, 3, 5}
```

Because duplicates aren't allowed, only one of the 2s appears in the set:

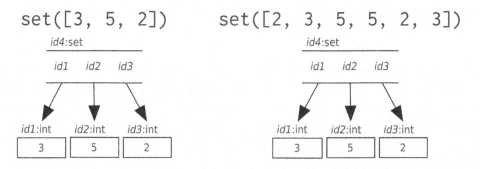

Function set expects at most one argument. You can't pass several values as separate arguments:

```
>>> set(2, 3, 5)
Traceback (most recent call last):
  File "<stdin>", line 1, in <module>
TypeError: set expected at most 1 arguments, got 3
```

In addition to lists, there are a couple of other types that can be used as arguments to function set. One is a set:

```
>>> vowels = {'a', 'e', 'a', 'a', 'i', 'o', 'u', 'u'}
>>> vowels
{'i', 'a', 'u', 'e', 'o'}
>>> set(vowels)
{'i', 'a', 'u', 'e', 'o'}
>>> set({5, 3, 1})
{1, 3, 5}
```

Another such type is range from *Generating Ranges of Numbers*, on page 150. In the following code a set is created with the values 0 to 4 inclusive:

```
>>> set(range(5))
{0, 1, 2, 3, 4}
```

In Section 11.2, *Storing Data Using Tuples*, on page 204, you will learn about the tuple type, another type of sequence, that can also be used as an argument to function set.

Set Operations

In mathematics, set operations include union, intersection, add, and remove. In Python, these are implemented as methods (for a complete list, see Table 13, *Set Operations*, on page 202). We'll show you these in action.

Sets are mutable, which means you can change what is in a set object. The methods add, remove, and clear all modify what is in a set. The letter y is sometimes considered to be a vowel; here we add it to our set of vowels:

```
>>> vowels = {'a', 'e', 'i', 'o', 'u'}
>>> vowels
{'o', 'u', 'a', 'e', 'i'}
>>> vowels.add('y')
>>> vowels
{'u', 'y', 'e', 'a', 'o', 'i'}
```

Other methods, such as intersection and union, return new sets based on their arguments.

In the following code, we show all of these methods in action:

```
>>> ten = set(range(10))
>>> lows = {0, 1, 2, 3, 4}
>>> odds = {1, 3, 5, 7, 9}
>>> lows.add(9)
>>> lows
{0, 1, 2, 3, 4, 9}
>>> lows.difference(odds)
{0, 2, 4}
>>> lows.intersection(odds)
{1, 3, 9}
>>> lows.issubset(ten)
True
>>> lows.issuperset(odds)
False
>>> lows.remove(0)
>>> lows
{1, 2, 3, 4, 9}
>>> lows.symmetric_difference(odds)
{2, 4, 5, 7}
>>> lows.union(odds)
{1, 2, 3, 4, 5, 7, 9}
>>> lows.clear()
>>> lows
set()
```

Method	Description
S.add(v)	Adds item v to a set S—this has no effect if v is already in S.
S.clear()	Removes all items from set S
S.difference(other)	Returns a set with items that occur in set S but not in set other
S.intersection(other)	Returns a set with items that occur both in sets S and other
S.issubset(other)	Returns True if and only if all of set S's items are also in set other
S.issuperset(other)	Returns True if and only if set S contains all of set other's items
S.remove(v)	Removes item v from set S
S.symmetric_difference(other)	Returns a set with items that are in exactly one of sets S and other—any items that are in both sets are *not* included in the result.
S.union(other)	Returns a set with items that are either in set S or other (or in both)

Table 13—Set Operations

Many of the tasks performed by methods can also be accomplished using operators. If acids and bases are two sets, for example, then acids | bases creates a new set containing their union (that is, all the elements from both acids and bases), while acids <= bases tests whether all the values in acids are also in bases. Some of the operators that sets support are listed in Table 14, *Set Operators*.

Method Call	Operator
set1.difference(set2)	set1 - set2
set1.intersection(set2)	set1 & set2
set1.issubset(set2)	set1 <= set2
set1.issuperset(set2)	set1 >= set2
set1.union(set2)	set1	set2
set1.symmetric_difference(set2)	set1 ^ set2

Table 14—Set Operators

The following code shows the set operations in action:

```
>>> lows = set([0, 1, 2, 3, 4])
>>> odds = set([1, 3, 5, 7, 9])
>>> lows - odds              # Equivalent to lows.difference(odds)
{0, 2, 4}
>>> lows & odds              # Equivalent to lows.intersection(odds)
{1, 3}
>>> lows <= odds             # Equivalent to lows.issubset(odds)
False
>>> lows >= odds             # Equivalent to lows.issuperset(odds)
False
>>> lows | odds              # Equivalent to lows.union(odds)
{0, 1, 2, 3, 4, 5, 7, 9}
>>> lows ^ odds              # Equivalent to lows.symmetric_difference(odds)
{0, 2, 4, 5, 7, 9}
```

Arctic Birds

To see how sets are used, suppose you have a file used to record observations of birds in the Canadian Arctic and you want to know which species have been observed. The observations file, observations.txt, has one species per line:

```
canada goose
canada goose
long-tailed jaeger
canada goose
snow goose
canada goose
long-tailed jaeger
canada goose
northern fulmar
```

The program below reads each line of the file, strips off the leading and trailing whitespace, and adds the species on that line to the set:

```
>>> observations_file = open('observations.txt')
>>> birds_observed = set()
>>> for line in observations_file:
...     bird = line.strip()
...     birds_observed.add(bird)
...
>>> birds_observed
{'long-tailed jaeger', 'canada goose', 'northern fulmar', 'snow goose'}
```

The resulting set contains four species. Since sets don't contain duplicates, calling the add method with a species already in the set had no effect.

You can loop over the values in a set. In the code below, a for loop is used to print each species:

```
>>> for species in birds_observed:
...     print(species)
...
long-tailed jaeger
canada goose
northern fulmar
snow goose
```

Looping over a set works exactly like a loop over a list, except that the order in which items are encountered is arbitrary: there is no guarantee that they will come out in the order in which they were added, in alphabetical order, in order by length, or in any other order.

11.2 Storing Data Using Tuples

Lists aren't the only kind of ordered sequence in Python. You've already learned about one of the others: strings (see Chapter 4, *Working with Text*, on page 65). Formally, a string is an immutable sequence of characters. The characters in a string are ordered and a string can be indexed and sliced like a list to create new strings:

```
>>> rock = 'anthracite'
>>> rock[9]
'e'
>>> rock[0:3]
'ant'
>>> rock[-5:]
'acite'
>>> for character in rock[:5]:
...     print(character)
...
```

a
n
t
h
r

Python also has an immutable sequence type called a *tuple*. Tuples are written using parentheses instead of brackets; like strings and lists, they can be subscripted, sliced, and looped over:

```
>>> bases = ('A', 'C', 'G', 'T')
>>> for base in bases:
...     print(base)
...
A
C
G
T
```

There's one small catch: although () represents the empty tuple, a tuple with one element is *not* written as (x) but as (x,) (with a trailing comma). This is done to avoid ambiguity. If the trailing comma weren't required, (5 + 3) could mean either 8 (under the normal rules of arithmetic) or the tuple containing only the value 8:

```
>>> (8)
8
>>> type((8))
<class 'int'>
>>> (8,)
(8,)
>>> type((8,))
<class 'tuple'>
>>> (5 + 3)
8
>>> (5 + 3,)
(8,)
```

Unlike lists, once a tuple is created, it cannot be mutated:

```
>>> life = (['Canada', 76.5], ['United States', 75.5], ['Mexico', 72.0])
>>> life[0] = life[1]
Traceback (most recent call last):
  File "<stdin>", line 1, in ?
TypeError: object does not support item assignment
```

However, the objects inside it *can* still be mutated:

```
>>> life = (['Canada', 76.5], ['United States', 75.5], ['Mexico', 72.0])
>>> life[0][1] = 80.0
>>> life
(['Canada', 80.0], ['United States', 75.5], ['Mexico', 72.0])
```

Rather than saying that a tuple cannot change, it is more accurate to say this: the references contained in a tuple cannot be changed after the tuple has been created, though the objects referred to may themselves be mutated.

Here is an example that explores what is mutable and what isn't. We'll build the same tuple as in the previous example, but we'll do it in steps. First let's create three lists:

```
>>> canada = ['Canada', 76.5]
>>> usa = ['United States', 75.5]
>>> mexico = ['Mexico', 72.0]
```

That builds this memory model:

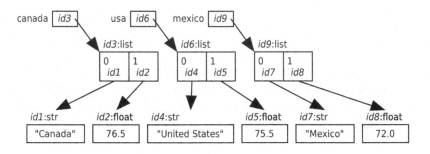

We'll create a tuple using those variables:

```
>>> life = (canada, usa, mexico)
```

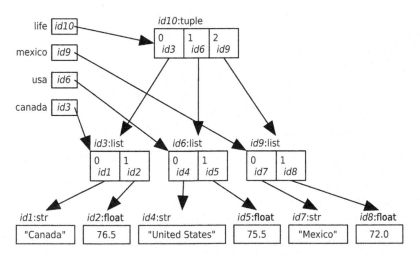

The most important thing to notice is that none of the four variables know about the others. The tuple object contains three references, one for each of the country lists.

Now let's change what variable mexico refers to:

```
>>> mexico = ['Mexico', 72.5]
>>> life
(['Canada', 76.5], ['United States', 75.5], ['Mexico', 72.0])
```

Notice that the tuple that variable life refers to hasn't changed. Here's the new picture:

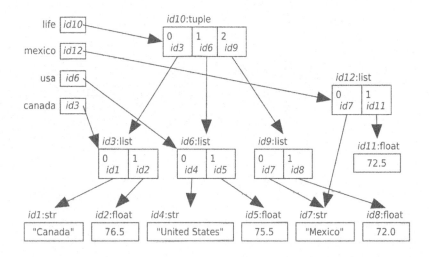

life[0] will always refer to the same list object—we can't change the memory address stored in life[0]—but we can mutate that list object; and because variable canada also refers to that list, it sees the mutation (see Figure 10, *Mutating the List Object*, on page 208).

```
>>> life[0][1] = 80.0
>>> canada
['Canada', 80.0]
```

We hope that it is clear how essential it is to thoroughly understand variables and references and how collections contain references to objects and not to variables.

Assigning to Multiple Variables Using Tuples

You can assign to multiple variables at the same time:

```
>>> (x, y) = (10, 20)
>>> x
10
>>> y
20
```

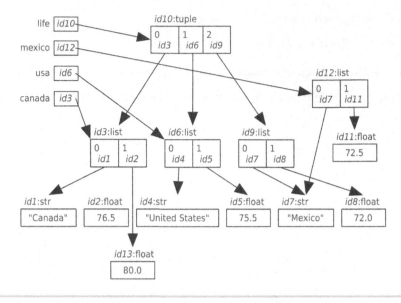

Figure 10—Mutating the List Object

As with a normal assignment statement (see *Assignment Statement*, on page 18), Python first evaluates all expressions on the right side of the = symbol, and then it assigns those values to the variables on the left side.

Python uses the comma as a tuple constructor, so we can leave off the parentheses:

```
>>> 10, 20
(10, 20)
>>> x, y = 10, 20
>>> x
10
>>> y
20
```

In fact, multiple assignment will work with lists and sets as well. Python will happily pull apart information out of any collection:

```
>>> [[w, x], [[y], z]] = [{10, 20}, [(30,), 40]]
>>> w
10
>>> x
20
>>> y
30
>>> z
40
```

Any depth of nesting will work as long as the structure on the right can be translated into the structure on the left.

One of the most common uses of multiple assignment is to swap the values of two variables:

```
>>> s1 = 'first'
>>> s2 = 'second'
>>> s1, s2 = s2, s1
>>> s1
'second'
>>> s2
'first'
```

This works because the expressions on the right side of operator = are evaluated before assigning to the variables on the left side.

11.3 Storing Data Using Dictionaries

Here is the same bird-watching observation file that we saw in *Arctic Birds*, on page 203:

```
canada goose
canada goose
long-tailed jaeger
canada goose
snow goose
canada goose
long-tailed jaeger
canada goose
northern fulmar
```

Suppose we want to know how often each species was seen. Our first attempt uses a list of lists, in which each inner list has two items. The item at index 0 of the inner list contains the species, and the item at index 1 contains the number of times it has been seen so far. To build this list, we iterate over the lines of the observations file. For each line, we iterate over the list, looking for the species on that line. If we find that the species occurs in the list, we add one to the number of times it has been observed:

```
>>> observations_file = open('observations.txt')
>>> bird_counts = []
>>> for line in observations_file:
...     bird = line.strip()
...     found = False
...     # Find bird in the list of bird counts.
...     for entry in bird_counts:
...         if entry[0] == bird:
...             entry[1] = entry[1] + 1
...             found = True
```

```
...         if not found:
...             bird_counts.append([bird, 1])
...
>>> observations_file.close()
>>> for entry in bird_counts:
...         print(entry[0], entry[1])
...
canada goose 5
long-tailed jaeger 2
snow goose 1
northern fulmar 1
```

The code above uses a Boolean variable, found. Once a species is read from the file, found is assigned False. The program then iterates over the list, looking for that species at index 0 of one of the inner lists. If the species occurs in an inner list, found is assigned True. At the end of the loop over the list, if found still refers to False it means that this species is not yet present in the list and so it is added, along with the number of observations of it, which is currently 1.

The code above works, but there are two things wrong with it. The first is that it is complex. The more nested loops our programs contain, the harder they are to understand, fix, and extend. The second is that it is inefficient. Suppose we were interested in beetles instead of birds and that we had millions of observations of tens of thousands of species. Scanning the list of names each time we want to add one new observation would take a long, long time, even on a fast computer (a topic we will return to in Chapter 13, *Searching and Sorting*, on page 237).

Can you use a set to solve both problems at once? Sets can look up values in a single step; why not combine each bird's name and the number of times it has been seen into a two-valued tuple and put those tuples in a set?

The problem with this idea is that you can look for values only if you know what those values are. In this case, you won't. You will know only the name of the species, not how many times it has already been seen.

The right approach is to use another data structure called a *dictionary*. Also known as a *map*, a dictionary is an unordered mutable collection of key/value pairs. In plain English, Python's dictionaries are like dictionaries that map words to definitions. They associate a key (like a word) with a value (such as a definition). The keys form a set. Any particular key can appear once at most in a dictionary; and like the elements in sets, keys must be immutable (though the values associated with them don't have to be).

Dictionaries are created by putting key/value pairs inside braces (each key is followed by a colon and then by its value):

```
>>> bird_to_observations = {'canada goose': 3, 'northern fulmar': 1}
>>> bird_to_observations
{'northern fulmar': 1, 'canada goose': 3}
```

We chose variable name bird_to_observations since this variable refers to a dictionary where each key is a bird and each value is the number of observations of that bird. In other words, the dictionary maps birds to observations. Here is a picture of the resulting dictionary:

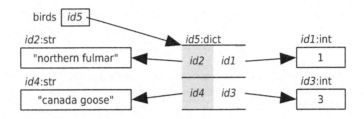

To get the value associated with a key, we put the key in square brackets, much like indexing into a list:

```
>>> bird_to_observations['northern fulmar']
1
```

Indexing a dictionary with a key it doesn't contain produces an error, just like an out-of-range index for a list does:

```
>>> bird_to_observations['canada goose']
3
>>> bird_to_observations['long-tailed jaeger']
Traceback (most recent call last):
  File "<stdin>", line 1, in <module>
KeyError: 'long-tailed jaeger'
```

The empty dictionary is written {} (this is why we can't use this notation for the empty set). It doesn't contain any key/value pairs, so indexing into it always results in an error.

Updating and Checking Membership

To update the value associated with a key, you use the same notation as for lists, except you use a key instead of an index. If the key is already in the dictionary, this assignment statement changes the value associated with it. If the key isn't present, the key/value pair is added to the dictionary:

```
>>> bird_to_observations = {}
>>>
>>> # Add a new key/value pair, 'snow goose': 33.
>>> bird_to_observations['snow goose'] = 33
>>>
```

```
>>> # Add a new key/value pair, 'eagle': 999.
>>> bird_to_observations['eagle'] = 999
>>> bird_to_observations
{'eagle': 999, 'snow goose': 33}
>>>
>>> # Change the value associated with key 'eagle' to 9.
>>> bird_to_observations['eagle'] = 9
>>> bird_to_observations
{'eagle': 9, 'snow goose': 33}
```

To remove an entry from a dictionary, use del d[k], where d is the dictionary and k is the key being removed. Only entries that are present can be removed; trying to remove one that isn't there results in an error:

```
>>> bird_to_observations = {'snow goose': 33, 'eagle': 9}
>>> del bird_to_observations['snow goose']
>>> bird_to_observations
{'eagle': 9}
>>> del bird_to_observations['gannet']
Traceback (most recent call last):
  File "<stdin>", line 1, in <module>
KeyError: 'gannet'
```

To test whether a key is in a dictionary, we can use the in operator:

```
>>> bird_to_observations = {'eagle': 999, 'snow goose': 33}
>>> if 'eagle' in bird_to_observations:
...     print('eagles have been seen')
...
eagles have been seen
>>> del bird_to_observations['eagle']
>>> if 'eagle' in bird_to_observations:
...     print('eagles have been seen')
...
>>>
```

The in operator only checks the keys of a dictionary. In the example above, 33 in birds evaluates to False, since 33 is a value, not a key.

Looping Over Dictionaries

Like the other collections you've seen, you can loop over dictionaries. The general form of a for loop over a dictionary is as follows:

```
for «variable» in «dictionary»:
    «block»
```

For dictionaries, the loop variable is assigned each key from the dictionary in turn:

```
>>> bird_to_observations = {'canada goose': 183, 'long-tailed jaeger': 71,
...                         'snow goose': 63, 'northern fulmar': 1}
>>> for bird in bird_to_observations:
...     print(bird, bird_to_observations[bird])
...
long-tailed jaeger 71
canada goose 183
northern fulmar 1
snow goose 63
```

Notice that long-tailed jaegar 71 is printed first, but in the assignment statement, the first key/value pair listed is 'canada goose': 183. As with the items in a set, Python loops over the keys in the dictionary in an arbitrary order. There is no guarantee they will be seen alphabetically or in the order they were added to the dictionary.

When Python loops over a dictionary, it assigns the keys to the loop variable. It's a lot easier to go from a dictionary key to the associated value than it is to take the value and find the associated key.

Dictionary Operations

Like lists, tuples, and sets, dictionaries are objects. Their methods are described in Table 15, *Dictionary Methods*, on page 214. The following code shows how the methods can be used:

```
>>> scientist_to_birthdate = {'Newton' : 1642, 'Darwin' : 1809,
...                           'Turing' : 1912}
>>> scientist_to_birthdate.keys()
dict_keys(['Darwin', 'Newton', 'Turing'])
>>> scientist_to_birthdate.values()
dict_values([1809, 1642, 1912])
>>> scientist_to_birthdate.items()
dict_items([('Darwin', 1809), ('Newton', 1642), ('Turing', 1912)])
>>> scientist_to_birthdate.get('Newton')
1642
>>> scientist_to_birthdate.get('Curie', 1867)
1867
>>> scientist_to_birthdate
{'Darwin': 1809, 'Newton': 1642, 'Turing': 1912}
>>> researcher_to_birthdate = {'Curie' : 1867, 'Hopper' : 1906,
...                            'Franklin' : 1920}
>>> scientist_to_birthdate.update(researcher_to_birthdate)
>>> scientist_to_birthdate
{'Hopper': 1906, 'Darwin': 1809, 'Turing': 1912, 'Newton': 1642,
 'Franklin': 1920, 'Curie': 1867}
>>> researcher_to_birthdate
{'Franklin': 1920, 'Hopper': 1906, 'Curie': 1867}
>>> researcher_to_birthdate.clear()
>>> researcher_to_birthdate
{}
```

Method	Description
D.clear()	Removes all key/value pairs from dictionary D.
D.get(k)	Returns the value associated with key k, or None if the key isn't present. (Usually you'll want to use D[k] instead.)
D.get(k, v)	Returns the value associated with key k, or a default value v if the key isn't present.
D.keys()	Returns dictionary D's keys as a set-like object—entries are guaranteed to be unique.
D.items()	Returns dictionary D's (key, value) pairs as set-like objects.
D.pop(k)	Removes key k from dictionary D and returns the value that was associated with k—if k isn't in D, an error is raised.
D.pop(k, v)	Removes key k from dictionary D and returns the value that was associated with k; if k isn't in D , returns v.
D.setdefault(k)	Returns the value associated with key k in D.
D.setdefault(k, v)	Returns the value associated with key k in D; if k isn't a key in D, adds the key k with the value v to D and returns v.
D.values()	Returns dictionary D's values as a list-like object—entries may or may not be unique.
D.update(other)	Updates dictionary D with the contents of dictionary other; for each key in other, if it is also a key in D, replaces that key in D's value with the value from other; for each key in other, if that key isn't in D, adds that key/value pair to D.

Table 15—Dictionary Methods

As you can see from this output, the keys and values methods return the dictionary's keys and values, respectively, while items returns the (key, value) pairs. Like the range object that you learned about previously, these are virtual sequences over which we can loop. Similarly, function list can be applied to them to create lists of keys/values or key/value tuples.

Because dictionaries usually map values from one concept (scientists, in our example) to another (birthdays), it's common to use variable names linking the two—hence, scientist_to_birthdate.

One common use of items is to loop over the keys and values in a dictionary together:

```
for key, value in dictionary.items():
    # Do something with the key and value
```

For example, the format above can be used to loop over the scientists and their birth years:

```
>>> scientist_to_birthdate = {'Newton' : 1642, 'Darwin' : 1809,
...                           'Turing' : 1912}
>>> for scientist, birthdate in scientist_to_birthdate.items():
...     print(scientist, 'was born in', birthdate)
...
Turing was born in 1912
Darwin was born in 1809
Newton was born in 1642
```

Instead of a single loop variable, there are two. The two parts of each of the two-item tuples returned by the method items is associated with a variable. Variable scientist refers to the first item in the tuple, which is the key, and birthdate refers to the second item, which is the value.

Dictionary Example

Back to birdwatching once again. Like before, we want to count the number of times each species has been seen. To do this, we create a dictionary that is initially empty. Each time we read an observation from a file, we check to see whether we have encountered that bird before—that is, whether the bird is already a key in our dictionary. If it is, we add 1 to the value associated with it. If it isn't, we add the bird as a key to the dictionary with the value 1. Here is the program that does this:

```
>>> observations_file = open('observations.txt')
>>> bird_to_observations = {}
>>> for line in observations_file:
...     bird = line.strip()
...     if bird in bird_to_observations:
...         bird_to_observations[bird] = bird_to_observations[bird] + 1
...     else:
...         bird_to_observations[bird] = 1
...
>>> observations_file.close()
>>>
>>> # Print each bird and the number of times it was seen.
... for bird, observations in bird_to_observations.items():
...     print(bird, observations)
...
snow goose 1
long-tailed jaeger 2
canada goose 5
northern fulmar 1
```

This program can be shortened by using the method dict.get, which saves three lines:

```
>>> observations_file = open('observations.txt')
>>> bird_to_observations = {}
>>> for line in observations_file:
...     bird = line.strip()
...     bird_to_observations[bird] = bird_to_observations.get(bird, 0) + 1
...
>>> observations_file.close()
```

Using the get method makes the program shorter, but some programmers find it harder to understand at a glance. If the first argument to get is not a key in the dictionary, it returns 0; otherwise it returns the value associated with that key. After that, 1 is added to that value. The dictionary is updated to associate that sum with the key that bird refers to.

Instead of printing the birds' names in whatever arbitrary order they are accessed by the loop, you can create a list of the dictionary's keys, sort that list alphabetically, and then loop over the sorted list. This way, the entries appear in a sensible order:

```
>>> sorted_birds = sorted(bird_to_observations.keys())
>>> for bird in sorted_birds:
...     print(bird, bird_to_observations[bird])
...
canada goose 5
long-tailed jaeger 2
northern fulmar 1
snow goose 1
```

If order matters, then an ordered sequence like lists or tuples should be used instead of sets and dictionaries.

11.4 Inverting a Dictionary

You might want to print the birds in another order—in order of the number of observations, for example. To do this, you need to *invert* the dictionary; that is, create a new dictionary in which you use the values as keys and the keys as values. This is a little trickier than it first appears. There's no guarantee that the values are unique, so you have to handle what are called *collisions*. For example, if you invert the dictionary {'a': 1, 'b': 1, 'c': 1}, a key would be 1, but it's not clear what the value associated with it would be.

Since you'd like to keep all of the data from the original dictionary, you may need to use a collection, such as a list, to keep track of the values associated with a key. If we go this route, the inverse of the dictionary shown earlier would be {1: ['a', 'b', 'c']}. Here's a program to invert the dictionary of birds to observations:

```
>>> bird_to_observations
{'canada goose': 5, 'northern fulmar': 1, 'long-tailed jaeger': 2,
'snow goose': 1}
>>>
>>> # Invert the dictionary
>>> observations_to_birds_list = {}
>>> for bird, observations in bird_to_observations.items():
...     if observations in observations_to_birds_list:
...         observations_to_birds_list[observations].append(bird)
...     else:
...         observations_to_birds_list[observations] = [bird]
...
>>> observations_to_birds_list
{1: ['northern fulmar', 'snow goose'], 2: ['long-tailed jaeger'],
5: ['canada goose']}
```

The program above loops over each key/value pair in the original dictionary, bird_to_observations. If that value is not yet a key in the inverted dictionary, observations_to_birds_list, it is added as a key and its value is a single-item list containing the key associated with it in the original dictionary. On the other hand, if that value is already a key, then the key associated with it in the original dictionary is appended to its list of values.

Now that the dictionary is inverted, you can print each key and all of the items in its value list:

```
>>> # Print the inverted dictionary
... observations_sorted = sorted(observations_to_birds_list.keys())
>>> for observations in observations_sorted:
...     print(observations, ':', end=" ")
...     for bird in observations_to_birds_list[observations]:
...         print(' ', bird, end=" ")
...     print()
...
1 :    northern fulmar   snow goose
2 :    long-tailed jaeger
5 :    canada goose
```

The outer loop passes over each key in the inverted dictionary, and the inner loop passes over each of the items in the values list associated with that key.

11.5 Using the In Operator on Tuples, Sets, and Dictionaries

As with lists, the in operator can be applied to tuples and sets to check whether an item is a member of the collection:

```
>>> odds = set([1, 3, 5, 7, 9])
>>> 9 in odds
True
```

```
>>> 8 in odds
False
>>> '9' in odds
False
>>> evens = (0, 2, 4, 6, 8)
>>> 4 in evens
True
>>> 11 in evens
False
```

When used on a dictionary, in checks whether a value is a key in the dictionary:

```
>>> bird_to_observations = {'canada goose': 183, 'long-tailed jaeger': 71,
...        'snow goose': 63, 'northern fulmar': 1}
>>> 'snow goose' in bird_to_observations
True
>>> 183 in bird_to_observations
False
```

Notice that the values in the dictionary are ignored; the in operator only looks at the keys.

11.6 Comparing Collections

You've now seen strings, lists, sets, tuples, and dictionaries. They all have their uses. Here is a table comparing them:

Collection	Mutable?	Ordered?	Use When...
str	No	Yes	You want to keep track of text.
list	Yes	Yes	You want to keep track of an ordered sequence that you want to update.
tuple	No	Yes	You want to build an ordered sequence that you know won't change or that you want to use as a key in a dictionary or as a value in a set.
set	Yes	No	You want to keep track of values, but order doesn't matter, and you don't want to keep duplicates. The values must be immutable.
dictionary	Yes	No	You want to keep a mapping of keys to values. The keys must be immutable.

Table 16—Features of Python Collections

11.7 A Collection of New Information

In this chapter, you learned the following:

• Sets are used in Python to store unordered collections of unique values. They support the same operations as sets in mathematics.

• Tuples are another kind of Python sequence. Tuples are ordered sequences like lists, except they are immutable.

• Dictionaries are used to store unordered collections of key/value pairs. The keys must be immutable, but the values need not be.

• Looking things up in sets and dictionaries is much faster than searching through lists. If you have a program that is doing the latter, consider changing your choice of data structures.

11.8 Exercises

Here are some exercises for you to try on your own. Solutions are available at http://pragprog.com/titles/gwpy2/practical-programming.

1. Write a function called find_dups that takes a list of integers as its input argument and returns a set of those integers that occur two or more times in the list.

2. Python's set objects have a method called pop that removes and returns an arbitrary element from the set. If the set gerbils contains five cuddly little animals, for example, calling gerbils.pop() five times will return those animals one by one, leaving the set empty at the end. Use this to write a function called mating_pairs that takes two equal-sized sets called males and females as input and returns a set of pairs; each pair must be a tuple containing one male and one female. (The elements of males and females may be strings containing gerbil names or gerbil ID numbers—your function must work with both.)

3. The PDB file format is often used to store information about molecules. A PDB file may contain zero or more lines that begin with the word AUTHOR (which may be in uppercase, lowercase, or mixed case), followed by spaces or tabs, followed by the name of the person who created the file. Write a function that takes a list of filenames as an input argument and returns the set of all author names found in those files.

4. The keys in a dictionary are guaranteed to be unique, but the values are not. Write a function called count_values that takes a single dictionary as an argument and returns the number of distinct values it contains. Given the input {'red': 1, 'green': 1, 'blue': 2}, for example, it should return 2.

5. After doing a series of experiments, you have compiled a dictionary showing the probability of detecting certain kinds of subatomic particles. The particles' names are the dictionary's keys, and the probabilities are the values: {'neutron': 0.55, 'proton': 0.21, 'meson': 0.03, 'muon': 0.07, 'neutrino': 0.14}. Write a function that takes a single dictionary of this kind as input and returns the particle that is least likely to be observed. Given the dictionary shown earlier, for example, the function would return 'meson'.

6. Write a function called count_duplicates that takes a dictionary as an argument and returns the number of values that appear two or more times.

7. A *balanced color* is one whose red, green, and blue values add up to 1.0. Write a function called is_balanced that takes a dictionary whose keys are 'R', 'G', and 'B' and whose values are between 0 and 1 as input and returns True if they represent a balanced color.

8. Write a function called dict_intersect that takes two dictionaries as arguments and returns a dictionary that contains only the key/value pairs found in both of the original dictionaries.

9. Programmers sometimes use a dictionary of dictionaries as a simple database. For example, to keep track of information about famous scientists, you might have a dictionary where the keys are strings and the values are dictionaries, like this:

```
{
    'jgoodall'  : {'surname'  : 'Goodall',
                   'forename' : 'Jane',
                   'born'     : 1934,
                   'died'     : None,
                   'notes'    : 'primate researcher',
                   'author'   : ['In the Shadow of Man',
                                 'The Chimpanzees of Gombe']},
    'rfranklin' : {'surname'  : 'Franklin',
                   'forename' : 'Rosalind',
                   'born'     : 1920,
                   'died'     : 1957,
                   'notes'    : 'contributed to discovery of DNA'},


    'rcarson'   : {'surname'  : 'Carson',
                   'forename' : 'Rachel',
                   'born'     : 1907,
                   'died'     : 1964,
                   'notes'    : 'raised awareness of effects of DDT',
                   'author'   : ['Silent Spring']}
}
```

Write a function called db_headings that returns the set of keys used in *any* of the inner dictionaries. In this example, the function should return set('author', 'forename', 'surname', 'notes', 'born', 'died').

10. Write another function called db_consistent that takes a dictionary of dictionaries in the format described in the previous question and returns True if and only if every one of the inner dictionaries has exactly the same keys. (This function would return False for the previous example, since Rosalind Franklin's entry doesn't contain the 'author' key.)

11. A *sparse vector* is a vector whose entries are almost all zero, like [1, 0, 0, 0, 0, 0, 3, 0, 0, 0]. Storing all those zeros in a list wastes memory, so programmers often use dictionaries instead to keep track of just the nonzero entries. For example, the vector shown earlier would be represented as {0:1, 6:3}, because the vector it is meant to represent has the value 1 at index 0 and the value 3 at index 6.

    a. The sum of two vectors is just the element-wise sum of their elements. For example, the sum of [1, 2, 3] and [4, 5, 6] is [5, 7, 9]. Write a function called sparse_add that takes two sparse vectors stored as dictionaries and returns a new dictionary representing their sum.

    b. The dot product of two vectors is the sum of the products of corresponding elements. For example, the dot product of [1, 2, 3] and [4, 5, 6] is 4+10+18, or 32. Write another function called sparse_dot that calculates the dot product of two sparse vectors.

    c. Your boss has asked you to write a function called sparse_len that will return the length of a sparse vector (just as Python's len returns the length of a list). What do you need to ask her before you can start writing it?

## CHAPTER 12

Designing Algorithms

An *algorithm* is a set of steps that accomplishes a task, such as the steps involved in synthesizing caffeine. Each function in a program, as well as the program itself, is an algorithm that is written in a programming language like Python. Writing a program directly in Python, without careful planning, can waste hours, days, or even weeks of effort. Instead, programmers often write algorithms in a combination of English and mathematics and then translate it into Python.

In this chapter, you'll learn an algorithm-writing technique called *top-down design*. You start by describing your solution in English and then mark the phrases that correspond directly to Python statements. Those that don't correspond are then rewritten in more detail in English, until everything in your description can be written in Python.

Top-down design is easy to describe, but doing it requires a little practice. Often, parts of an algorithm written in English will be tricky to translate into Python; in fact, an implementation may *look* reasonable but will contain bugs. This is common in many fields. In mathematics, for example, the first versions of "proofs" often handle common cases well but fail for odd cases (*Proofs and Refutations [Lak76]*). Mathematicians deal with this by looking for counterexamples, and programmers (good programmers, at least) deal with it by testing their code as they write it.

In this chapter, we have skipped the discussion of testing our code to make sure it works. In fact, the first versions we wrote had minor bugs in them, and we found them only by doing thorough testing. We will talk more about testing in Chapter 15, *Testing and Debugging*, on page 297.

12.1 Searching for the Smallest Values

This section will explore how to find the index of the smallest items in an unsorted list using three quite different algorithms. We'll go through a top-down design using each approach.

To start, suppose we have data showing the number of humpback whales sighted off the coast of British Columbia over the past ten years:

809   834   477   478   307   122   96   102   324   476

The first value, 809, represents the number of sightings ten years ago; the last one, 476, represents the number of sightings last year.

We want to know how changes in fishing practices have impacted the whales' numbers. Our first question is, what was the lowest number of sightings during those years? This code tells us just that:

```
>>> counts = [809, 834, 477, 478, 307, 122, 96, 102, 324, 476]
>>> min(counts)
96
```

If we want to know in which year the population bottomed out, we can use index to find the position of the minimum:

```
>>> counts = [809, 834, 477, 478, 307, 122, 96, 102, 324, 476]
>>> low = min(counts)
>>> min_index = counts.index(low)
>>> print(min_index)
6
```

And here is a more succinct version:

```
>>> counts = [809, 834, 477, 478, 307, 122, 96, 102, 324, 476]
>>> counts.index(min(counts))
6
```

Now, what if we want to find the indices of the *two* smallest values? Lists don't have a method to do this directly, so we'll have to design an algorithm ourselves and then translate it to a Python function.

Here is the header for a function that does this.

```
def find_two_smallest(L):
    """ (list of int) -> tuple of (int, int)

    Return a tuple of the indices of the two smallest values in list L.

    >>> find_two_smallest([809, 834, 477, 478, 307, 122, 96, 102, 324, 476])
    (6, 7)
    """
```

As you may recall from Section 3.6, *Designing New Functions: A Recipe*, on page 47, the next step in the function design recipe is to write the function body.

There are at least three ways we could do this, each of which will be subjected to top-down design. We'll start by giving a very high-level description of each. Each of these descriptions is the first step in doing a top-down design for that approach.

- *Find, remove, find.* Find the index of the minimum, remove that item from the list, and find the index of the new minimum item in the list. After we have the second index, we need to put back the value we removed and, if necessary, adjust the second index to account for that reinsertion.

- *Sort, identify minimums, get indices.* Sort the list, get the two smallest numbers, and then find their indices in the original list.

- *Walk through the list.* Examine each value in the list in order, keep track of the two smallest values found so far, and update these values when a new smaller value is found.

The first two algorithms mutate the list, either by removing an item or by sorting the list. It is vital that our algorithms put things back the way we found them, or the people who call our functions are going to be annoyed with us.

While you are investigating these algorithms in the next few pages, consider this question: *Which one is the fastest?*

Find, Remove, Find

Here is the algorithm again, rewritten with one instruction per line and explicitly discussing the parameter L:

```
def find_two_smallest(L):
    """ (list of int) -> tuple of (int, int)

    Return a tuple of the indices of the two smallest values in list L.

    >>> find_two_smallest([809, 834, 477, 478, 307, 122, 96, 102, 324, 476])
    (6, 7)
    """
    # Find the index of the minimum item in L
    # Remove that item from the list
    # Find the index of the new minimum item in the list
    # Put the smallest item back in the list
    # If necessary, adjust the second index
    # Return the two indices
```

To address the first step, Find the index of the minimum item in *L*, we skim the output produced by calling help(list) and find that there are no methods that do exactly that. We'll refine it:

```
def find_two_smallest(L):
    """ (see above) """

    # Get the minimum item in L              <-- This line is new
    # Find the index of that minimum item    <-- This line is new
    # Remove that item from the list
    # Find the index of the new minimum item in the list
    # Put the smallest item back in the list
    # If necessary, adjust the second index
    # Return the two indices
```

Those first two statements match Python functions and methods: min does the first, and list.index does the second. (There are other ways; for example, we could have written a loop to do the search.)

We see that list.remove does the third, and the refinement of "Find the index of the new minimum item in the list" is also straightforward.

Notice that we've left some of our English statements in as comments, which makes it easier to understand *why* the Python code does what it does:

```
def find_two_smallest(L):
    """ (see above) """

    # Find the index of the minimum and remove that item
    smallest = min(L)
    min1 = L.index(smallest)
    L.remove(smallest)

    # Find the index of the new minimum
    next_smallest = min(L)
    min2 = L.index(next_smallest)

    # Put the smallest item back in the list
    # If necessary, adjust the second index
    # Return the two indices
```

Since we removed the smallest item, we need to put it back. Also, when we remove a value, the indices of the following values shift down by one.

So, since smallest has been removed, if we want to get the indices of the two lowest values in the *original* list, we might need to add 1 to min2:

```python
def find_two_smallest(L):
    """ (see above) """

    # Find the index of the minimum and remove that item
    smallest = min(L)
    min1 = L.index(smallest)
    L.remove(smallest)

    # Find the index of the new minimum
    next_smallest = min(L)
    min2 = L.index(next_smallest)

    # Put smallest back into L
    # Fix min2 in case it was affected by the reinsertion:
    # If min1 comes before min2, add 1 to min2
    # Return the two indices
```

That's enough refinement (finally!) to do it all in Python:

```python
def find_two_smallest(L):
    """ (list of int) -> tuple of (int, int)

    Return a tuple of the indices of the two smallest values in list L.

    >>> find_two_smallest([809, 834, 477, 478, 307, 122, 96, 102, 324, 476])
    (6, 7)
    """

    # Find the index of the minimum and remove that item
    smallest = min(L)
    min1 = L.index(smallest)
    L.remove(smallest)

    # Find the index of the new minimum
    next_smallest = min(L)
    min2 = L.index(next_smallest)

    # Put smallest back into L
    L.insert(min1, smallest)

    # Fix min2 in case it was affected by the reinsertion
    if min1 <= min2:
        min2 += 1

    return (min1, min2)
```

That seems like a lot of work, and it is. Even if you go right to code, you'll be thinking through all those steps. But by writing them down first, you have a much greater chance of getting it right with a minimum amount of work.

Sort, Identify Minimums, Get Indices

Here is the second algorithm rewritten with one instruction per line.

```python
def find_two_smallest(L):
    """ (list of int) -> tuple of (int, int)

    Return a tuple of the indices of the two smallest values in list L.

    >>> find_two_smallest([809, 834, 477, 478, 307, 122, 96, 102, 324, 476])
    (6, 7)
    """

    # Sort a copy of L
    # Get the two smallest numbers
    # Find their indices in the original list L
    # Return the two indices
```

That looks straightforward: we can use built-in function sorted, which returns a copy of the list with the items in order from smallest to largest. We could have used method list.sort to sort L, but that breaks a fundamental rule: never mutate the contents of parameters unless the docstring says to.

```python
def find_two_smallest(L):
    """ (see above) """

    # Get a sorted copy of the list so that the two smallest items are at the
    # front
    temp_list = sorted(L)
    smallest = temp_list[0]
    next_smallest = temp_list[1]

    # Find their indices in the original list L
    # Return the two indices
```

Now we can find the indices and return them the same way we did in find-remove-find:

```python
def find_two_smallest(L):
    """ (list of int) -> tuple of (int, int)

    Return a tuple of the indices of the two smallest values in list L.

    >>> find_two_smallest([809, 834, 477, 478, 307, 122, 96, 102, 324, 476])
    (6, 7)
    """

    # Get a sorted copy of the list so that the two smallest items are at the
    # front
    temp_list = sorted(L)
    smallest = temp_list[0]
```

```
    next_smallest = temp_list[1]

    # Find the indices in the original list L
    min1 = L.index(smallest)
    min2 = L.index(next_smallest)

    return (min1, min2)
```

Walk Through the List

Our last algorithm starts the same way as for the first two:

```
def find_two_smallest(L):
    """ (list of int) -> tuple of (int, int)

    Return a tuple of the indices of the two smallest values in list L.

    >>> find_two_smallest([809, 834, 477, 478, 307, 122, 96, 102, 324, 476])
    (6, 7)
    """

    # Examine each value in the list in order
    # Keep track of the indices of the two smallest values found so far
    # Update these values when a new smaller value is found
    # Return the two indices
```

We'll move the second line before the first one because it describes the whole process; it isn't a single step. Also, when we see phrases like *each value*, we think of iteration; the third line is part of that iteration, so we'll indent it:

```
def find_two_smallest(L):
    """ (see above) """

    # Keep track of the indices of the two smallest values found so far
    # Examine each value in the list in order
    #     Update these values when a new smaller value is found
    # Return the two indices
```

Every loop has three parts: an initialization section to set up the variables we'll need, a loop condition, and a loop body. Here, the initialization will set up min1 and min2, which will be the indices of the smallest two items encountered so far. A natural choice is to set them to the first two items of the list:

```
def find_two_smallest(L):
    """ (see above) """

    # Set min1 and min2 to the indices of the smallest and next-smallest
    # values at the beginning of L
    # Examine each value in the list in order
    #     Update these values when a new smaller value is found
    # Return the two indices
```

We can turn that first line into a couple lines of code; we've left our English version in as a comment:

```python
def find_two_smallest(L):
    """ (see above) """

    # Set min1 and min2 to the indices of the smallest and next-smallest
    # Values at the beginning of L
    if L[0] < L[1]:
        min1, min2 = 0, 1
    else:
        min1, min2 = 1, 0

    # Examine each value in the list in order
    #     Update these values when a new smaller value is found
    # Return the two indices
```

We have a couple of choices now. We can iterate with a for loop over the values, a for loop over the indices, or a while loop over the indices. Since we're trying to find indices and we want to look at all of the items in the list, we'll use a for loop over the indices—and we'll start at index 2 because we've examined the first two values already. At the same time, we'll refine the statement in the body of the loop to mention min1 and min2.

```python
def find_two_smallest(L):
    """ (see above) """

    # Set min1 and min2 to the indices of the smallest and next-smallest
    # values at the beginning of L
    if L[0] < L[1]:
        min1, min2 = 0, 1
    else:
        min1, min2 = 1, 0

    # Examine each value in the list in order
    for i in range(2, len(values)):
    #     Update min1 and/or min2 when a new smaller value is found
    # Return the two indices
```

Now for the body of the loop. We'll pick apart "update min1 and/or min2 when a new smaller value is found." Here are the possibilities:

- If L[i] is smaller than both min1 and min2, then we have a new smallest item; so min1 currently holds the second smallest, and min2 currently holds the third smallest. We need to update both of them.
- If L[i] is larger than min1 and smaller than min2, we have a new second smallest.
- If L[i] is larger than both, we skip it.

```python
def find_two_smallest(L):
    """ (see above) """

    # Set min1 and min2 to the indices of the smallest and next-smallest
    # values at the beginning of L
    if L[0] < L[1]:
        min1, min2 = 0, 1
    else:
        min1, min2 = 1, 0

    # Examine each value in the list in order
    for i in range(2, len(L)):
        #
        #     L[i] is smaller than both min1 and min2, in between, or
        #     larger than both:
        #     If L[i] is smaller than min1 and min2, update them both
        #     If L[i] is in between, update min2
        #     If L[i] is larger than both min1 and min2, skip it

    return (min1, min2)
```

All of those are easily translated to Python; in fact, we don't even need code for the "larger than both" case:

```python
def find_two_smallest(L):

    """ (list of int) -> tuple of (int, int)
    Return a tuple of the indices of the two smallest values in list L.

    >>> find_two_smallest([809, 834, 477, 478, 307, 122, 96, 102, 324, 476])
    (6, 7)
    """

    # Set min1 and min2 to the indices of the smallest and next-smallest
    # values at the beginning of L
    if L[0] < L[1]:
        min1, min2 = 0, 1
    else:
        min1, min2 = 1, 0

    # Examine each value in the list in order
    for i in range(2, len(L)):
        # L[i] is smaller than both min1 and min2, in between, or
        # larger than both

        # New smallest?
        if L[i] < L[min1]:
            min2 = min1
            min1 = i
```

```
    # New second smallest?
    elif L[i] < L[min2]:
        min2 = i

return (min1, min2)
```

12.2 Timing the Functions

Profiling a program means measuring how long it takes to run and how much memory it uses. These two measures—time and space—are fundamental to the theoretical study of algorithms. They are also pretty important from a pragmatic point of view. Fast programs are more useful than slow ones, and programs that need more memory than what your computer has aren't particularly useful at all.

This section introduces one way to time how long code takes to run. You'll see how to run the three functions we developed to find the two lowest values in a list on 1,400 monthly readings of air pressure in Darwin, Australia, from 1882 to 1998.[1]

Module time contains functions related to time. One of these functions is perf_counter, which returns a time in seconds. We can call it before and after the code we want to time and take the difference to find out how many seconds have elapsed. We multiply by 1000 in order to convert from seconds to milliseconds:

```
import time

t1 = time.perf_counter()

# Code to time goes here

t2 = time.perf_counter()
print('The code took {:.2f}ms'.format((t2 - t1) * 1000.))
```

We'll want to time all three of our find_two_smallest functions. Rather than copying and pasting the timing code three times, we'll write a function that takes another function as a parameter as well as the list to search in. This timing function will return how many milliseconds it takes to execute a call on the function. After the timing function is the main program that reads the file of sea level pressures and then calls the timing function with each of the find_two_smallest functions:

---

1. See http://www.stat.duke.edu/~mw/ts_data_sets.html.

```python
import time
import find_remove_find5
import sort_then_find3
import walk_through7

def time_find_two_smallest(find_func, lst):
    """ (function, list) -> float

    Return how many seconds find_func(lst) took to execute.
    """

    t1 = time.perf_counter()
    find_func(lst)
    t2 = time.perf_counter()
    return (t2 - t1) * 1000.0

if __name__ == '__main__':
    # Gather the sea level pressures
    sea_levels = []
    sea_levels_file = open('sea_levels.txt', 'r')
    for line in sea_levels_file:
        sea_levels.append(float(line))
    sea_levels_file.close()

    # Time each of the approaches
    find_remove_find_time = time_find_two_smallest(
        find_remove_find5.find_two_smallest, sea_levels)

    sort_get_minimums_time = time_find_two_smallest(
        sort_then_find3.find_two_smallest, sea_levels)

    walk_through_time = time_find_two_smallest(
        walk_through7.find_two_smallest, sea_levels)

    print('"Find, remove, find" took {:.2f}ms.'.format(find_remove_find_time))
    print('"Sort, get minimums" took {:.2f}ms.'.format(
        sort_get_minimums_time))
    print('"Walk through the list" took {:.2f}ms.'.format(walk_through_time))
```

The execution times were as follows:

Algorithm	Running Time (ms)
Find, remove, find	0.09ms
Sort, identify, index	0.30ms
Walk through the list	0.28ms

Notice how small these times are. No human being can notice the difference between values that are less than a millisecond; if this code never has to process lists with more than 1,400 values, we would be justified in choosing an implementation based on simplicity or clarity rather than on speed.

But what if we wanted to process millions of values? Find-remove-find outperforms the other two algorithms on 1,400 values, but how much does that tell us about how each will perform on data sets that are a thousand times larger? That will be covered in Chapter 13, *Searching and Sorting*, on page 237.

12.3 At a Minimum, You Saw This

In this chapter, you learned the following:

- The most effective way to design algorithms is to use top-down design, in which goals are broken down into subgoals until the steps are small enough to be translated directly into a programming language.

- Almost all problems have more than one correct solution. Choosing between them often involves a trade-off between simplicity and performance.

- The performance of a program can be characterized by how much time and memory it uses. This can be determined experimentally by profiling its execution. One way to profile time is with function perf_counter from module time.

12.4 Exercises

Here are some exercises for you to try on your own. Solutions are available at http://pragprog.com/titles/gwpy2/practical-programming.

1. A DNA sequence is a string made up of the letters *A*, *T*, *G*, and *C*. To find the complement of a DNA sequence, *A*s are replaced by *T*s, *T*s by *A*s, *G*s by *C*s, and *C*s by *G*s. For example, the complement of AATTGCCGT is TTAACGGCA.

   a. Write an outline in English of the algorithm you would use to find the complement.
   b. Review your algorithm. Will any characters be changed to their complement and then changed back to their original value? If so, rewrite your outline. Hint: Convert one character at a time, rather than all of the *A*s, *T*s, *G*s, or *C*s at once.
   c. Using the algorithm that you have developed, write a function named complement that takes a DNA sequence (a str) and returns the complement of it.

2. In this exercise, you'll develop a function that finds the minimum or maximum value in a list, depending on the caller's request.

a. Write a loop (including initialization) to find both the minimum value in a list and that value's index in one pass through the list.

b. Write a function named min_index that takes one parameter (a list) and returns a tuple containing the minimum value in the list and that value's index in the list.

c. You might also want to find the maximum value and its index. Write a function named min_or_max_index that has two parameters: a list and a bool. If the Boolean parameter refers to True, the function returns a tuple containing the minimum and its index; and if it refers to False, it returns a tuple containing the maximum and its index.

3. In *The Readline Technique*, on page 179, you learned how to read some files from the Time Series Data Library. In particular, you learned about the Hopedale data set, which describes the number of colored fox fur pelts produced from 1834 to 1842. This file contains one value per year per line.

a. Write an outline in English of the algorithm you would use to read the values from this data set to compute the average number of pelts produced per year.

b. Translate your algorithm into Python by writing a function named hopedale_average that takes a filename as a parameter and returns the average number of pelts produced per year.

4. Write a set of doctests for the find-two-smallest functions. Think about what kinds of data are interesting, long lists or short lists, and what order the items are in. Here is one list to test with: [1, 2]. What other interesting ones are there?

5. What happens if the functions to find the two smallest values in a list are passed a list of length one? What should happen, and why? How about length zero? Modify one of the docstrings to describe what happens.

6. This one is a fun challenge.

Edsgar Dijkstra is known for his work on programming languages. He came up with a neat problem that he called the Dutch National Flag problem: given a list of strings, each of which is either 'red', 'green', or 'blue' (each is repeated several times in the list), rearrange the list so that the strings are in the order of the Dutch national flag—all the 'red' strings first, then all the 'green' strings, then all the 'blue' strings.

Write a function called dutch_flag that takes a list and solves this problem.

## CHAPTER 13

Searching and Sorting

A huge part of computer science involves studying how to organize, store, and retrieve data. The amount of data is growing exponentially: according to IBM, 90 percent of the data in the world has been generated in the past two years.[1] There are many ways to organize and process data, and you need to develop an understanding of how to analyze how good your approach is. This chapter introduces you to some tools and concepts that you can use to tell whether a particular approach is faster or slower than another.

As you know, there are many solutions to each programming problem. If a problem involves a large amount of data, a slow algorithm will mean the problem can't be solved in a reasonable amount of time, even with an incredibly powerful computer. This chapter includes several examples of both slower and faster algorithms. Try running them yourself: experiencing just how slow (or fast) something is has a much more profound effect on your understanding than the data we include in this chapter.

Searching and sorting data are fundamental parts of programming. There are several ways to do both of them. In this chapter, we will develop several algorithms for searching and sorting lists, and then we will use them to explore what it means for one algorithm to be faster than another. As a bonus, this approach will give you another set of examples of how there are many solutions to any problem, and that the approach you take to solving a problem will dictate which solution you come up with.

13.1 Searching a List

As you have already seen in Table 10, *List Methods*, on page 141, Python lists have a method called index that searches for a particular item:

---

1.   http://www-01.ibm.com/software/data/bigdata/

```
index(...)
    L.index(value, [start, [stop]]) -> integer -- return first index of value
```

List method index starts at the front of the list and examines each item in turn. For reasons that will soon become clear, this technique is called *linear search*. Linear search is used to find an item in an *unsorted* list. If there are duplicate values, our algorithms will find the leftmost one:

```
>>> ['d', 'a', 'b', 'a'].index('a')
1
```

We're going to write several versions of linear search in order to demonstrate how to compare different algorithms that all solve the same problem.

After we do this analysis, we will see that we can search a *sorted* list much faster than we can search an unsorted list.

An Overview of Linear Search

Linear search starts at index 0 and looks at each item one by one. At each index, we ask this question: Is the value we are looking for at the current index? We'll show three variations of this. All of them use a loop of some kind, and they are all implementations of this function:

```
def linear_search(lst, value):
    """ (list, object) -> int

    Return the index of the first occurrence of value in lst, or return
    -1 if value is not in lst.

    >>> linear_search([2, 5, 1, -3], 5)
    1
    >>> linear_search([2, 4, 2], 2)
    0
    >>> linear_search([2, 5, 1, -3], 4)
    -1
    >>> linear_search([], 5)
    -1
    """

    # examine the items at each index i in lst, starting at index 0:
    #    is lst[i] the value we are looking for?  if so, stop searching.
```

The algorithm in the function body describes what every variation will do to look for the value.

We've found it to be helpful to have a picture of how linear search works. (We will use pictures throughout this chapter for both searching and sorting.)

Because all of our versions examine index 0 first, then index 1, then 2, and so on, that means that partway through our searching process we have this situation:

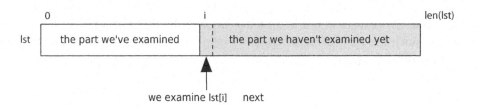

There is a part of the list that we've examined and another part that remains to be examined. We use variable i to mark the current index.

Here's a concrete example of where we are searching for a value in a list that starts like this: [2, -3, 5, 9, 8, -6, 4, 15, ...]. We don't know how long the list is, but let's say that after six iterations we have examined items at indices 0, 1, 2, 3, 4, and 5. Index 6 is the index of the next item to examine:

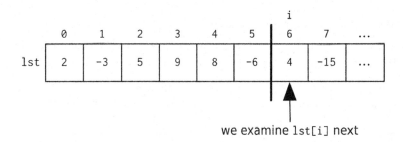

That vertical line divides the list in two: the part we have examined and the part we haven't. Because we stop when we find the value, we know that the value isn't in the first part:

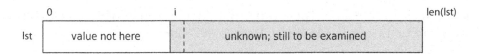

This picture is sometimes called an *invariant* of linear search. An invariant is something that remains unchanged throughout a process. But variable i is changing—how can that picture be an invariant?

Here is a word version of the picture:

```
lst[0:i] doesn't contain value, and 0 <= i <= len(lst)
```

This version says that we know that value wasn't found before index i and that i is somewhere between 0 and the length of the list. If our code matches that word version, that word version is an invariant of the code, and so is the picture version.

We can use invariants to come up with the initial values of our variables. For example, with linear search, at the very beginning the entire list is unknown —we haven't examined anything:

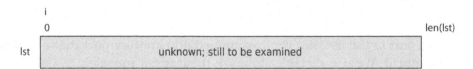

Variable i refers to 0 at the beginning, because then the section with the label value not here is empty; further, list[0:0] is an empty list, which is exactly what we want according to the word version of the invariant. So the initial value of i should be 0 in all of our versions of linear search.

The While Loop Version of Linear Search

Let's develop our first version of linear search. We need to refine our comments to get them closer to Python:

```
Examine every index i in lst, starting at index 0:
    Is lst[i] the value we are looking for?  if so, stop searching
```

Here's a refinement:

```
i = 0  # The index of the next item in lst to examine

While the unknown section isn't empty, and lst[i] isn't
the value we are looking for:
    add 1 to i
```

That's easier to translate. The unknown section is empty when i == len(lst), so it isn't empty as long as i != len(lst). Here is the code:

```python
def linear_search(lst, value):
    """ (list, object) -> int

    Return the index of the first occurrence of value in lst, or return
    -1 if value is not in lst.

    >>> linear_search([2, 5, 1, -3], 5)
    1
    >>> linear_search([2, 4, 2], 2)
    0
```

```
>>> linear_search([2, 5, 1, -3], 4)
-1
>>> linear_search([], 5)
-1
"""

i = 0  # The index of the next item in lst to examine.

# Keep going until we reach the end of lst or until we find value.
while i != len(lst) and lst[i] != value:
    i = i + 1

# If we fell off the end of the list, we didn't find value.
if i == len(lst):
    return -1
else:
    return i
```

This version uses variable i as the current index and marches through the values in lst, stopping in one of two situations: when we have run out of values to examine or when we find the value we are looking for.

The first check in the loop condition, i != len(lst), makes sure that we still have values to look at; if we were to omit that check, then if value isn't in lst, we would end up trying to access lst[len(lst)]. This would result in an IndexError.

The second check, lst[i] != value, causes the loop to exit when we find value. The loop body increments i; we enter the loop when we haven't reached the end of lst, and when lst[i] isn't the value we are looking for.

At the end, we return i's value, which is either the index of value (if the second loop check evaluated to False) or -1 if value wasn't in list.

The For Loop Version of Linear Search

The first version evaluates two Boolean subexpressions each time through the loop. But the first check, i != len(lst), is almost unnecessary: it evaluates to True almost every time through the loop, so the only effect it has is to make sure we don't attempt to index past the end of the list. We can instead exit the function as soon as we find the value:

```
i = 0  # The index of the next item in lst to examine

For each index i in lst:
    If lst[i] is the value we are looking for:
        return i

If we get here, value was not in lst, so we return -1
```

In this version, we use Python's for loop to examine each index.

```python
def linear_search(lst, value):
    """ (list, object) -> int

    … Exactly the same docstring goes here …
    """

    for i in range(len(lst)):
        if lst[i] == value:
            return i

    return -1
```

With this version, we no longer need the first check because the for loop controls the number of iterations. This for loop version is significantly faster than our first version; we'll see in a bit how much faster.

Sentinel Search

The last linear search we will study is called *sentinel search*. (A sentinel is a guard whose job it is to stand watch.) Remember that one problem with the while loop linear search is that we check i != len(lst) every time through the loop even though it can never evaluate to False except when value is not in lst. So we'll play a trick: we'll add value to the end of lst before we search. That way we are guaranteed to find it! We also need to remove it before the function exits so that the list looks unchanged to whoever called this function:

```
Set up the sentinel: append value to the end of lst

i = 0  # The index of the next item in lst to examine

While lst[i] isn't the value we are looking for:
    Add 1 to i

Remove the sentinel

return i
```

Let's translate that to Python:

```python
def linear_search(lst, value):
    """ (list, object) -> int

    … Exactly the same docstring goes here …
    """

    # Add the sentinel.
    lst.append(value)
```

```
    i = 0

    # Keep going until we find value.
    while lst[i] != value:
        i = i + 1

    # Remove the sentinel.
    lst.pop()

    # If we reached the end of the list we didn't find value.
    if i == len(lst):
        return -1
    else:
        return i
```

All three of our linear search functions are correct. Which one you prefer is largely a matter of taste: some programmers dislike returning in the middle of a loop, so they won't like the second version. Others dislike modifying parameters in any way, so they won't like the third version. Still others will dislike that extra check that happens in the first version.

Timing the Searches

Here is a program that we used to time the three searches on a list with about ten million values:

```
import time
import linear_search_1
import linear_search_2
import linear_search_3

def time_it(search, L, v):
    """ (function, list, object) -> number
    Time how long it takes to run function search to find
    value v in list L.
    """

    t1 = time.perf_counter()
    search(L, v)
    t2 = time.perf_counter()
    return (t2 - t1) * 1000.0

def print_times(v, L):
    """ (object, list) -> NoneType

    Print the number of milliseconds it takes for linear_search(v, L)
    to run for list.index, the while loop linear search, the for loop
    linear search, and sentinel search.
    """
```

```
# Get list.index's running time.
t1 = time.perf_counter()
L.index(v)
t2 = time.perf_counter()
index_time = (t2 - t1) * 1000.0

# Get the other three running times.
while_time = time_it(linear_search_1.linear_search, L, v)
for_time = time_it(linear_search_2.linear_search, L, v)
sentinel_time = time_it(linear_search_3.linear_search, L, v)

print("{0}\t{1:.2f}\t{2:.2f}\t{3:.2f}\t{4:.2f}".format(
        v, while_time, for_time, sentinel_time, index_time))

L = list(range(10000001))  # A list with just over ten million values

print_times(10, L)  # How fast is it to search near the beginning?
print_times(5000000, L)  # How fast is it to search near the middle?
print_times(10000000, L)  # How fast is it to search near the end?
```

This program makes use of function perf_counter in built-in module time. Function time_it will call whichever search function it's given on v and L and returns how long that search took. Function print_times calls time_it with the various linear search functions we have been exploring and prints those search times.

Linear Search Running Time

The running times of the three linear searches with that of Python's list.index are compared in Table 17, *Running Times for Linear Search (in milliseconds)*. This comparison used a list of 10,000,001 items and three test cases: an item near the front, an item roughly in the middle, and the last item. Except for the first case, where the speeds differ by very little, our while loop linear search takes about thirteen times as long as the one built into Python, and the for loop search and sentinel search take about five and seven times as long, respectively.

Case	while	for	sentinel	list.index
First	0.01	0.01	0.01	0.01
Middle	1261	515	697	106
Last	2673	1029	1394	212

Table 17—Running Times for Linear Search (in milliseconds)

What is more interesting is the way the *running times* of these functions increase with the number of items they have to examine. Roughly speaking, when they have to look through twice as much data, every one of them takes twice as long. This is reasonable because indexing a list, adding 1 to an integer, and evaluating the loop control expression require the computer to do a fixed amount of work. Doubling the number of times the loop has to be executed therefore doubles the total number of operations, which in turn should double the total running time. This is why this kind of search is called *linear*: the time to do it grows linearly with the amount of data being processed.

13.2 Binary Search

Is there a faster way to find values than by doing a linear search? The answer is yes, we can do much better, provided the list is sorted. To understand how, think about finding a name in a phone book. You open the book in the middle, glance at a name on the page, and immediately know which half to look in next. After checking only two names, you have eliminated $\frac{3}{4}$ of the numbers in the phone book. Even in a large city like Toronto, whose phone book has hundreds of thousands of entries, finding a name takes only a few steps.

This technique is called *binary search*, because each step divides the remaining data into two equal parts and discards one of the two halves. To figure out how fast it is, think about how big a list can be searched in a fixed number of steps. One step divides two values; two steps divide four; three steps divide $2^3 = 8$, four divide $2^4 = 16$, and so on. Turning this around, N values can be searched in roughly $\log_2 N$ steps.

More exactly, N values can be searched in ceiling($\log_2 N$) steps, where ceiling() is the ceiling function that rounds a value up to the nearest integer. As shown in Table 18, *Logarithmic Growth*, this increases much less quickly than the time needed for linear search.

Searching *N* Items	Worst Case—Linear Search	Worst Case—Binary Search
100	100	7
1000	1000	10
10,000	10,000	14
100,000	100,000	17
1,000,000	1,000,000	20
10,000,000	10,000,000	24

Table 18—Logarithmic Growth

The key to binary search is to keep track of three parts of the list: the left part, which contains values that are smaller than the value we are searching for; the right part, which contains values that are equal to or larger than the value we are searching for; and the middle part, which contains values that we haven't yet examined—the unknown section. (If there are duplicate values, we want to return the index of the leftmost one (as we did with linear search), which is why the "equal to" section belongs on the right.)

We'll use two variables to keep track of the boundaries: i will mark the index of the first unknown value, and j will mark the index of the last unknown value:

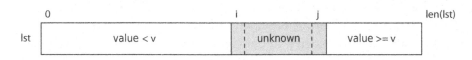

At the beginning of the algorithm, the unknown section makes up the entire list, so we will set i to 0 and j to the length of the list minus one:

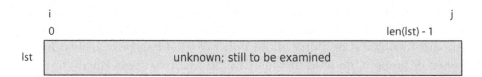

We are done when that unknown section is empty—when we've examined every item in the list. This happens when i == j + 1—when the values *cross*. (When i == j, there is still one item left in the unknown section.) Here is a picture of what the values are when the unknown section is empty:

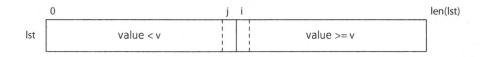

To make progress, we will set either i or j to near the middle of the range between them. Let's call this index m, which is at (i + j) // 2. (Notice the use of integer division: we are calculating an index, so we need an integer.)

Think for a moment about the value at m. If it is less than v, we need to move i up, while if it is greater than v, we should move j down. But where exactly do we move them?

When we move i up, we don't want to set it to the midpoint exactly, because L[m] isn't included in the range; instead, we set it to one past the middle, in other words, to m + 1.

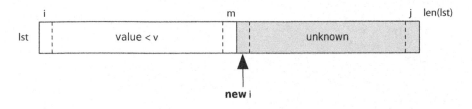

Similarly, when we move j down, we move it to m - 1:

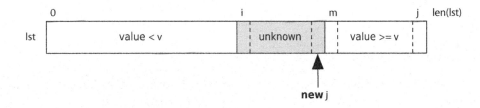

The completed function is as follows:

```python
def binary_search(L, v):
    """ (list, object) -> int

    Return the index of the first occurrence of value in L, or return
    -1 if value is not in L.

    >>> binary_search([1, 3, 4, 4, 5, 7, 9, 10], 1)
    0
    >>> binary_search([1, 3, 4, 4, 5, 7, 9, 10], 4)
    2
    >>> binary_search([1, 3, 4, 4, 5, 7, 9, 10], 5)
    4
    >>> binary_search([1, 3, 4, 4, 5, 7, 9, 10], 10)
    7
    >>> binary_search([1, 3, 4, 4, 5, 7, 9, 10], -3)
    -1
    >>> binary_search([1, 3, 4, 4, 5, 7, 9, 10], 11)
    -1
    >>> binary_search([1, 3, 4, 4, 5, 7, 9, 10], 2)
    -1
    >>> binary_search([], -3)
    -1
    >>> binary_search([1], 1)
    0
    """

    # Mark the left and right indices of the unknown section.
    i = 0
    j = len(L) - 1
```

```
    while i != j + 1:
        m = (i + j) // 2
        if L[m] < v:
            i = m + 1
        else:
            j = m - 1

    if 0 <= i < len(L) and L[i] == v:
        return i
    else:
        return -1

if __name__ == '__main__':
    import doctest
    doctest.testmod()
```

There are a lot of tests because the algorithm is quite complicated and we wanted to test pretty thoroughly. Our tests cover these cases:

- The value is the first item.
- The value occurs twice. We want the index of the first one.
- The value is in the middle of the list.
- The value is the last item.
- The value is smaller than everything in the list.
- The value is larger than everything in the list.
- The value isn't in the list, but it is larger than some and smaller than others.
- The list has no items.
- The list has one item.

In Chapter 15, *Testing and Debugging*, on page 297, you'll learn a different testing framework that allows you to write tests in a separate Python file (thus making docstrings shorter and easier to read; only a couple of examples are necessary), and you'll learn strategies for coming up with your own test cases.

Binary Search Running Time

Binary search is *much* more complicated to write and understand than linear search. Is it fast enough to make the extra effort worthwhile? To find out, we can compare it to list.index. As before, we search for the first, middle, and last items in a list with about ten million elements. (See Table 19, *Running Times for Binary Search*, on page 249.)

The results are impressive. Binary search is up to several thousand times faster than its linear counterpart when searching ten million items. Most importantly, if we double the number of items, binary search takes only one more iteration, while the time for list.index nearly doubles.

Case	list.index	binary_search	Ratio
First	0.007	0.02	0.32
Middle	105	0.02	5910
Last	211	0.02 (Wow!)	11661

Table 19—Running Times for Binary Search

Note also that although the time taken for linear search grows in step with the index of the item found, there is no such pattern for binary search. No matter where the item is, it takes the same number of steps.

Built-In Binary Search

The Python standard library's bisect module includes binary search functions that are slightly faster than our binary search. Function bisect_left returns the index where an item should be inserted in a list to keep it in sorted order, assuming it is sorted to begin with. insort_left actually does the insertion.

The word *left* in the name signals that these functions find the leftmost (lowest index) position where they can do their jobs; the complementary functions bisect_right and insort_right find the rightmost.

There's a problem, though: binary search assumes that the list is sorted, and sorting is time and memory intensive. When does it make sense to sort the list before we search?

13.3 Sorting

Now let's look at a slightly harder problem. The following table[2] shows the number of acres burned in forest fires in Canada from 1918 to 1987. What were the worst years?

563	7590	1708	2142	3323	6197	1985	1316	1824	472
1346	6029	2670	2094	2464	1009	1475	856	3027	4271
3126	1115	2691	4253	1838	828	2403	742	1017	613
3185	2599	2227	896	975	1358	264	1375	2016	452
3292	538	1471	9313	864	470	2993	521	1144	2212
2212	2331	2616	2445	1927	808	1963	898	2764	2073
500	1740	8592	10856	2818	2284	1419	1328	1329	1479

Table 20—Acres Lost to Forest Fires in Canada (in thousands), 1918–1987

---

2. http://robjhyndman.com/tsdldata/annual/canfire.dat: Number of acres burned in forest fires in Canada, 1918–1987.

One way to find out how much forest was destroyed in the *N* worst years is to sort the list and then take the last *N* values, as shown in the following code:

```
def find_largest(n, L):
    """ (int, list) -> list

    Return the n largest values in L in order from smallest to largest.

    >>> L = [3, 4, 7, -1, 2, 5]
    >>> find_largest(3, L)
    [4, 5, 7]
    """

    copy = sorted(L)
    return copy[-n:]
```

This algorithm is short, clean, and easy to understand, but it relies on a bit of black magic. How *does* function sorted (and also method list.sort) work, anyway? And how efficient are they?

It turns out that many sorting algorithms have been developed over the years, each with its own strengths and weaknesses. Broadly speaking, they can be divided into two categories: those that are simple but inefficient and those that are efficient but harder to understand and implement. We'll examine two of the former kind. The rest rely on techniques that are more advanced; we'll show you one of these, rewritten to use only material seen so far.

Both of the simple sorting algorithms keep track of two sections in the list being sorted. The section at the front contains values that are now in sorted order; the section at the back contains values that have yet to be sorted. Here is the main part of the invariant that we will use for our two simple sorts:

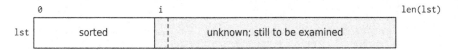

One of the two algorithms has an additional property in its invariant: the items in the sorted section must be smaller than all the items in the unknown section.

Both of these sorting algorithms will work their way through the list, making the sorted section one item longer on each iteration. We'll see that there are two ways to do this. Here is an outline for our code:

```
i = 0  # The index of the first unknown item in lst; lst[:i] is sorted
while i != len(L):
    # Do something to incorporate L[i] into the sorted section

    i = i + 1
```

Most Python programmers would probably write the loop header as for i in range(len(L)) rather than incrementing i explicitly in the body of the loop. We're doing the latter here to explicitly initialize i (to set up the loop invariant) and to show the increment separately from the work this particular algorithm is doing. The "do something…" part is where the two simple sorting algorithms will differ.

Selection Sort

Selection sort works by searching the unknown section for the smallest item and moving it to the index i. Here is our algorithm:

```
i = 0  # The index of the first unknown item in lst

# lst[:i] is sorted and those items are smaller than those in list[i:]
while i != len(L):
    # Find the index of the smallest item in lst[i:]
    # Swap that smallest item with the item at index i
    i = i + 1
```

As you can probably guess from this description, selection sort works by repeatedly finding the next smallest item in the unsorted section and placing it at the end of the sorted section. This works because we are selecting the items in order. On the first iteration, i is 0, and lst[0:] is the entire list. That means that on the first iteration we select the smallest item and move it to the front. On the second iteration we select the second-smallest item and move it to the second spot, and so on. (See Figure 11, *First few steps in selection sort*, on page 252.)

In a file named sorts.py, we have started writing a selection sort function, partially in English, as shown in the following code:

```
def selection_sort(L):
    """ (list) -> NoneType

    Reorder the items in L from smallest to largest.

    >>> L = [3, 4, 7, -1, 2, 5]
    >>> selection_sort(L)
    >>> L
    [-1, 2, 3, 4, 5, 7]
    """

    i = 0
    while i != len(L):
        # Find the index of the smallest item in L[i:]
        # Swap that smallest item with L[i]
        i = i + 1
```

We can replace the second comment with a single line of code.

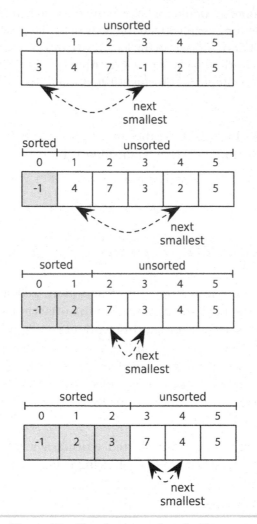

Figure 11—First few steps in selection sort

```python
def selection_sort(L):
    """ (list) -> NoneType

    Reorder the items in L from smallest to largest.

    >>> L = [3, 4, 7, -1, 2, 5]
    >>> selection_sort(L)
    >>> L
    [-1, 2, 3, 4, 5, 7]
    """

    i = 0
```

```
    while i != len(L):
        # Find the index of the smallest item in L[i:]
        L[i], L[smallest] = L[smallest], L[i]
        i = i + 1
```

Now all that's left is finding the index of the smallest item in L[i:]. This is complex enough that it's worth putting it in a function of its own:

```
def find_min(L, b):
    """ (list, int) -> int

    Precondition: L[b:] is not empty.
    Return the index of the smallest value in L[b:].

    >>> find_min([3, -1, 7, 5], 0)
    1
    >>> find_min([3, -1, 7, 5], 1)
    1
    >>> find_min([3, -1, 7, 5], 2)
    3
    """

    smallest = b  # The index of the smallest so far.
    i = b + 1
    while i != len(L):
        if L[i] < L[smallest]:
            # We found a smaller item at L[i].
            smallest = i

        i = i + 1

    return smallest

def selection_sort(L):
    """ (list) -> NoneType

    Reorder the items in L from smallest to largest.

    >>> L = [3, 4, 7, -1, 2, 5]
    >>> selection_sort(L)
    >>> L
    [-1, 2, 3, 4, 5, 7]
    """

    i = 0
    while i != len(L):
        smallest = find_min(L, i)
        L[i], L[smallest] = L[smallest], L[i]
        i = i + 1
```

Function find_min examines each item in L[b:], keeping track of the index of the minimum item so far in variable smallest. Whenever it finds a smaller item, it updates smallest. (Because it is returning the index of the smallest value, it won't work if L[b:] is empty; hence the precondition.)

This is complicated enough that a couple of doctests may not test enough. Here's a list of test cases for sorting:

- An empty list
- A list of length 1
- A list of length 2 (this is the shortest case where items move)
- An already-sorted list
- A list with all the same values
- A list with duplicates

Here are our expanded doctests:

```
def selection_sort(L):
    """ (list) -> NoneType

    Reorder the items in L from smallest to largest.

    >>> L = [3, 4, 7, -1, 2, 5]
    >>> selection_sort(L)
    >>> L
    [-1, 2, 3, 4, 5, 7]
    >>> L = []
    >>> selection_sort(L)
    >>> L
    []
    >>> L = [1]
    >>> selection_sort(L)
    >>> L
    [1]
    >>> L = [2, 1]
    >>> selection_sort(L)
    >>> L
    [1, 2]
    >>> L = [1, 2]
    >>> selection_sort(L)
    >>> L
    [1, 2]
    >>> L = [3, 3, 3]
    >>> selection_sort(L)
    >>> L
    [3, 3, 3]
    >>> L = [-5, 3, 0, 3, -6, 2, 1, 1]
    >>> selection_sort(L)
    >>> L
```

```
[-6, -5, 0, 1, 1, 2, 3, 3]
"""

i = 0

while i != len(L):
    smallest = find_min(L, i)
    L[i], L[smallest] = L[smallest], L[i]
    i = i + 1
```

As with binary search, the doctest is so long that, as documentation for the function, it obscures rather than helps clarify. Again, we'll see how to fix this in Chapter 15, *Testing and Debugging*, on page 297.

Insertion Sort

Like selection sort, *insertion sort* keeps a sorted section at the beginning of the list. Rather than scan all of the unsorted section for the next smallest item, though, it takes the next item from the unsorted section—the one at index i—and inserts it where it belongs in the sorted section, increasing the size of the sorted section by one.

```
i = 0  # The index of the first unknown item in lst; lst[:i] is sorted

while i != len(L):
    # Move the item at index i to where it belongs in lst[:i + 1]

    i = i + 1
```

The reason why we use lst[i + 1] is because the item at index i may be larger than everything in the sorted section, and if that is the case then the current item won't move.

In outline, this is as follows (save this in sorts.py as well):

```
def insertion_sort(L):
    """ (list) -> NoneType

    Reorder the items in L from smallest to largest.

    >>> L = [3, 4, 7, -1, 2, 5]
    >>> insertion_sort(L)
    >>> L
    [-1, 2, 3, 4, 5, 7]
    """

    i = 0
    while i != len(L):
        # Insert L[i] where it belongs in L[0:i+1].
        i = i + 1
```

This is exactly the same approach as for selection sort; the difference is in the comment in the loop. Like we did with selection sort, we'll write a helper function to do that work:

```python
def insert(L, b):
    """ (list, int) -> NoneType

    Precondition: L[0:b] is already sorted.
    Insert L[b] where it belongs in L[0:b + 1].

    >>> L = [3, 4, -1, 7, 2, 5]
    >>> insert(L, 2)
    >>> L
    [-1, 3, 4, 7, 2, 5]
    >>> insert(L, 4)
    >>> L
    [-1, 2, 3, 4, 7, 5]
    """

    # Find where to insert L[b] by searching backwards from L[b]
    # for a smaller item.
    i = b
    while i != 0 and L[i - 1] >= L[b]:
        i = i - 1

    # Move L[b] to index i, shifting the following values to the right.
    value = L[b]
    del L[b]
    L.insert(i, value)

def insertion_sort(L):
    """ (list) -> NoneType

    Reorder the items in L from smallest to largest.

    >>> L = [3, 4, 7, -1, 2, 5]
    >>> insertion_sort(L)
    >>> L
    [-1, 2, 3, 4, 5, 7]
    """

    i = 0

    while i != len(L):
        insert(L, i)
        i = i + 1
```

How does insert work? It works by finding out where L[b] belongs and then moving it. Where does it belong? It belongs after every value less than or equal to it and before every value that is greater than it. We need the check i != 0 in case L[b] is smaller than every value in L[0:b], which will place the current item at the beginning of the list. (See Figure 12, *First few steps in insertion sort*.) This passes all the tests we wrote earlier for selection sort.

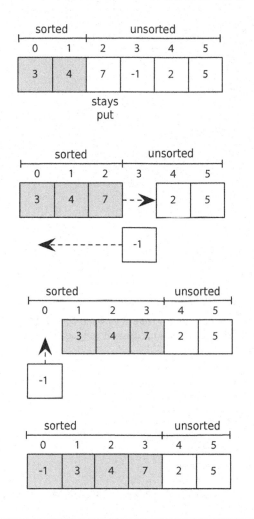

Figure 12—First few steps in insertion sort

Performance

We now have two sorting algorithms. Which should we use? Because both are not too difficult to understand, it's reasonable to decide based on how fast they are.

It's easy enough to write a program to compare their running times, along with that for list.sort:

```python
import time
import random
from sorts import selection_sort
from sorts import insertion_sort


def built_in(L):
    """ (list) -> NoneType

    Call list.sort --- we need our own function to do this so that we can
    treat it as we treat our own sorts.
    """

    L.sort()


def print_times(L):
    """ (list) -> NoneType

    Print the number of milliseconds it takes for selection sort, insertion
    sort, and list.sort to run.
    """

    print(len(L), end='\t')
    for func in (selection_sort, insertion_sort, built_in):
        if func in (selection_sort, insertion_sort) and len(L) > 10000:
            continue

        L_copy = L[:]
        t1 = time.perf_counter()
        func(L_copy)
        t2 = time.perf_counter()
        print("{0:7.1f}".format((t2 - t1) * 1000.), end='\t')

    print()  # Print a newline.

for list_size in [10, 1000, 2000, 3000, 4000, 5000, 10000]:
    L = list(range(list_size))
    random.shuffle(L)
    print_times(L)
```

The results are shown in Table 21, *Running Times for Selection, Insertion, and list.sort (in milliseconds)*, on page 259.

Something is very clearly wrong, because our sorting functions are thousands of times slower than the built-in function. What's more, the time required by our routines is growing faster than the size of the data. On a thousand items, for example, selection sort takes about 0.15 milliseconds per item, but on ten

List Length	Selection Sort	Insertion Sort	list.sort
1000	148	64	0.3
2000	583	268	0.6
3000	1317	594	0.9
4000	2337	1055	1.3
5000	3699	1666	1.6
10000	14574	6550	3.5

Table 21—Running Times for Selection, Insertion, and list.sort (in milliseconds)

thousand items, it needs about 1.45 milliseconds per item—slightly more than a tenfold increase! What is going on?

To answer this, we examine what happens in the inner loops of our two algorithms. On the first iteration of selection sort, the inner loop examines *every* element to find the smallest. On the second iteration, it looks at all but one; on the third, it looks at all but two, and so on.

If there are N items in the list, then the number of iterations of the inner loop, in total, is roughly $N + (N - 1) + (N - 2) + ... + 1$, or $N(N + 1)/2$. Putting it another way, the number of steps required to sort N items is roughly proportional to $N^2 + N$. For large values of N, we can ignore the second term and say that the time needed by selection sort grows as the square of the number of values being sorted. And indeed, examining the timing data further shows that doubling the size of the list increases the running time by four.

The same analysis can be used for insertion sort, since it also examines one element on the first iteration, two on the second, and so on. (It's just examining the already sorted values rather than the unsorted values.)

So why is insertion sort slightly faster? The reason is that, on average, only half of the values need to be scanned in order to find the location in which to insert the new value, while with selection sort, *every* value in the unsorted section needs to be examined in order to select the smallest one. But, wow, list.sort is *so* much faster!

13.4 More Efficient Sorting Algorithms

The analysis of selection and insertion sort begs the question, how can list.sort be so much more efficient? The answer is the same as it was for binary search: by taking advantage of the fact that some values are already sorted.

A First Attempt

Consider the following function:

```python
import bisect

def bin_sort(values):
    """ (list) -> list

    Return a sorted version of the values.  (This does not mutate values.)
    >>> L = [3, 4, 7, -1, 2, 5]
    >>> bin_sort(L)
    [-1, 2, 3, 4, 5, 7]
    """

    result = []
    for v in values:
        bisect.insort_left(result, v)

    return result
```

This code uses bisect.insort_left to figure out where to put each value from the original list into a new list that is kept in sorted order. As we have already seen, doing this takes time proportional to $\log_2 N$, where N is the length of the list. Since N values have to be inserted, the overall running time ought to be $N \log_2 N$.

As shown in the following table, this grows much more slowly with the length of the list than N^2.

N	N^2	$N \log_2 N$
10	100	3.32
100	10,000	6.64
1000	1,000,000	9.96

Table 22—Sorting Times

Unfortunately, there's a flaw in this analysis. It's correct to say that bisect.insort_left needs only $\log_2 N$ time to figure out where to insert a value, but actually inserting it takes time as well. To create an empty slot in the list, we have to move all the values above that slot up one place. On average, this means copying half of the list's values, so the cost of insertion is proportional to N. Since there are N values to insert, our total time is $N(N + \log_2 N)$. For large values of N, this is once again roughly proportional to N^2.

13.5 Mergesort: A Faster Sorting Algorithm

There are several well-known, fast sorting algorithms; mergesort, quicksort, and heapsort are the ones you are most likely to encounter in a future CS course. Most of them involve techniques that we haven't taught you yet, but mergesort can be written to be more accessible. Mergesort is built around the idea that taking two sorted lists and merging them is proportional to the number of items in both lists. The running time for mergesort is $N \log_2 N$.

We'll start with very small lists and keep merging them until we have a single sorted list.

Merging Two Sorted Lists

Given two sorted lists L1 and L2, we can produce a new sorted list by running along L1 and L2 and comparing pairs of elements. (We'll see how to produce these two sorted lists in a bit.)

Here is the code for merge:

```
def merge(L1, L2):
    """ (list, list) -> list

    Merge sorted lists L1 and L2 into a new list and return that new list.
    >>> merge([1, 3, 4, 6], [1, 2, 5, 7])
    [1, 1, 2, 3, 4, 5, 6, 7]
    """

    newL = []
    i1 = 0
    i2 = 0

    # For each pair of items L1[i1] and L2[i2], copy the smaller into newL.
    while i1 != len(L1) and i2 != len(L2):
        if L1[i1] <= L2[i2]:
            newL.append(L1[i1])
            i1 += 1
        else:
            newL.append(L2[i2])
            i2 += 1

    # Gather any leftover items from the two sections.
    # Note that one of them will be empty because of the loop condition.
    newL.extend(L1[i1:])
    newL.extend(L2[i2:])
    return newL
```

i1 and i2 are the indices into L1 and L2, respectively; in each iteration, we compare L1[i1] to L2[i2] and copy the smaller item to the resulting list. At the end of the loop, we have run out of items in one of the two lists, and the two extend calls will append the rest of the items to the result.

Mergesort

Here is the header for mergesort:

```
def mergesort(L):
    """ (list) -> NoneType

    Reorder the items in L from smallest to largest.

    >>> L = [3, 4, 7, -1, 2, 5]
    >>> mergesort(L)
    >>> L
    [-1, 2, 3, 4, 5, 7]
    """
```

Mergesort uses function merge to do the bulk of the work. Here is the algorithm, which creates and keeps track of a list of lists:

- Take list L and make a list of one-item lists from it.
- As long as there are two lists left to merge, merge them, and append the new list to the list of lists.

The first step is straightforward:

```
# Make a list of 1-item lists so that we can start merging.
workspace = []
for i in range(len(L)):
    workspace.append([L[i]])
```

The second step is trickier. If we remove the two lists, then we'll run into the same problem that we ran into in bin_sort: all the following lists will need to shift over, which takes time proportional to the number of lists.

Instead, we'll keep track of the index of the next two lists to merge. Initially, they will be at indices 0 and 1, and then 2 and 3, and so on:

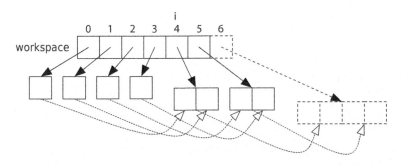

Here is our refined algorithm:

- Take list L and make a list of one-item lists from it.
- Start index i off at 0.
- As long as there are two lists (at indices i and i + 1), merge them, append the new list to the list of lists, and increment i by 2.

With that, we can go straight to code:

```
def mergesort(L):
    """ (list) -> NoneType

    Reorder the items in L from smallest to largest.

    >>> L = [3, 4, 7, -1, 2, 5]
    >>> mergesort(L)
    >>> L
    [-1, 2, 3, 4, 5, 7]
    """

    # Make a list of 1-item lists so that we can start merging.
    workspace = []
    for i in range(len(L)):
        workspace.append([L[i]])

    # The next two lists to merge are workspace[i] and workspace[i + 1].
    i = 0
    # As long as there are at least two more lists to merge, merge them.
    while i < len(workspace) - 1:
        L1 = workspace[i]
        L2 = workspace[i + 1]
        newL = merge(L1, L2)
        workspace.append(newL)
        i += 2

    # Copy the result back into L.
    if len(workspace) != 0:
        L[:] = workspace[-1][:]
```

Notice that since we're always making new lists, we need to copy the last of the merged lists back into the parameter L.

Mergesort Analysis

Mergesort, it turns out, is $N \log_2 N$, where N is the number of items in L. The following diagram shows the one-item lists getting merged into two-item lists, then four-item lists, and so on until there is one N-item list. (See Section 13.5, *Mergesort: A Faster Sorting Algorithm*, on page 261.)

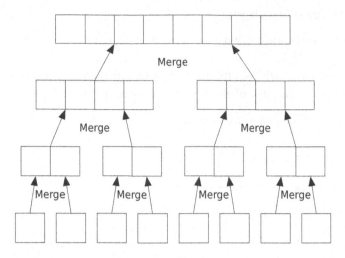

The first part of the function, creating the list of one-item lists, takes N iterations, one for each item.

The second loop, in which we continually merge lists, will take some care to analyze. We'll start with the very last iteration, in which we are merging two lists with about $^N/_2$ items. As we've seen, function merge copies each element into its result exactly once, so with these two lists, this merge step takes roughly N steps.

On the previous iteration, there are two lists of size $^N/_4$ to merge into one of the two lists of size $^N/_2$, and on the iteration before that there are another two lists of size $^N/_2$ to merge into the second list of size $^N/_2$. Each of these two merges takes roughly $^N/_2$ steps, so the two together take roughly N steps total.

On the iteration before that, there are a total of eight lists of size $^N/_8$ to merge into the four lists of size $^N/_4$. Four merges of this size together also take roughly N steps.

We can subdivide a list with N items a total of $\log_2 N$ times using an analysis much like we used for binary search. Since at each "level" there are a total of N items to be merged, each of these $\log_2 N$ levels takes roughly N steps. Hence, mergesort takes time proportional to $N \log_2 N$.

That's an awful lot of code to sort a list! There are shorter and clearer versions; but again, they rely on techniques that we haven't yet introduced.

Despite all the code and our somewhat messy approach (it creates a *lot* of sublists), mergesort turns out to be much, much faster than selection sort and insertion sort. More importantly, it grows at the same rate as the built-in sort:

List Length	Selection Sort	Insertion Sort	Mergesort	list.sort
1000	148	64	7	0.3
2000	583	268	15	0.6
3000	1317	594	23	0.9
4000	2337	1055	32	1.3
5000	3699	1666	41	1.6
10000	14574	6550	88	3.5

Table 23—Running Times for Selection, Insertion, Merge, and list.sort (in milliseconds)

13.6 Sorting Out What You Learned

In this chapter, you learned the following:

- An invariant describes the data being used in a loop. The initial values for the variables used in the loop will establish the invariant, and the work done inside the loop will make progress toward the solution. When the loop terminates, the invariant is still true, but the solution will have been reached.

- Linear search is the simplest way to find a value in a list; but on average, the time required is directly proportional to the length of the list.

- Binary search is much faster—the average time is proportional to the logarithm of the list's length—but it works only if the list is in sorted order.

- Similarly, the average running time of simple sorting algorithms like selection sort is proportional to the square of the input size N, while the running time of more complex sorting algorithms grows as $N \log_2 N$.

- Looking at how the running time of an algorithm grows as a function of the size of its inputs is the standard way to analyze and compare the algorithm's efficiency.

- Selection sort and insertion sort have almost the same invariant; the only difference is that with selection sort, the sorted section contains values that are smaller than all the values in the unsorted section. The two algorithms differ by how they make progress: selection sort selects the next-smallest item to put at the end of the sorted section, while insertion sort inserts the next item into the sorted section.

Big-Oh and All That

Our method of analyzing the performance of searching and sorting algorithms might seem like hand-waving, but there is actually a well-developed mathematical theory behind it. If f and g are functions, then the expression $f(x) = O(g(x))$ is read "f is big-oh of g" and means that for sufficiently large values of x, $f(x)$ is bounded above by some constant multiple of $g(x)$, or equivalently that function g gives us an upper bound on the values of function f. Computer scientists use this to group algorithms into families, such as those sorting functions that execute in N^2 time and those that execute in $N \log_2 N$ time.

These distinctions have important practical applications. In particular, one of the biggest puzzles in theoretical computer science today is whether two families of algorithms (called P and NP for reasons that we won't go into here) are the same or not. Almost everyone thinks they aren't, but no one has been able to prove it (despite the offer of a million-dollar prize for the first correct proof). If it turns out that they *are* the same, then many of the algorithms used to encrypt data in banking and military applications (as well as on the Web) will be much more vulnerable to attack than expected.

13.7 Exercises

Here are some exercises for you to try on your own. Solutions are available at http://pragprog.com/titles/gwpy2/practical-programming.

1. All three versions of linear search start at index 0. Rewrite all three to search from the end of the list instead of from the beginning. Make sure you test them.

2. For the new versions of linear search: if there are duplicate values, which do they find?

3. Binary search is significantly faster than the built-in search but requires that the list is sorted. As you know, the running time for the best sorting algorithm is on the order of $N \log_2 N$, where N is the length of the list. If we search a lot of times on the same list of data, it makes sense to sort it once before doing the searching. Roughly how many times do we need to search in order to make sorting and then searching faster than using the built-in search?

4. Given the unsorted list [6, 5, 4, 3, 7, 1, 2], show what the contents of the list would be after each iteration of the loop as it is sorted using the following:
   a. Selection sort
   b. Insertion sort

5. Another sorting algorithm is *bubble sort*. Bubble sort involves keeping a sorted section at the end of the list. The list is traversed, pairs of elements are compared, and larger elements are swapped into the higher position. This is repeated until all elements are sorted.

    a. Using the English description of bubble sort, write an outline of the bubble sort algorithm in English.

    b. Continue using top-down design until you have a Python algorithm.

    c. Turn it into a function called bubble_sort(L).

    d. Try it out on the test cases from selection_sort.

6. In the description of bubble sort in the previous exercise, the sorted section of the list was at the end of the list. In this exercise, bubble sort will maintain the sorted section at the beginning of the list. Make sure that you are still implementing bubble sort!

    a. Rewrite the English description of bubble sort from the previous exercise with the necessary changes so that the sorted elements are at the beginning of the list instead of at the end.

    b. Using your English description of bubble sort, write an outline of the bubble sort algorithm in English.

    c. Write function bubble_sort_2(L).

    d. Try it out on the test cases from selection_sort.

7. Modify the timing program to compare bubble sort with insertion and selection sort. Explain the results.

8. The analysis of bin_sort said, "Since N values have to be inserted, the overall running time is $N \log_2 N$." Point out a flaw in this reasoning, and explain whether it affects the overall conclusion.

9. There are at least two ways to come up with loop conditions. One of them is to answer the question, "When is the work done?" and then negate it. In function merge in *Merging Two Sorted Lists*, on page 261, the answer is, "When we run out of items in one of the two lists," which is described by this expression: i1 == len(L1) or i2 == len(L2). Negating this leads to our condition i1 != len(L1) and i2 != len(L2).

Another way to come up with a loop condition is to ask, "What are the valid values of the loop index?" In function merge, the answer to this is 0

<= i1 < len(L1) and 0 <= i2 < len(L2); since i1 and i2 start at zero, we can drop the comparisons with zero, giving us i1 < len(L1) and i2 < len(L2).

Is there another way to do it? Have you tried both approaches? Which do you prefer?

10. In function mergesort in *Mergesort*, on page 262, there are two calls to extend. They are there because when the preceding loop ends, one of the two lists still has items in it that haven't been processed. Rewrite that loop so that these extend calls aren't needed.

## CHAPTER 14

Object-Oriented Programming

Imagine you've been hired to help write a program to keep track of books in a bookstore. Every record about a book would probably include the title, authors, publisher, price, and ISBN, which stands for International Standard Book Number, a unique identifier for a book.

Read this code and try to guess what it prints:

```
python_book = Book(
    'Practical Programming',
    ['Campbell', 'Gries', 'Montojo'],
    'Pragmatic Bookshelf',
    '978-1-93778-545-1',
    25.0)

survival_book = Book(
    "New Programmer's Survival Manual",
    ['Carter'],
    'Pragmatic Bookshelf',
    '978-1-93435-681-4',
    19.0)

print('{0} was written by {1} authors and costs ${2}'.format(
    python_book.title, python_book.num_authors(), python_book.price))

print('{0} was written by {1} authors and costs ${2}'.format(
    survival_book.title, survival_book.num_authors(), survival_book.price))
```

You might guess that this code creates two book objects, one called *Practical Programming* and one called *New Programmer's Survival Manual.* You might even guess the output:

```
Practical Programming was written by 3 authors and costs $25.0
New Programmer's Survival Manual was written by 1 authors and costs $19.0
```

There's a problem, though: this code doesn't run. Python doesn't have a Book type. And that is what this chapter is about: how to define and use your own types.

14.1 Understanding a Problem Domain

In our book example, we wrote the code based on what we *wanted* to do with books. The idea of a Book type comes from the *problem domain*: keeping track of books in a bookstore. We thought about this problem domain and figured out what features of a book we cared about.

We might have decided to keep track of the number of pages, the date it was published, and much more; what you decide to keep track of depends exactly on what your program is supposed to do.

It's common to define multiple related types. For example, if this code was part of an online store, we might also have an Inventory type, perhaps a ShoppingCart type, and much more.

Object-oriented programming revolves around defining and using new types. As you learned in Section 7.1, *Modules, Classes, and Methods*, on page 115, a class is how Python represents a type. Object-oriented programming involves at least these phases:

1. *Understanding the problem domain.* This step is crucial: you need to know what your customer wants (your boss, perhaps a friend or business contact, perhaps yourself) before you can write a program that does what the customer wants.

2. *Figuring out what type(s) you might want.* A good starting point is to read the description of the problem domain and look for the main nouns and noun phrases.

3. *Figuring out what features you want your type to have.* Here you should write some code that *uses* the type you're thinking about, much like we did with the Book code at the beginning of this chapter. This is a lot like the Examples step in the function design recipe, where you decide what the code that you're about to write should do.

4. *Writing a class that represents this type.* You now need to tell Python about your type. To do this, you will write a class, including a set of methods inside that class. (You will use the function design recipe as you design and implement each of your methods.)

5. *Testing your code.* Your methods will have been tested separately as you followed the function design recipe, but it's important to think about how the various methods will interact.

14.2 Function "Isinstance," Class Object, and Class Book

Function isinstance reports whether an object is an *instance* of a class—that is, whether an object has a particular type:

```
>>> isinstance('abc', str)
True
>>> isinstance(55.2, str)
False
```

'abc' is an instance of str, but 55.2 is not.

Python has a class called object. Every other class is based on it:

```
>>> help(object)
Help on class object in module builtins:

class object
 |  The most base type
```

Function isinstance reports that both 'abc' and 55.2 are instances of class object:

```
>>> isinstance(55.2, object)
True
>>> isinstance('abc', object)
True
```

Even classes and functions are instances of object:

```
>>> isinstance(str, object)
True
>>> isinstance(max, object)
True
```

What's happening here is that every class in Python is *derived* from class object, and so every instance of every class is an object.

Using object-oriented lingo, we say that class object is the *superclass* of class str, and class str is a *subclass* of class object. The superclass information is available in the help documentation for a type:

```
>>> help(int)
Help on class int in module builtins:

class int(object)
```

Here we see that class SyntaxError is a subclass of class Exception:

```
>>> help(SyntaxError)
Help on class SyntaxError in module builtins:

class SyntaxError(Exception)
```

Class object has the following *attributes* (attributes are variables inside a class that refer to methods, functions, variables, or even other classes):

```
>>> dir(object)
['__class__', '__delattr__', '__dir__', '__doc__', '__eq__', '__format__',
'__ge__', '__getattribute__', '__gt__', '__hash__', '__init__', '__le__',
'__lt__', '__ne__', '__new__', '__reduce__', '__reduce_ex__', '__repr__',
'__setattr__', '__sizeof__', '__str__', '__subclasshook__']
```

Every class in Python, including ones that you define, automatically *inherits* these attributes from class object: they are automatically part of every class. More generally, every subclass inherits the features of its superclass. This is a powerful tool: it helps avoid a lot of duplicate code and makes interactions between related types consistent.

Let's try this out. Here is the simplest class that we can write:

```
>>> class Book:
...         """Information about a book."""
...
```

Just as keyword def tells Python that we're defining a new function, keyword class signals that we're defining a new type.

Much like str is a type, Book is a type:

```
>>> type(str)
<class 'type'>
>>> type(Book)
<class 'type'>
```

Our Book class isn't empty, either, because it has inherited all the attributes of class object:

```
>>> dir(Book)
['__class__', '__delattr__', '__dict__', '__dir__', '__doc__', '__eq__',
'__format__', '__ge__', '__getattribute__', '__gt__', '__hash__', '__init__',
'__le__', '__lt__', '__module__', '__ne__', '__new__', '__qualname__',
'__reduce__', '__reduce_ex__', '__repr__', '__setattr__', '__sizeof__',
'__str__', '__subclasshook__', '__weakref__']
```

If you look carefully, you'll see that this list is nearly identical to the output for dir(object). There are four extra attributes in class Book; every subclass of class object automatically has these attributes in addition to the inherited ones:

```
'__dict__', '__module__', '__qualname__', '__weakref__'
```

We'll get to those attributes later on in this chapter in *What Are Those Special Attributes?*, on page 283. First, let's create a Book object and give that Book a title and a list of authors:

```
>>> ruby_book = Book()
>>> ruby_book.title = 'Programming Ruby'
>>> ruby_book.authors = ['Thomas', 'Fowler', 'Hunt']
```

The first assignment statement creates a Book object and then assigns that object to variable ruby_book. The second assignment statement creates a title variable *inside* the Book object; that variable refers to the string 'Programming Ruby'. The third assignment statement creates variable authors, also inside the Book object, which refers to the list of strings ['Thomas', 'Fowler', 'Hunt'].

Variables title and authors are called *instance variables* because they are variables inside an instance of a class. We can access these instance variables through variable ruby_book:

```
>>> ruby_book.title
'Programming Ruby'
>>> ruby_book.authors
['Thomas', 'Fowler', 'Hunt']
```

In the expression ruby_book.title, Python finds variable ruby_book, then sees the dot and goes to the memory location of the Book object, and then looks for variable title. Here is a picture:

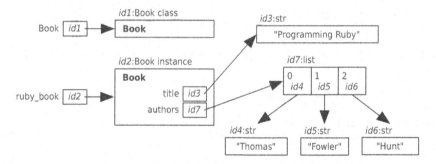

We can even get help on our Book class:

```
>>> help(Book)
Help on class Book in module __main__:

class Book(builtins.object)
 |  Information about a book.
 |
 |  Data descriptors defined here:
 |
 |  __dict__
 |      dictionary for instance variables (if defined)
 |
 |  __weakref__
 |      list of weak references to the object (if defined)
```

The first line tells us that we asked for help on class Book. After that is the header for class Book; the (builtins.object) part tells us that Book is a subclass of class object. The next line shows the Book docstring. Last is a section called "data descriptors," which are special pieces of information that Python keeps with every user-defined class that it uses for its own purposes. Again, we'll get to those in *What Are Those Special Attributes?*, on page 283.

14.3 Writing a Method in Class Book

As you saw in Chapter 7, *Using Methods*, on page 115, there are two ways to call a method. One way is to access the method through the class, and the other is to use object-oriented syntax. These two calls are equivalent:

```
>>> str.capitalize('browning')
'Browning'
>>> 'browning'.capitalize()
'Browning'
```

We'd like to be able to write similar code involving class Book. For example, we might want to be able to ask how many authors a Book has:

```
>>> Book.num_authors(ruby_book)
3
>>> ruby_book.num_authors()
3
```

To get this to work, we'll define a method called num_authors inside Book. Here it is:

```
class Book:
    """Information about a book."""

    def num_authors(self):
        """ (Book) -> int

        Return the number of authors of this book.
        """

        return len(self.authors)
```

Book method num_authors looks just like a function except that it has a parameter called self. The type contract states that self refers to a Book. Assuming this class is defined in the file book.py, we can import it, create a Book object, and call num_authors in two different ways:

```
>>> import book
>>> ruby_book = book.Book()
>>> ruby_book.title = 'Programming Ruby'
>>> ruby_book.authors = ['Thomas', 'Fowler', 'Hunt']
>>> book.Book.num_authors(ruby_book)
3
```

```
>>> ruby_book.num_authors()
3
```

Let's take a close look at the first call on method num_authors:

```
>>> book.Book.num_authors(ruby_book)
```

The book part says to look in the imported module. In that module is class Book. Inside Book is method num_authors. The argument to the call, ruby_book, is passed to parameter self.

Python treats the second call on num_authors exactly as it did the first; the first call is equivalent to this one:

```
>>> ruby_book.num_authors()
```

The second version is much more common because it lists the object first; we think of that version as asking the book how many authors it has. Thinking of method calls this way can really help develop an object-oriented mentality.

In the ruby_book example, we assigned the title and the list of authors after the Book object was created. That approach isn't scalable; we don't want to have to type those extra assignment statements every time we create a Book. Instead, we'll write a method that does this for us as we create the Book. This is a special method and is called _init_. We'll also include the publisher, ISBN, and price as parameters of _init_:

```
class Book:
    """Information about a book, including title, list of authors,
    publisher, ISBN, and price.
    """

    def __init__(self, title, authors, publisher, isbn, price):
        """ (Book, str, list of str, str, str, number) -> NoneType

        Create a new book entitled title, written by the people in authors,
        published by publisher, with ISBN isbn and costing price dollars.

        >>> python_book = Book( \
                'Practical Programming', \
                ['Campbell', 'Gries', 'Montojo'], \
                'Pragmatic Bookshelf', \
                '978-1-93778-545-1', \
                25.0)
        >>> python_book.title
        'Practical Programming'
        >>> python_book.authors
        ['Campbell', 'Gries', 'Montojo']
        >>> python_book.publisher
```

```
        'Pragmatic Bookshelf'
        >>> python_book.ISBN
        '978-1-93778-545-1'
        >>> python_book.price
        25.0
        """

        self.title = title
        # Copy the authors list in case the caller modifies that list later.
        self.authors = authors[:]
        self.publisher = publisher
        self.ISBN = isbn
        self.price = price

    def num_authors(self):
        """ (Book) -> int

        Return the number of authors of this book.

        >>> python_book = Book( \
                'Practical Programming', \
                ['Campbell', 'Gries', 'Montojo'], \
                'Pragmatic Bookshelf', \
                '978-1-93778-545-1', \
                25.0)
        >>> python_book.num_authors()
        3
        """

        return len(self.authors)
```

Notice that we can include doctests for methods just as we do for functions.

This module contains a single (complicated) statement: the class definition. When Python executes this module, it creates a class object and assigns it to variable Book:

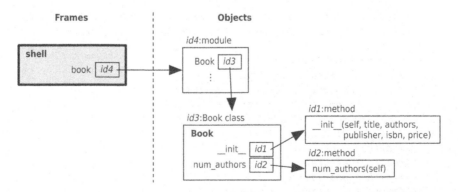

What's in an Object?

Methods belong to classes. Instance variables belong to objects. If we try to access an instance variable as we do a method, we get an error:

```
>>> import book
>>> book.Book.title
Traceback (most recent call last):
  File "<stdin>", line 1, in <module>
AttributeError: type object 'Book' has no attribute 'title'
>>> dir(book.Book)
['__class__', '__delattr__', '__dict__', '__dir__', '__doc__', '__eq__',
[''__format__', '__ge__', '__getattribute__', '__gt__', '__hash__',
[''__init__', '__le__', '__lt__', '__module__', '__ne__', '__new__',
[''__qualname__', '__reduce__', '__reduce_ex__', '__repr__', '__setattr__',
[''__sizeof__', '__str__', '__subclasshook__', '__weakref__', 'num_authors']
```

Instances of class Book contain instance variables and also have access to the methods in Book:

```
>>> python_book = book.Book(
...         'Practical Programming',
...         ['Campbell', 'Gries', 'Montojo'],
...         'Pragmatic Bookshelf',
...         '978-1-93778-545-1',
...         25.0)
>>> dir(python_book)
['ISBN', '__class__', '__delattr__', '__dict__', '__dir__', '__doc__',
[''__eq__', '__format__', '__ge__', '__getattribute__', '__gt__', '__hash__',
[''__init__', '__le__', '__lt__', '__module__', '__ne__', '__new__',
[''__qualname__', '__reduce__', '__reduce_ex__', '__repr__', '__setattr__',
[''__sizeof__', '__str__', '__subclasshook__', '__weakref__', 'authors',
[''num_authors', 'price', 'publisher', 'title']
```

Notice that ISBN, authors, price, publisher, and title are all available in the object as instance variables in addition to the contents of class Book.

Method _init_ is called whenever a Book object is created. Its purpose is to initialize the new object; this method is sometimes called a *constructor*. Here are the steps that Python follows when creating an object:

1. It creates an object at a particular memory address.
2. It calls method _init_, passing in the new object into the parameter self.
3. It produces that object's memory address.

Let's try it out in the shell:

```
>>> import book
>>> python_book = book.Book(
...         'Practical Programming',
...         ['Campbell', 'Gries', 'Montojo'],
...         'Pragmatic Bookshelf',
...         '978-1-93778-545-1',
```

```
...           25.0)
>>> python_book.title
'Practical Programming'
>>> python_book.authors
['Campbell', 'Gries', 'Montojo']
>>> python_book.publisher
'Pragmatic Bookshelf'
>>> python_book.ISBN
'978-1-93778-545-1'
>>> python_book.price
25.0
```

The following picture gives a picture of the memory model that results from this code.

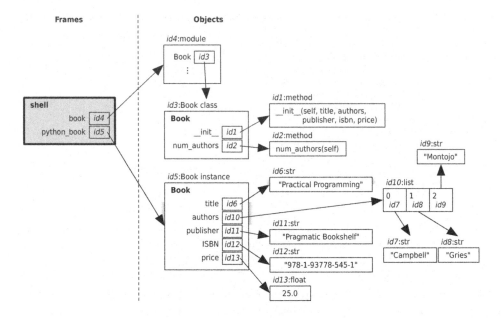

Let's trace method call python_book.num_authors(). (As a reminder, this is equivalent to Book.num_authors(python_book).)

Python first finds the object that python_book refers to and calls its method num_authors. There are no explicit arguments, so Python only passes in the Book object that python_book refers to, assigning that object to the self parameter. (See Figure 13, *Calling a method*, on page 279.)

The return statement, return len(self.authors), is then executed. The expression, len(self.authors), is a function call. Python evaluates the argument, self.authors, by finding the object that self refers to and then, in that object, finds instance

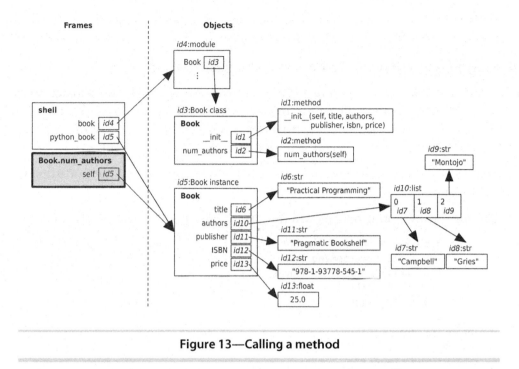

Figure 13—Calling a method

variable authors. This is a list, and the length of that list is the value that Python returns, as shown here:

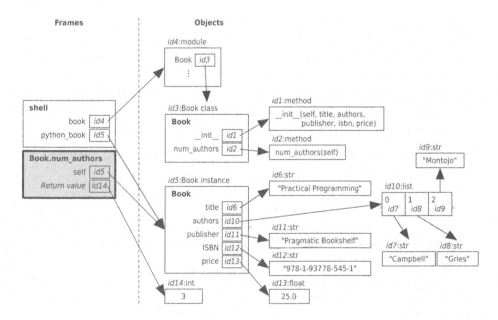

With constructors, methods, and instance variables in hand, we can now create classes that look and work like those that come with Python itself.

14.4 Plugging into Python Syntax: More Special Methods

In Section 7.4, *What Are Those Underscores?*, on page 123, you learned that some Python syntax, such as + or ==, triggers method calls. For example, when Python sees 'abc' + '123', it turns that into 'abc'.__add__('123'). When we call print(obj), then obj.__str__() is called to find out what string to print.

You can do this too. All you need to do is define these special methods inside your classes.

The output Python produces when we print a Book isn't particularly useful:

```
>>> python_book = Book(
...     'Practical Programming',
...     ['Campbell', 'Gries', 'Montojo'],
...     'Pragmatic Bookshelf',
...     '978-1-93778-545-1',
...     25.0)
>>> print(python_book)
<book.Book object at 0x59f410>
```

This is the default behavior for converting objects to strings: it just shows us where the object is in memory. This is the behavior defined in class object's method __str__, which our Book class has inherited.

If we want to present a more useful string, we need to explore two more special methods, __str__ and __repr__. __str__ is called when an informal, human-readable version of an object is needed, and __repr__ is called when unambiguous, but possibly less-readable, output is desired. In particular, __str__ is called when print is used, and it is also called by function str and by string method format. Method __repr__ is called when you ask for the value of a variable in the Python shell, and it is also called when a collection such as list is printed.

Let's define method Book.__str__ to provide useful output; this method goes inside class Book, along with __init__ and num_authors:

```
def __str__(self):
    """ (Book) -> str

    Return a human-readable string representation of this Book.
    """

    return """Title: {0}
Authors: {1}
Publisher: {2}
ISBN: {3}
```

```
Price: ${4}""".format(
    self.title, ', '.join(self.authors), self.publisher, self.ISBN, self.price)
```

Printing a Book now gives more useful information:

```
>>> python_book = Book(
...         'Practical Programming',
...         ['Campbell', 'Gries', 'Montojo'],
...         'Pragmatic Bookshelf',
...         '978-1-93778-545-1',
...         25.0)
>>> print(python_book)
Title: Practical Programming
Authors: Campbell, Gries, Montojo
Publisher: Pragmatic Bookshelf
ISBN: 978-1-93778-545-1
Price: $25.0
```

Method _repr_ is called to get an unambiguous string representation of an object. The string should include the type of the object as well as the values of any instance variables—ideally, if we were to evaluate the string, it would create an object that is equivalent to the one that owns method _repr_. We will show an example of _repr_ in Section 14.6, *A Case Study: Molecules, Atoms, and PDB Files*, on page 288.

The operator == triggers a call on method _eq_. This method is defined in class object, and so class Book has inherited it; object's _eq_ produces True exactly when an object is compared to itself. That means that even if two objects contain identical information they will not be considered equal:

```
>>> python_book_1 = book.Book(
...     'Practical Programming',
...     ['Campbell', 'Gries', 'Montojo'],
...     'Pragmatic Bookshelf',
...     '978-1-93778-545-1',
...     25.0)
>>> python_book_2 = book.Book(
...     'Practical Programming',
...     ['Campbell', 'Gries', 'Montojo'],
...     'Pragmatic Bookshelf',
...     '978-1-93778-545-1',
...     25.0)
>>> python_book_1 == python_book_2
False
>>> python_book_1 == python_book_1
True
>>> python_book_2 == python_book_2
True
```

We can *override* an inherited method by defining a new version in our subclass. This replaces the inherited method so that it is no longer used. As an example, we'll define method Book._eq_ to compare two books for equality. Because ISBNs are unique, we can compare using them; we'll add this method to class Book:

```
def __eq__(self, other):
    """ (Book, Book) -> bool

    Return True iff this book and other have the same ISBN.
    """

    return self.ISBN == other.ISBN
```

Here is our new method _eq_ in action:

```
>>> python_book_1 = book.Book(
...     'Practical Programming', ['Campbell', 'Gries', 'Montojo'],
...     'Pragmatic Bookshelf', '978-1-93778-545-1', 25.0)
>>> python_book_2 = book.Book(
...     'Practical Programming', ['Campbell', 'Gries', 'Montojo'],
...     'Pragmatic Bookshelf', '978-1-93778-545-1', 25.0)
>>> survival_book = book.Book(
...     "New Programmer's Survival Manual", ['Carter'],
...     'Pragmatic Bookshelf', '978-1-93435-681-4', 19.0)
>>> python_book_1 == python_book_2
True
>>> python_book_1 == survival_book
False
```

Here, then, are the lookup rules for a method call obj.method(...):

1. Look in the current object's class. If we find a method with the right name, use it.

2. If we didn't find it, look in the superclass. Continue up the class hierarchy until the method is found.

Python has lots of other special methods; the official Python website gives a full list.

14.5 A Little Bit of OO Theory

Classes and objects are two of programming's power tools. They let good programmers do a lot in very little time, but with them, bad programmers can create a real mess. This section will introduce some underlying theory that will help you design reliable, reusable object-oriented software.

What Are Those Special Attributes?

In Section 14.2, *Function "Isinstance," Class Object, and Class Book*, on page 271, we encountered these four special class attributes:

`'__dict__', '__module__', '__qualname__', '__weakref__'`

Every class that you have defined contains these four attributes, plus several more.

The first one, `__dict__`, unsurprisingly refers to a dictionary. What you might find surprising is that this dictionary is used to keep track of the instance variables and their values! Here it is for our running python_book example:

```
>>> python_book.__dict__
{'publisher': 'Pragmatic Bookshelf', 'ISBN': '978-1-93778-545-1',
 'title': 'Practical Programming', 'price': 25.0,
 'authors': ['Campbell', 'Gries', 'Montojo']}
```

Whenever you assign to an instance variable, it changes the contents of the object's dictionary. You can even change it yourself directly, although we *don't* recommend it.

Here are brief descriptions of some of the other special attributes of classes:

Variable `__module__` refers to the module object in which the class of the object was defined.

Variable `__weakref__` is used by Python to manage when the memory for an object can be reused.

Variables `__name__` and `__qualname__` refer to strings containing the simple and fully qualified names of classes, respectively; their values are usually identical, except when a class is defined inside another class, in which case the fully qualified name contains both the outer class name and the inner class name.

Variable `__class__` refers to an object's class object.

There are several more special attributes, and they are all used by Python to properly manage information about a program as it executes.

Encapsulation

To *encapsulate* something means to enclose it in some kind of container. In programming, *encapsulation* means keeping data and the code that uses it in one place and hiding the details of exactly how they work together. For example, each instance of class file keeps track of what file on the disk it is reading or writing and where it currently is in that file. The class hides the details of how this is done so that programmers can use it without needing to know the details of how it was implemented.

Polymorphism

Polymorphism means "having more than one form." In programming, it means that an expression involving a variable can do different things depending on the type of the object to which the variable refers. For example, if obj refers to a string, then obj[1:3] produces a two-character string. If obj refers to a list, on the other hand, the same expression produces a two-element list. Similarly, the expression left + right can produce a number, a string, or a list, depending on the types of left and right.

Polymorphism is used throughout modern programs to cut down on the amount of code programmers need to write and test. It lets us write a generic function to count nonblank lines:

```python
def non_blank_lines(thing):
    """Return the number of nonblank lines in thing."""

    count = 0
    for line in thing:
        if line.strip():
            count += 1
    return count
```

And then we can apply it to a list of strings, a file, a web page on a site halfway around the world (see Section 10.4, *Files over the Internet*, on page 181), or a single string wrapped up in class StringIO to look like a file. Each of those four types knows how to be the subject of a loop; in other words, each one knows how to produce its "next" element as long as there is one and then say "all done." That means that instead of writing four functions to count interesting lines or copying the lines into a list and then applying one function to that list, we can apply one function to all those types directly.

Inheritance

Giving one class the same methods as another is one way to make them polymorphic, but it suffers from the same flaw as initializing an object's instance variables from outside the object. If a programmer forgets just one line of code, the whole program can fail for reasons that will be difficult to track down. A better approach is to use a third fundamental feature of object-oriented programming called *inheritance*, which allows you to recycle code in yet another way.

Whenever you create a class, you are using inheritance: your new class automatically inherits all of the attributes of class object, much like a child inherits attributes from his or her parents. You can also declare that your new class is a subclass of some other class.

Here is an example. Let's say we're managing people at a university. There are students and faculty. (This is a gross oversimplification for purposes of illustrating inheritance; we're ignoring administrative staff, caretakers, food providers, and more.)

Both students and faculty have names, postal addresses, and email addresses; each student also has a student number, a list of courses taken, and a list of courses he or she is currently taking. Each faculty member has a faculty number and a list of courses he or she is currently teaching. (Again, this is a simplification.)

We'll have a Faculty class and a Student class. We need both of them to have names, addresses, and email addresses, but duplicate code is generally a bad thing; so we'll avoid it by also defining a class, perhaps called Member, and keeping track of those features in Member. Then we'll make both Faculty and Student subclasses of Member:

```python
class Member:
    """ A member of a university. """

    def __init__(self, name, address, email):
        """ (Member, str, str, str) -> NoneType

        Create a new member named name, with home address and email address.
        """

        self.name = name
        self.address = address
        self.email = email


class Faculty(Member):
    """ A faculty member at a university. """

    def __init__(self, name, address, email, faculty_num):
        """ (Faculty, str, str, str) -> NoneType

        Create a new faculty named name, with home address, email address,
        faculty number faculty_num, and empty list of courses.
        """

        super().__init__(name, address, email)
        self.faculty_number = faculty_num
        self.courses_teaching = []
```

```
class Student(Member):
    """ A student member at a university. """

    def __init__(self, name, address, email, student_num):
        """ (Student, str, str, str, str) -> NoneType

        Create a new student named name, with home address, email address,
        student number student_num, an empty list of courses taken, and an
        empty list of current courses.
        """

        super().__init__(name, address, email)
        self.student_number = student_num
        self.courses_taken = []
        self.courses_taking = []
```

Both class headers—class Faculty(Member): and class Student(Member):—tell Python that Faculty and Student are subclasses of class Member. That means that they inherit all of the attributes of class Member.

The first line of both Faculty._init_ and Student._init_ call function super, which produces a reference to the superclass part of the object, Member. That means that both of those first lines call method _init_, which was inherited from class Member. Notice that we just pass the relevant parameters in as arguments to this call, just as we would with any method call.

If we import these into the shell, we can create both faculty and students:

```
>>> paul = Faculty('Paul Gries', 'Ajax', 'pgries@cs.toronto.edu', '1234')
>>> paul.name
Paul Gries
>>> paul.email
pgries@cs.toronto.edu
>>> paul.faculty_number
1234
>>> jen = Student('Jen Campbell', 'Toronto', 'campbell@cs.toronto.edu',
...               '4321')
>>> jen.name
Jen Campbell
>>> jen.email
campbell@cs.toronto.edu
>>> jen.student_number
4321
```

Both the Faculty and Student objects have inherited the features defined in class Member.

Often, you'll want to *extend* the behavior inherited from a superclass. As an example, we might write a _str_ method inside class Member:

```
def __str__(self):
    """ (Member) -> str

    Return a string representation of this Member.

    >>> member = Member('Paul', 'Ajax', 'pgries@cs.toronto.edu')
    >>> member.__str__()
    'Paul\\nAjax\\npgries@cs.toronto.edu'
    """

    return '{}\n{}\n{}'.format(self.name, self.address, self.email)
```

With this method added to class Member, both Faculty and Student inherit it:

```
>>> paul = Faculty('Paul', 'Ajax', 'pgries@cs.toronto.edu', '1234')
>>> str(paul)
'Paul\nAjax\npgries@cs.toronto.edu'
>>> print(paul)
Paul
Ajax
pgries@cs.toronto.edu
```

That isn't quite enough though: for class Faculty, we want to *extend* what the Member's _str_ does, adding the faculty number and the list of courses the faculty member is teaching, and a Student string should include the equivalent student-specific information.

We'll use super again to access the inherited Member._str_ method and to append the Faculty-specific information:

```
def __str__(self):
    """ (Faculty) -> str

    Return a string representation of this Faculty.

    >>> faculty = Faculty('Paul', 'Ajax', 'pgries@cs.toronto.edu', '1234')
    >>> faculty.__str__()
    'Paul\\nAjax\\npgries@cs.toronto.edu\\n1234\\nCourses: '
    """

    member_string = super().__str__()

    return '''{}\n{}\nCourses: {}'''.format(
        member_string,
        self.faculty_number,
        ' '.join(self.courses_teaching))
```

With this, we get the desired output:

```
>>> paul = Faculty('Paul', 'Ajax', 'pgries@cs.toronto.edu', '1234')
>>> str(paul)
```

```
'Paul\nAjax\npgries@cs.toronto.edu\n1234\nCourses: '
>>> print(paul)
Paul
Ajax
pgries@cs.toronto.edu
1234
Courses:
```

14.6 A Case Study: Molecules, Atoms, and PDB Files

Molecular graphic visualization tools allow for interactive exploration of molecular structures. Most read PDB-formatted files, which we describe in Section 10.7, *Multiline Records*, on page 191. For example, Jmol (in the following graphic) is a Java-based open source 3D viewer for these structures.

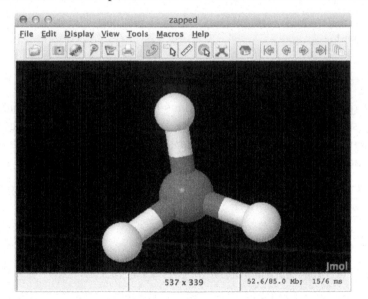

In a molecular visualizer, every atom, molecule, bond, and so on has a location in 3D space, usually defined as a *vector*, which is an arrow from the origin to where the structure is. All of these structures can be rotated and translated.

A vector is usually represented by x, y, and z coordinates that specify how far along the x-axis, y-axis, and z-axis the vector extends.

Here is how ammonia can be specified in PDB format:

```
COMPND     AMMONIA
ATOM     1  N  0.257  -0.363   0.000
ATOM     2  H  0.257   0.727   0.000
ATOM     3  H  0.771  -0.727   0.890
ATOM     4  H  0.771  -0.727  -0.890
END
```

In our simplified PDB format, a molecule is made up of numbered atoms. In addition to the number, an atom has a symbol and (x, y, z) coordinates. For example, one of the atoms in ammonia is nitrogen, with symbol N at coordinates (0.257, -0.363, 0.0). In the following sections, we will look at how we could translate these ideas into object-oriented Python.

Class Atom

We might want to create an atom like this using information we read from the PDB file:

```
nitrogen = Atom(1, "N", 0.257, -0.363, 0.0)
```

To do this, we'll need a class called Atom with a constructor that creates all the appropriate instance variables:

```
class Atom:
    """ An atom with a number, symbol, and coordinates. """

    def __init__(self, num, sym, x, y, z):
        """ (Atom, int, str, number, number, number) -> NoneType

        Create an Atom with number num, string symbol sym, and float
        coordinates (x, y, z).
        """

        self.number = num
        self.center = (x, y, z)
        self.symbol = sym
```

To inspect an Atom, we'll want to provide _repr_ and _str_ methods:

```
def __str__(self):
    """ (Atom) -> str

    Return a string representation of this Atom in this format:

        (SYMBOL, X, Y, Z)
    """

    return '({0}, {1}, {2}, {3})'.format(
        self.symbol, self.center[0], self.center[1], self.center[2])

def __repr__(self):
    """ (Atom) -> str

    Return a string representation of this Atom in this format:

        Atom(NUMBER, "SYMBOL", X, Y, Z)
    """
```

```
    return 'Atom({0}, "{1}", {2}, {3}, {4})'.format(
        self.number, self.symbol,
        self.center[0], self.center[1], self.center[2])
```

We'll use those later when we define a class for molecules.

In visualizers, one common operation is translation, or moving an atom to a different location. We'd like to be able to write this in order to tell the nitrogen atom to move up by 0.2 units:

```
nitrogen.translate(0, 0, 0.2)
```

This code works as expected if we add the following method to class Atom:

```
def translate(self, x, y, z):
    """ (Atom, number, number, number) -> NoneType

    Move this Atom by adding (x, y, z) to its coordinates.
    """

    self.center = (self.center[0] + x,
                   self.center[1] + y,
                   self.center[2] + z)
```

Class Molecule

Remember that we read PDB files one line at a time. When we reach the line containing COMPND AMMONIA, we know that we're building a complex structure: a molecule with a name and a list of atoms. Here's the start of a class for this, including an add method that adds an Atom to the molecule:

```
class Molecule:
    """A molecule with a name and a list of Atoms. """

    def __init__(self, name):
        """ (Molecule, str) -> NoneType

        Create a Molecule named name with no Atoms.
        """

        self.name = name
        self.atoms = []

    def add(self, a):
        """ (Molecule, Atom) -> NoneType

        Add a to my list of Atoms.
        """

        self.atoms.append(a)
```

As we read through the ammonia PDB information, we add atoms as we find them; here is the code from Section 10.7, *Multiline Records*, on page 191, rewritten to return a Molecule object instead of a list of lists:

```python
from molecule import Molecule
from atom import Atom

def read_molecule(r):
    """ (reader) -> Molecule

    Read a single molecule from r and return it,
    or return None to signal end of file.
    """
    # If there isn't another line, we're at the end of the file.
    line = r.readline()
    if not line:
        return None

    # Name of the molecule: "COMPND    name"
    key, name = line.split()

    # Other lines are either "END" or "ATOM num kind x y z"
    molecule = Molecule(name)
    reading = True

    while reading:
        line = r.readline()
        if line.startswith('END'):
            reading = False
        else:
            key, num, kind, x, y, z = line.split()
            molecule.add(Atom(num, kind, float(x), float(y), float(z)))

    return molecule
```

If we compare the two versions, we can see the code is nearly identical. It's just as easy to read the new version as the old—more so even, because it includes type information. Here are the _str_ and _repr_ methods:

```python
def __str__(self):
    """ (Molecule) -> str

    Return a string representation of this Molecule in this format:
        (NAME, (ATOM1, ATOM2, ...))
    """

    res = ''
    for atom in self.atoms:
        res = res + str(atom) + ', '
```

```
    # Strip off the last comma.
    res = res[:-2]
    return '({0}, ({1}))'.format(self.name, res)


def __repr__(self):
    """ (Molecule) -> str

    Return a string representation of this Molecule in this format:
       Molecule("NAME", (ATOM1, ATOM2, ...))
    """

    res = ''
    for atom in self.atoms:
        res = res + repr(atom) + ', '

    # Strip off the last comma.
    res = res[:-2]
    return 'Molecule("{0}", ({1}))'.format(self.name, res)
```

We'll add a translate method to Molecule to make it easier to move:

```
def translate(self, x, y, z):
    """ (Molecule, number, number, number) -> NoneType

    Move this Molecule, including all Atoms, by (x, y, z).
    """

    for atom in self.atoms:
        atom.translate(x, y, z)
```

And here we'll call it:

```
ammonia = Molecule("AMMONIA")
ammonia.add(Atom(1, "N", 0.257, -0.363, 0.0))
ammonia.add(Atom(2, "H", 0.257, 0.727, 0.0))
ammonia.add(Atom(3, "H", 0.771, -0.727, 0.890))
ammonia.add(Atom(4, "H", 0.771, -0.727, -0.890))
ammonia.translate(0, 0, 0.2)
```

14.7 Classifying What You've Learned

In this chapter, you learned the following:

- In object-oriented languages, new types are defined by creating classes. Classes support encapsulation; in other words, they combine data and the operations on it so that other parts of the program can ignore implementation details.

- Classes also support polymorphism. If two classes have methods that work the same way, instances of those classes can replace one another without the rest of the program being affected. This enables "plug-and-play" programming, in which one piece of code can perform different operations depending on the objects it is operating on.

- Finally, new classes can be defined by inheriting features from existing ones. The new class can override the features of its parent and/or add entirely new features.

- When a method is defined in a class, its first argument must be a variable that represents the object the method is being called on. By convention, this argument is called self.

- Some methods have special predefined meanings in Python; to signal this, their names begin and end with two underscores. Some of these methods are called when constructing objects (_init_) or converting them to strings (_str_ and _repr_); others, like _add_ and _sub_, are used to imitate arithmetic.

14.8 Exercises

Here are some exercises for you to try on your own. Solutions are available at http://pragprog.com/titles/gwpy2/practical-programming.

1. In this exercise, you will implement class Country, which represents a country with a name, a population, and an area.

   a. Here is a sample interaction from the Python shell:

   ```
   >>> canada = Country('Canada', 34482779, 9984670)
   >>> canada.name
   'Canada'
   >>> canada.population
   34482779
   >>> canada.area
   9984670
   ```

   The code above cannot be executed yet because class Country does not exist. Define Country with a constructor (method _init_) that has four parameters: a country, its name, its population, and its area.

   b. Consider this code:

   ```
   >>> canada = Country('Canada', 34482779, 9984670)
   >>> usa = Country('United States of America', 313914040, 9826675)
   >>> canada.is_larger(usa)
   True
   ```

   In class Country, define a method named is_larger that takes two Country objects and returns True if and only if the first has a larger area than the second.

c. Consider this code:

```
>>> canada.population_density()
3.4535722262227995
```

In class Country, define a method named population_density that returns the population density of the country (people per square km).

d. Consider this code:

```
>>> usa = Country('United States of America', 313914040, 9826675)
>>> print(usa)
United States of America has a population of 313914040 and is 9826675
square km.
```

In class Country, define a method named _str_ that returns a string representation of the country in the format shown above.

e. After you have written _str_, this session shows that a _repr_ method would be useful:

```
>>> canada = Country('Canada', 34482779, 9984670)
>>> canada
<exercise_country.Country object at 0x7f2aba30b550>
>>> print(canada)
Canada has population 34482779 and is 9984670 square km.
>>> [canada]
[<exercise_country.Country object at 0x7f2aba30b550>]
>>> print([canada])
[<exercise_country.Country object at 0x7f2aba30b550>]
```

Define the _repr_ method in Country to produce a string that behaves like this:

```
>>> canada = Country('Canada', 34482779, 9984670)
>>> canada
Country('Canada', 34482779, 9984670)
>>> [canada]
[Country('Canada', 34482779, 9984670)]
```

2. In this exercise, you will implement a Continent class, which represents a continent with a name and a list of countries. Class Continent will use class Country from the previous exercise. If Country is defined in another module, you'll need to import it.

a. Here is a sample interaction from the Python shell:

```
>>> canada = country.Country('Canada', 34482779, 9984670)
>>> usa = country.Country('United States of America', 313914040,
...                        9826675)
>>> mexico = country.Country('Mexico', 112336538, 1943950)
```

```
>>> countries = [canada, usa, mexico]
>>> north_america = Continent('North America', countries)
>>> north_america.name
'North America'
>>> for country in north_america.countries:
    print(country)

Canada has a population of 34482779 and is 9984670 square km.
United States of America has a population of 313914040 and is 9826675
square km.
Mexico has a population of 112336538 and is 1943950 square km.
>>>
```

The code above cannot be executed yet, because class Continent does not exist. Define Continent with a constructor (method _init_) that has three parameters: a continent, its name, and its list of Country objects.

b. Consider this code:

```
>>> north_america.total_population()
460733357
```

In class Continent, define a method named total_population that returns the sum of the populations of the countries on this continent.

c. Consider this code:

```
>>> print(north_america)
North America
Canada has a population of 34482779 and is 9984670 square km.
United States of America has a population of 313914040 and is 9826675
square km.
Mexico has a population of 112336538 and is 1943950 square km.
```

In class Continent, define a method named _str_ that returns a string representation of the continent in the format shown above.

3. In this exercise, you'll write _str_ and _repr_ methods for several classes.

a. In class Student, write a _str_ method that includes all the Member information and in addition includes the student number, the list of courses taken, and the list of current courses.

b. Write _repr_ methods in classes Member, Student, and Faculty.

Create a few Student and Faculty objects and call str and repr on them to verify that your code does what you want it to.

4. Write a class called Nematode to keep track of information about *C. elegans*, including a variable for the body length (in millimeters; they are about 1 mm in length), gender (either hermaphrodite or male), and age (in days).

    Include methods _init_, _repr_, and _str_.

5. Consider this code:

```
>>> segment = LineSegment(Point(1, 1), Point(3, 2))
>>> segment.slope()
0.5
>>> segment.length()
2.23606797749979
```

    In this exercise, you will write two classes, Point and LineSegment, so that you can run the code above and get the same results.

    a. Write a Point class with an _init_ method that takes two numbers as parameters.

    b. In the same file, write a LineSegment class whose constructor takes two Points as parameters. The first Point should be the start of the segment.

    c. Write a slope method in the class LineSegment that computes the slope of the segment. (Hint: The slope of a line is rise over run.)

    d. Write a length method in class LineSegment that computes the length of the segment. (Hint: Use x ** n to raise x to the nth power. To compute the square root, raise a number to the (1/2) power or use math.sqrt.)

## CHAPTER 15

Testing and Debugging

How can you tell whether the programs you write work correctly? Following the function design recipe from Section 3.6, *Designing New Functions: A Recipe*, on page 47, you include an example call or two in the docstring. The last step of the recipe is calling your function to make sure that it returns what you expect. But are one or two calls enough? If not, how many do you need? How do you pick the arguments for those function calls? In this chapter, you will learn how to choose good test cases and how to test your code using Python's unittest module.

Finally, what happens if your tests fail, revealing a bug? (See Section 1.3, *What's a Bug?*, on page 4.) How can you tell where the problem is in your code? In this chapter, you'll also learn how to find and fix bugs in your programs.

15.1 Why Do You Need to Test?

Quality assurance, or QA, checks that software is working correctly. Over the last fifty years, programmers have learned that quality isn't some kind of magic pixie dust that you can sprinkle on a program after it has been written. Quality has to be designed in, and software must be tested and retested to check that it meets standards.

The good news is that putting effort into QA actually makes you more productive overall. The reason can be seen in the graphic of Boehm's curve shown in Figure 14, *Boehm's curve: the later a bug is discovered, the more expensive it is to fix*, on page 298. The later you find a bug, the more expensive it is to fix, so catching bugs early reduces overall effort.

Most good programmers today don't just test their software while writing it; they build their tests so that other people can rerun them months later and a dozen time zones away. This takes a little more time up front but makes

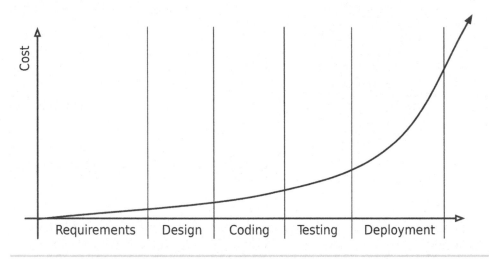

Figure 14—Boehm's curve: the later a bug is discovered, the more expensive it is to fix

programmers more productive overall, since every hour invested in preventing bugs saves two, three, or ten frustrating hours tracking bugs down.

In Section 6.3, *Testing Your Code Semiautomatically*, on page 110, you learned how to run tests using Python's doctest module. As part of the function design recipe (see Section 3.6, *Designing New Functions: A Recipe*, on page 47), you learned to include example calls on your function in the docstring. You can then use module doctest to execute those function calls and have it compare the output you expect with the actual output produced by that function call.

15.2 Case Study: Testing above_freezing

The first function that we'll test is above_freezing from Section 6.3, *Testing Your Code Semiautomatically*, on page 110:

```
def above_freezing(celsius):
    """ (number) -> bool

    Return True iff temperature celsius degrees is above freezing.

    >>> above_freezing(5.2)
    True
    >>> above_freezing(-2)
    False
    """

    return celsius > 0
```

In that section, we ran the example calls from the docstring using doctest. But we're missing a test: what happens if the temperature is zero? In the next section, we'll write another version of this function that behaves differently at zero and we'll discuss how our current set of tests is incomplete.

Choosing Test Cases for above_freezing

Before writing our testing code, we must decide which test cases to use. Function above_freezing takes one argument, a number, so for each test case, we need to choose the value of that argument. There are billions of numbers to choose from and we can't possibly test them all, so how do we decide which values to use? For above_freezing, there are two categories of numbers: values below freezing and values above freezing. We'll pick one value from each category to use in our test cases.

Looking at it another way, this particular function returns a Boolean, so we need at least two tests: one that causes the function to return True and another that causes it to return False. In fact, that's what we already did in our example function calls in the docstring.

In above_freezing's docstring, the first example call uses 5.2 as the value of the argument, and that value is above freezing so the function should return True. This test case represents the temperatures that are above freezing. We chose that value from among the billions of possible positive floating-point values; any one of them would work just as well. For example, we could have used 100.6, 29, 357.32, or any other number greater than 0 to represent the "above freezing" category. The second example call uses -2, which represents the temperatures that are below freezing. As before, we could have used -16, -294.3, -56.97, or any other value less than 0 to represent the "below freezing" category, but we chose to use -2. Again, our choice is arbitrary.

Are we missing any test case categories? Imagine that we had written our code using the >= operator instead of the > operator:

```
def above_freezing_v2(celsius):
    """ (number) -> bool

    Return True iff temperature celsius degrees is above freezing.

    >>> above_freezing_v2(5.2)
    True
    >>> above_freezing_v2(-2)
    False
    """

    return celsius >= 0
```

Both versions of the function produce the expected results for the two doc-string examples, but the code is different from before, and it won't produce the same result in all cases. We neglected to test one category of inputs: temperatures at the freezing mark. Test cases like the one at the freezing mark are often called *boundary cases* since they lie on the boundary between two different possible behaviors of the function (in this case, between temperatures above freezing and temperatures below freezing). Experience shows that boundary cases are much more likely to contain bugs than other cases, so it's always worth figuring out what they are and testing them.

Sometimes there are multiple boundary cases. For example, if we had a function that determined which state water was in—solid, liquid, or gas—then the two boundary cases would be the freezing point and the boiling point.

To summarize, the following table shows each category of inputs, the value we chose to represent that category, and the value that we expect the call on the function to return in that case:

Test Case Description	Argument Value	Expected Return Value
Temperatures above freezing	5.2	True
Temperatures below freezing	-2	False
Temperatures at freezing	0	False

Table 24—Test Cases for above_freezing

Now that all categories of inputs are covered, we need to run the third test. Running the third test in the Python shell reveals that the value returned by above_freezing_v2 isn't False, which is what we expected:

```
>>> above_freezing(0)
False
>>> above_freezing_v2(0)
True
```

It took three test cases to cover all the categories of inputs for this function, but three isn't a magic number. The three tests had to be carefully chosen. If the three tests had all fallen into the same category (say, temperatures above freezing: 5, 70, and 302) they wouldn't have been sufficient. It's the quality of the tests that matters, not the quantity.

Testing above_freezing Using Unittest

Once you decide which test cases are needed, you can use one of two approaches that you've learned about so far to actually test the code. The first is to call the functions and read the results yourself to see if they match what you expected. The second is to run the functions from the docstring using module doctest. The latter approach is preferable because the comparison of the actual value returned by the function to the value we expect to be returned is done by the program and not by a human, so it's faster and less error prone.

In this section, we'll introduce another of Python's modules, unittest. A *unit test* exercises just one isolated component of a program. Like we did with doctest, we'll use module unittest to test each function in our module independently from the others. This approach contrasts with *system testing*, which looks at the behavior of the system as a whole, just as its eventual users will.

In *Inheritance*, on page 284, you learned how to write classes that inherit code from others. Now you'll write test classes that inherit from class unittest.TestCase. Our first test class tests function above_freezing:

```python
import unittest
import temperature


class TestAboveFreezing(unittest.TestCase):
    """Tests for temperature.above_freezing."""

    def test_above_freezing_above(self):
        """Test a temperature that is above freezing."""

        expected = True
        actual = temperature.above_freezing(5.2)
        self.assertEqual(expected, actual,
            "The temperature is above freezing.")

    def test_above_freezing_below(self):
        """Test a temperature that is below freezing."""

        expected = False
        actual = temperature.above_freezing(-2)
        self.assertEqual(expected, actual,
            "The temperature is below freezing.")

    def test_above_freezing_at_zero(self):
        """Test a temperature that is at freezing."""

        expected = False
        actual = temperature.above_freezing(0)
        self.assertEqual(expected, actual,
            "The temperature is at the freezing mark.")

unittest.main()
```

The name of our new class is TestAboveFreezing, and it's saved in the file test_above_freezing.py. The class has three of its own methods, one per each test case. Each test case follows this pattern:

```
expected = «the value we expect will be returned»
actual = «call on the function being tested»
self.assertEqual(expected, actual,
    "Error message in case of failure")
```

In each test method, there is a call on method assertEqual, which has been inherited from class unittest.TestCase. To *assert* something is to claim that it is true; here we are asserting that the expected value and the actual value should be equal. Method assertEqual compares its first two arguments (which are the expected return value and the actual return value from calling the function being tested) to see whether they are equal. If they aren't equal, the third argument, a string, is displayed as part of the failure message.

At the bottom of the file, the call on unittest.main() executes every method that begins with the name test.

When the program in test_above_freezing.py is executed, the following results are produced:

```
...
----------------------------------------------------------------------
Ran 3 tests in 0.000s

OK
```

The first line of output has three dots, one dot per test method. A dot indicates that a test was run successfully—that the test case *passed*.

The summary after the dashed line tells you that unittest found and ran three tests, that it took less than a millisecond to do so, and that everything was successful (OK).

If our faulty function above_freezing_v2 was renamed above_freezing and our test_above_freezing unit test program was rerun, instead of three passes (as indicated by the three dots), there would be two passes and a failure:

```
.F.
======================================================================
FAIL: test_above_freezing_at (__main__.TestAboveFreezing)
Test a temperature that is at freezing.
----------------------------------------------------------------------
Traceback (most recent call last):
  File "test_above_freezing.py", line 33, in test_above_freezing_at
    "The temperature is at the freezing mark.")
AssertionError: False != True : The temperature is at the freezing mark.
```

```
------------------------------------------------------------------
Ran 3 tests in 0.001s
```

FAILED (failures=1)

The F indicates that a test case *failed*. The error message tells you that the failure happened in method test_above_freezing_at_zero. The error is an AssertionError, which indicates that when we asserted that the expected and actual value should be equal, we were wrong.

The expression False != True comes from our call on assertEqual: variable expected was False, variable actual was True, and of course those aren't equal. Additionally, the string that was passed as the third argument to assertEqual is part of that error message: "The temperature is at the freezing mark."

Notice that the three calls on assertEqual were placed in three separate methods. We could have put them all in the same method, but that method would have been considered a single test case. That is, when the module was run, we would see only one result: if any of the three calls on assertEqual failed, the entire test case would have failed. Only when all three passed would we see the coveted dot.

As a rule, each test case you design should be implemented in its own test method.

Now that you've seen both doctest and unittest, which should you use? We prefer unittest, for several reasons:

- For large test suites, it is nice to have the testing code in a separate file rather than in a very long docstring.

- Each test case can be in a separate method, so the tests are independent of each other. With doctest, the changes to objects made by one test persist for the subsequent test, so more care needs to be taken to properly set up the objects for each doctest test case to make sure they are independent.

- Because each test case is in a separate method, we can write a docstring that describes the test case tested so that other programmers understand how the test cases differ from each other.

- The third argument to assertEqual is a string that appears as part of the error message produced by a failed test, which is helpful for providing a better description of the test case. With doctest, there is no straightforward way to customize the error messages.

15.3 Case Study: Testing running_sum

In Section 15.2, *Case Study: Testing above_freezing*, on page 298, we tested a program that involved only immutable types. In this section, you'll learn how to test functions involving mutable types, like lists and dictionaries.

Suppose we need to write a function that modifies a list so that it contains a running sum of the values in it. For example, if the list is [1, 2, 3], the list should be mutated so that the first value is 1, the second value is the sum of the first two numbers, 1 + 2, and the third value is the sum of the first three numbers, 1 + 2 + 3, so we expect that the list [1, 2, 3] will be modified to be [1, 3, 6].

Following the function design recipe (see Section 3.6, *Designing New Functions: A Recipe*, on page 47), here is a file named sums.py that contains the completed function with one (passing) example test:

```
def running_sum(L):
    """ (list of number) -> NoneType

    Modify L so that it contains the running sums of its original items.

    >>> L = [4, 0, 2, -5, 0]
    >>> running_sum(L)
    >>> L
    [4, 4, 6, 1, 1]
    """

    for i in range(len(L)):
        L[i] = L[i - 1] + L[i]
```

The structure of the test in the docstring is different from what you've seen before. Because there is no return statement, running_sum returns None. Writing a test that checks whether None is returned isn't enough to know whether the function call worked as expected. You also need to check whether the list passed to the function is mutated in the way you expect it to be. To do this, we follow these steps:

- Create a variable that refers to a list.
- Call the function, passing that variable as an argument to it.
- Check whether the list that the variable refers to was mutated correctly.

Following those steps, we created a variable, L, that refers to the list [4, 0, 2, -5, 0], called running_sum(L), and confirmed that L now refers to [4, 4, 6, 1, 1].

Although this test case passes, it doesn't guarantee that the function will always work—and in fact there is a bug. In the next section, we'll design a set of test cases to more thoroughly test this function and discover the bug.

Choosing Test Cases for running_sum

Function running_sum has one parameter, which is a list of number. For our test cases, we need to decide both on the size of the list and the values of the items. For size, we should test with the empty list, a short list with one item and another with two items (the shortest case where two numbers interact), and a longer list with several items.

When passed either the empty list or a list of length one, the modified list should be the same as the original.

When passed a two-number list, the first number should be unchanged and the second number should be changed to be the sum of the two original numbers.

For longer lists, things get more interesting. The values can be negative, positive, or zero, so the resulting values might be bigger than, the same as, or less than they were originally. We'll divide our test of longer lists into four cases: all negative values, all zero, all positive values, and a mix of negative, zero, and positive values. The resulting tests are shown in the table:

Test Case Description	List Before	List After
Empty list	[]	[]
One-item list	[5]	[5]
Two-item list	[2, 5]	[2, 7]
Multiple items, all negative	[-1, -5, -3, -4]	[-1, -6, -9, -13]
Multiple items, all zero	[0, 0, 0, 0]	[0, 0, 0, 0]
Multiple items, all positive	[4, 2, 3, 6]	[4, 6, 9, 15]
Multiple items, mixed	[4, 0, 2, -5, 0]	[4, 4, 6, 1, 1]

Table 25—Test Cases for running_sum

Now that we've decided on our test cases, the next step is to implement them using unittest.

Testing running_sumUsing Unittest

To test running_sum, we'll use this subclass of unittest.TestCase named TestRunningSum:

```python
import unittest
import sums as sums

class TestRunningSum(unittest.TestCase):
    """Tests for sums.running_sum."""

    def test_running_sum_empty(self):
        """Test an empty list."""

        argument = []
        expected = []
        sums.running_sum(argument)
        self.assertEqual(expected, argument, "The list is empty.")

    def test_running_sum_one_item(self):
        """Test a one-item list."""

        argument = [5]
        expected = [5]
        sums.running_sum(argument)
        self.assertEqual(expected, argument, "The list contains one item.")

    def test_running_sum_two_items(self):
        """Test a two-item list."""

        argument = [2, 5]
        expected = [2, 7]
        sums.running_sum(argument)
        self.assertEqual(expected, argument, "The list contains two items.")

    def test_running_sum_multi_negative(self):
        """Test a list of negative values."""

        argument = [-1, -5, -3, -4]
        expected = [-1, -6, -9, -13]
        sums.running_sum(argument)
        self.assertEqual(expected, argument,
            "The list contains only negative values.")

    def test_running_sum_multi_zeros(self):
        """Test a list of zeros."""

        argument = [0, 0, 0, 0]
        expected = [0, 0, 0, 0]
        sums.running_sum(argument)
        self.assertEqual(expected, argument, "The list contains only zeros.")

    def test_running_sum_multi_positive(self):
        """Test a list of positive values."""
```

```
        argument = [4, 2, 3, 6]
        expected = [4, 6, 9, 15]
        sums.running_sum(argument)
        self.assertEqual(expected, argument,
            "The list contains only positive values.")

    def test_running_sum_multi_mix(self):
        """Test a list containing mixture of negative values, zeros and
        positive values."""

        argument = [4, 0, 2, -5, 0]
        expected = [4, 4, 6, 1, 1]
        sums.running_sum(argument)
        self.assertEqual(expected, argument,
            "The list contains a mixture of negative values, zeros and"
                        + "positive values.")

unittest.main()
```

Next we run the tests and see that only three of them pass (the empty list, a list with several zeros, and a list with a mixture of negative values, zeros, and positive values):

```
..FF.FF
======================================================================
FAIL: test_running_sum_multi_negative (__main__.TestRunningSum)
Test a list of negative values.
----------------------------------------------------------------------
Traceback (most recent call last):
  File "test_running_sum.py", line 39, in test_running_sum_multi_negative
    "The list contains only negative values.")
AssertionError: Lists differ: [-1, -6, -9, -13] != [-5, -10, -13, -17]

First differing element 0:
-1
-5

- [-1, -6, -9, -13]
+ [-5, -10, -13, -17] : The list contains only negative values.


======================================================================
FAIL: test_running_sum_multi_positive (__main__.TestRunningSum)
Test a list of positive values.
----------------------------------------------------------------------
Traceback (most recent call last):
  File "test_running_sum.py", line 56, in test_running_sum_multi_positive
    "The list contains only positive values.")
AssertionError: Lists differ: [4, 6, 9, 15] != [10, 12, 15, 21]

First differing element 0:
```

```
4
10

- [4, 6, 9, 15]
+ [10, 12, 15, 21] : The list contains only positive values.

======================================================================
FAIL: test_running_sum_one_item (__main__.TestRunningSum)
Test a one-item list.
----------------------------------------------------------------------
Traceback (most recent call last):
  File "test_running_sum.py", line 22, in test_running_sum_one_item
    self.assertEqual(expected, argument, "The list contains one item.")
AssertionError: Lists differ: [5] != [10]

First differing element 0:
5
10

- [5]
+ [10] : The list contains one item.


======================================================================
FAIL: test_running_sum_two_items (__main__.TestRunningSum)
Test a two-item list.
----------------------------------------------------------------------
Traceback (most recent call last):
  File "test_running_sum.py", line 30, in test_running_sum_two_items
    self.assertEqual(expected, argument, "The list contains two items.")
AssertionError: Lists differ: [2, 7] != [7, 12]

First differing element 0:
2
7

- [2, 7]
+ [7, 12] : The list contains two items.


----------------------------------------------------------------------
Ran 7 tests in 0.002s

FAILED (failures=4)
```

The four that failed were a list with one item, a list with two items, a list with all negative values, and a list with all positive values. To find the bug, let's focus on the simplest test case, the single item list:

```
======================================================================
FAIL: test_running_sum_one_item (__main__.TestRunningSum)
Test a one-item list.
```

```
------------------------------------------------------------------
Traceback (most recent call last):
  File "/Users/campbell/pybook/gwpy2/Book/code/testdebug/test_running_sum.
  py", line 21, in test_running_sum_one_item
    self.assertEqual(expected, argument, "The list contains one item.")
AssertionError: Lists differ: [5] != [10]
First differing element 0:
5
10

- [5]
+ [10] : The list contains one item.
```

For this test, the list argument was [5]. After the function call, we expected
the list to be [5], but the list was mutated to become [10]. Looking back at the
function definition of running_sum, when i refers to 0, the for loop body executes
the statement L[0] = L[-1] + L[0]. L[-1] refers to the last element of the list—the
5—and L[0] refers to that same value. Oops! L[0] shouldn't be changed, since
the running sum of L[0] is simply L[0].

Looking at the other three failing tests, the failure messages indicate that the
first different elements are those at index 0. The same problem that we describe
for the single item list happened for these test cases as well.

So how did those other three tests pass? In those cases, L[-1] + L[0] produced
the same value that L[0] originally referred to. For example, for the list containing a mixture of values, [4, 0, 2, -5, 0], the item at index -1 happened to be 0, so
0 + 4 evaluated to 4, and that matched L[0]'s original value. Interestingly, the
simple single-item list test case revealed the problem, while the more complex
test case that involved a list of multiple values hid it!

To fix the problem, we can adjust the for loop header to start the running sum
from index 1 rather than from index 0:

```
def running_sum(L):
    """ (list of number) -> NoneType

    Modify L so that it contains the running sums of its original items.

    >>> L = [4, 0, 2, -5, 0]
    >>> running_sum(L)
    >>> L
    [4, 4, 6, 1, 1]
    """

    for i in range(1, len(L)):
        L[i] = L[i - 1] + L[i]
```

When the tests are rerun, all seven tests pass:

```
.......
----------------------------------------------------------------------
Ran 7 tests in 0.000s

OK
```

In the next section, you'll see some general guidelines for choosing test cases.

15.4 Choosing Test Cases

Having a set of tests that pass is good: it shows that your code does what it should in the situations you've thought of. However, for any large project there will be situations that *don't* occur to you. Tests can show the absence of many bugs, but it can't show that a program is fully correct.

It's important to make sure you have good *test coverage*: that your test cases cover important situations. In this section, we provide some heuristics that will help you come up with a fairly thorough set of test cases.

Now that you've seen two example sets of tests, we'll give you an overview of things to think about while you're developing tests for other functions. Some of them overlap and not all will apply in every situation, but they are all worth thinking about while you are figuring out what to test.

Think about size. When a test involves a collection such as a list, string, dictionary, or file, you need to do the following:

- Test the empty collection.
- Test a collection with one item in it.
- Test a general case with several items.
- Test the smallest interesting case, such as sorting a list containing two values.

Think about dichotomies. A *dichotomy* is a contrast between two things. Examples of dichotomies are empty/full, even/odd, positive/negative, and alphabetic/nonalphabetic. If a function deals with two or more different categories or situations, make sure you test all of them.

Think about boundaries. If a function behaves differently around a particular boundary or threshold, test exactly that boundary case.

Think about order. If a function behaves differently when values appear in different orders, identify those orders and test each one of them. For the sorting example mentioned above, you'll want one test case where the items are in order and one where they are not.

If you carefully plan your test cases according to these ideas and your code passes the tests, there's a very good chance that it will work for all other cases as well. Over time you'll commit fewer and fewer errors. Whenever you find an error, figure out why it happened; as you mentally catalog them, you'll subsequently become more conscious of them. And that's really the whole point of focusing on quality. The more you do it, the less likely it is for problems to arise.

15.5 Hunting Bugs

Bugs are discovered through testing and through program use, although the latter is what good testing can help avoid. Regardless of how they are discovered, tracking down and eliminating bugs in your programs is part of every programmer's life. This section introduces some techniques that can make debugging more efficient and give you more time to do the things you'd rather be doing.

Debugging a program is like diagnosing a medical condition. To find the cause, you start by working backward from the symptoms (or, in a program, its incorrect behavior), then you come up with a solution and test it to make sure it actually fixes the problem.

At least, that's the right way to do it. Many beginners make the mistake of skipping the diagnosis stage and trying to cure the program by changing things at random. Renaming a variable or swapping the order in which two functions are defined might actually fix the program, but millions of such changes are possible. Trying them one after another in no particular order can be an inefficient waste of many, many hours.

Here are some rules for tracking down the cause of a problem:

1. *Make sure you know what the program is supposed to do.* Sometimes this means doing the calculation by hand to see what the correct answer is. Other times it means reading the documentation (or the assignment handout) carefully or writing a test.

2. *Repeat the failure.* You can debug things only when they go wrong, so find a test case that makes the program fail reliably. Once you have one, try to find a simpler one; doing this often provides enough clues to allow you to fix the underlying problem.

3. *Divide and conquer.* Once you have a test that makes the program fail, try to find the first moment where something goes wrong. Examine the inputs to the function or block of code where the problem first becomes

visible. If those inputs are not what you expected, look at how they were created, and so on.

4. *Change one thing at a time, for a reason.* Replacing random bits of code on the off-chance they might be responsible for your problem is unlikely to do much good. (After all, you got it wrong the first time...) Each time you make a change, rerun your test cases immediately.

5. *Keep records.* After working on a problem for an hour, you won't be able to remember the results of the tests you've run. Like any other scientist, you should keep records. Some programmers use a lab notebook; others keep a file open in an editor. Whatever works for you, make sure that when the time comes to seek help, you can tell your colleagues exactly what you've learned.

15.6 Bugs We've Put in Your Ear

In this chapter, you learned the following:

- Finding and fixing bugs early reduces overall effort.

- When choosing test cases, you should consider size, dichotomies, boundary cases, and order.

- To test your functions, you can write subclasses of unittest's TestCase class. The advantages of using unittest include keeping the testing code separate from the code being tested, being able to keep the tests independent of one another, and being able to document each individual test case.

- To debug software, you have to know what it is supposed to do and be able to repeat the failure. Simplifying the conditions that make the program fail is an effective way to narrow down the set of possible causes.

15.7 Exercises

Here are some exercises for you to try on your own. Solutions are available at http://pragprog.com/titles/gwpy2/practical-programming.

1. Your lab partner claims to have written a function that replaces each value in a list with twice the preceding value (and the first value with 0). For example, if the list [1, 2, 3] is passed as an argument, the function is supposed to turn it into [0, 2, 4]. Here's the code:

```
def double_preceding(values):
    """ (list of number) -> NoneType

    Replace each item in the list with twice the value of the
```

```
preceding item, and replace the first item with 0.

>>> L = [1, 2, 3]
>>> double_preceding(L)
>>> L
[0, 2, 4]
"""
```

```
if values != []:
    temp = values[0]
    values[0] = 0
    for i in range(1, len(values)):
        values[i] = 2 * temp
        temp = values[i]
```

Although the example test passes, this code contains a bug. Write a set of unittest tests to identify the bug. Explain what the bug in this function is, and fix it.

2. Your job is to come up with tests for a function called line_intersect, which takes two lines as input and returns their intersection. More specifically:

    • Lines are represented as pairs of distinct points, such as [[0.0,0.0], [1.0, 3.0]] .

    • If the lines don't intersect, line_intersect returns None.

    • If the lines intersect in one point, line_intersect returns the point of intersection, such as [0.5, 0.75].

    • If the lines are coincident (that is, lie on top of each other), the function returns its first argument (that is, a line).

    What are the six most informative test cases you can think of? (That is, if you were allowed to run only six tests, which would tell you the most about whether the function was implemented correctly?)

    Write out the inputs and expected outputs of these six tests, and explain why you would choose them.

3. Using unittest, write four tests for a function called all_prefixes in a module called TestPrefixes.py that takes a string as its input and returns the set of all nonempty substrings that start with the first character. For example, given the string "lead" as input, all_prefixes would return the set {"l", "le", "lea", "lead"}.

4. Using unittest, write the five most informative tests you can think of for a function called is_sorted in a module called TestSorting.py that takes a list of

integers as input and returns True if they are sorted in nondecreasing order (as opposed to strictly increasing order, because of the possibility of duplicate values), and False otherwise.

5. The following function is broken. The docstring describes what it's supposed to do:

```
def find_min_max(values):
    """ (list) -> NoneType

    Print the minimum and maximum value from values.
    """

    min = None
    max = None
    for value in values:
        if value > max:
            max = value
        if value < min:
            min = value

    print('The minimum value is {0}'.format(min))
    print('The maximum value is {0}'.format(max))
```

What does it actually do? What line(s) do you need to change to fix it?

6. Suppose you have a data set of survey results where respondents can optionally give their age. Missing values are read in as None. Here is a function that computes the average age from that list.

```
def average(values):
    """ (list of number) -> number

    Return the average of the numbers in values.  Some items in values are
    None, and they are not counted toward the average.

    >>> average([20, 30])
    25.0
    >>> average([None, 20, 30])
    25.0
    """

    count = 0  # The number of values seen so far.
    total = 0  # The sum of the values seen so far.
    for value in values:
        if value is not None:
            total += value

        count += 1
```

```
    return total / count
```

Unfortunately it does not work as expected:

```
>>> import test_average
>>> test_average.average([None, 30, 20])
16.666666666666668
```

a. Using unittest, write a set of tests for function average in a module called test_average.py. The tests should cover cases involving lists with and without missing values.

b. Modify function average so it correctly handles missing values and passes all of your tests.

## CHAPTER 16

Creating Graphical User Interfaces

Most of the programs in previous chapters are not interactive. Once launched, they run to completion without giving us a chance to steer them or provide new input. The few that do communicate with us do so through the kind of text-only *command-line user interface*, or CLUI, that would have already been considered old-fashioned in the early 1980s.

As you already know, most modern programs interact with users via a *graphical user interface*, or GUI, which is made up of windows, menus, buttons, and so on. In this chapter, we will show you how to build simple GUIs using a Python module called tkinter. Along the way, we will introduce a different way of structuring programs called *event-driven programming*. A traditionally structured program usually has control over what happens when, but an event-driven program must be able to respond to input at unpredictable moments.

tkinter is one of several toolkits you can use to build GUIs in Python. It is the only one that comes with a standard Python installation.

16.1 Using Module Tkinter

Every tkinter program consists of these things:

- Windows, buttons, scrollbars, text areas, and other *widgets*—anything that you can see on the computer screen (Generally, the term *widget* means any useful object; in programming, it is short for "window gadget.")

- Modules, functions, and classes that manage the data that is being shown in the GUI—you are familiar with these; they are the tools you've seen so far in this book.

- An event manager that *listens* for events such as mouse clicks and keystrokes and reacts to these events by calling event handler functions

Here is a small but complete tkinter program:

```
import tkinter
window = tkinter.Tk()
window.mainloop()
```

Tk is a class that represents the *root window* of a tkinter GUI. This root window's mainloop method handles all the events for the GUI, so it's important to create only one instance of Tk.

Here is the resulting GUI:

The root window is initially empty; you'll see in the next section how to add widgets to it. If the window on the screen is closed, the window object is destroyed (though we can create a new root window by calling Tk() again). All of the applications we will create have only one root window, but additional windows can be created using the TopLevel widget.

The call on method mainloop doesn't exit until the window is destroyed (which happens when you click the appropriate widget in the title bar of the window), so any code following that call won't be executed until later:

```
import tkinter
window = tkinter.Tk()
window.mainloop()
print('Anybody home?')
```

When you try this code, you'll see that the call on function print doesn't get executed until after the window is destroyed. That means that if you want to make changes to the GUI after you have called mainloop, you need to do it in an event-handling function.

The following table gives a list of some of the available tkinter widgets:

Widget	Description
Button	A clickable button
Canvas	An area used for drawing or displaying images
Checkbutton	A clickable box that can be selected or unselected
Entry	A single-line text field that the user can type in
Frame	A container for widgets
Label	A single-line display for text
Listbox	A drop-down list that the user can select from
Menu	A drop-down menu
Message	A multiline display for text
Menubutton	An item in a drop-down menu
Text	A multiline text field that the user can type in
TopLevel	An additional window

Table 26—tkinter Widgets

16.2 Building a Basic GUI

Labels are widgets that are used to display short pieces of text. Here we create a Label that belongs to the root window—its *parent widget*—and we specify the text to be displayed by assigning it to the Label's text parameter.

```
import tkinter

window = tkinter.Tk()
label = tkinter.Label(window, text='This is our label.')
label.pack()

window.mainloop()
```

Here is the resulting GUI:

Method call label.pack() is crucial. Each widget has a method called pack that places it in its parent widget and then tells the parent to resize itself as necessary. If we forget to call this method, the child widget (in this case, Label) won't be displayed or will be displayed improperly.

Labels display text. Often, applications will want to update a label's text as the program runs to show things like the name of a file or the time of day. One way to do this is simply to assign a new value to the widget's text using method config:

```
import tkinter

window = tkinter.Tk()
label = tkinter.Label(window, text='First label.')
label.pack()
label.config(text='Second label.')
```

Run the previous code one line at a time from the Python shell to see how the label changes. (This code will not display the window at all if you run it as a program because we haven't called method mainloop.)

Using Mutable Variables with Widgets

Suppose you want to display a string, such as the current time or a score in a game, in several places in a GUI—the application's status bar, some dialog boxes, and so on. Calling method config on each widget every time there is new information isn't hard, but as the application grows, so too do the odds that we'll forget to update at least one of the widgets that's displaying the string. What we really want is a string that "knows" which widgets care about its value and can alert them itself when that value changes.

Python's strings, integers, floating-point numbers, and Booleans are immutable, so module tkinter provides one class for each of the immutable types: StringVar for str, IntVar for int, BooleanVar for bool, and DoubleVar for float. (The use of the word *double* is historical; it is short for "double-precision floating-point number.") These mutable types can be used instead of the immutable ones; here we show how to use a StringVar instead of a str:

```
import tkinter

window = tkinter.Tk()
data = tkinter.StringVar()
data.set('Data to display')
label = tkinter.Label(window, textvariable=data)
label.pack()

window.mainloop()
```

Notice that this time we assign to the textvariable parameter of the label rather than the text parameter.

The values in tkinter containers are set and retrieved using the methods set and get. Whenever a set method is called, it tells the label, and any other widgets it has been assigned to, that it's time to update the GUI.

There is one small trap here for newcomers: because of the way module tkinter is structured, you cannot create a StringVar or any other mutable variable until you have created the root Tk window.

Grouping Widgets with the Frame Type

A tkinter Frame is a container, much like the root window is a container. Frames are not directly visible on the screen; instead, they are used to organize other widgets. The following code creates a frame, puts it in the root window, and then adds three Labels to the frame:

```
import tkinter

window = tkinter.Tk()
frame = tkinter.Frame(window)
frame.pack()
first = tkinter.Label(frame, text='First label')
first.pack()
second = tkinter.Label(frame, text='Second label')
second.pack()
third = tkinter.Label(frame, text='Third label')
third.pack()

window.mainloop()
```

Note that we call pack on every widget; if we omit one of these calls, that widget will not be displayed.

Here is the resulting GUI:

In this particular case, putting the three Labels in a frame looks the same as when we put the Labels directly into the root window. However, with a more complicated GUI, we can use multiple frames to format the window's content and layout.

Here's an example with the same three Labels but with two frames instead of one. The second frame has a visual border around it:

```
import tkinter

window = tkinter.Tk()
frame = tkinter.Frame(window)
frame.pack()
frame2 = tkinter.Frame(window, borderwidth=4, relief=tkinter.GROOVE)
frame2.pack()
first = tkinter.Label(frame, text='First label')
first.pack()
```

```
second = tkinter.Label(frame2, text='Second label')
second.pack()
third = tkinter.Label(frame2, text='Third label')
third.pack()

window.mainloop()
```

We specify the border width using the borderwidth keyword argument (0 is the default) and the border style using relief (FLAT is the default). The other border styles are SUNKEN, RAISED, GROOVE, and RIDGE.

Here is the resulting GUI:

Getting Information from the User with the Entry Type

Two widgets let users enter text. The simplest one is Entry, which allows for a single line of text. If we associate a StringVar with the Entry, then whenever a user types anything into that Entry, the StringVar's value will automatically be updated to the contents of the Entry.

Here's an example that associates a single StringVar with both a Label and an Entry. When the user enters text in the Entry, the StringVar's contents will change. This will cause the Label to be updated, and so the Label will display whatever is currently in the Entry.

```
import tkinter
window = tkinter.Tk()

frame = tkinter.Frame(window)
frame.pack()
var = tkinter.StringVar()
label = tkinter.Label(frame, textvariable=var)
label.pack()
entry = tkinter.Entry(frame, textvariable=var)
entry.pack()
window.mainloop()
```

Here is the resulting GUI:

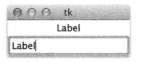

16.3 Models, Views, and Controllers, Oh My!

Using a StringVar to connect a text-entry box and a label is the first step toward separating *models* (How do we represent the data?), *views* (How do we display the data?), and *controllers* (How do we modify the data?), which is the key to building larger GUIs (as well as many other kinds of applications). This MVC design helps separate the parts of an application, which will make the application easier to understand and modify. The main goal of this design is to keep the representation of the data separate from the parts of the program that the user interacts with; that way, it is easier to make changes to the GUI code without affecting the code that manipulates the data.

As its name suggests, a view is something that displays information to the user, like Label. Many views, like Entry, also accept input, which they display immediately. The key is that they don't do anything else: they don't calculate average temperatures, move robot arms, or do any other calculations.

Models, on the other hand, store data, like a piece of text or the current inclination of a telescope. They also don't do calculations; their job is simply to keep track of the application's current state (and, in some cases, to save that state to a file or database and reload it later).

Controllers are the pieces that convert user input into calls on functions in the model that manipulate the data. The controller is what decides whether two gene sequences match well enough to be colored green or whether someone is allowed to overwrite an old results file. Controllers may update an application's models, which in turn can trigger changes to its views.

The following code shows what all of this looks like in practice. Here the model is kept track of by variable counter, which refers to an IntVar so that the view will update itself automatically. The controller is function click, which updates the model whenever a button is clicked. Four objects make up the view: the root window, a Frame, a Label that shows the current value of counter, and a button that the user can click to increment the counter's value:

```
import tkinter

# The controller.
def click():
    counter.set(counter.get() + 1)

if __name__ == '__main__':
    window = tkinter.Tk()
    # The model.
    counter = tkinter.IntVar()
    counter.set(0)
```

```
# The views.
frame = tkinter.Frame(window)
frame.pack()

button = tkinter.Button(frame, text='Click', command=click)
button.pack()

label = tkinter.Label(frame, textvariable=counter)
label.pack()

# Start the machinery!
window.mainloop()
```

The first two arguments used to construct the Button should be familiar by now. The third, command=click, tells it to call function click each time the user presses the button. This makes use of the fact that in Python a function is just another kind of object and can be passed as an argument like anything else.

Function click in the previous code does not have any parameters but uses variable counter, which is defined outside the function. Variables like this are called *global variables*, and their use should be avoided, since they make programs hard to understand. It would be better to pass any variables the function needs into it as parameters. We can't do this using the tools we have seen so far, because the functions that our buttons can call must not have any parameters. We will show you one way to avoid using global variables in the next section.

Using Lambda

The simple counter GUI shown earlier does what it's supposed to, but there is room for improvement. For example, suppose we want to be able to lower the counter's value as well as raise it.

Using only the tools we have seen so far, we could add another button and another controller function like this:

```
import tkinter

window = tkinter.Tk()

# The model.
counter = tkinter.IntVar()
counter.set(0)

# Two controllers.
def click_up():
    counter.set(counter.get() + 1)
```

```
def click_down():
    counter.set(counter.get() - 1)

# The views.
frame = tkinter.Frame(window)
frame.pack()
button = tkinter.Button(frame, text='Up', command=click_up)
button.pack()
button = tkinter.Button(frame, text='Down', command=click_down)
button.pack()
label = tkinter.Label(frame, textvariable=counter)
label.pack()

window.mainloop()
```

This seems a little clumsy, though. Functions click_up and click_down are doing almost the same thing; surely we ought to be able to combine them into one. While we're at it, we'll pass counter into the function explicitly rather than using it as a global variable:

```
# The model.
counter = tkinter.IntVar()
counter.set(0)

# One controller with parameters.
def click(variable, value):
    variable.set(variable.get() + value)
```

The problem with this is figuring out what to pass into the buttons, since we can't provide any arguments for the functions assigned to the buttons' command keyword arguments when creating those buttons. tkinter cannot read our minds—it can't magically know how many arguments our functions require or what values to pass in for them. For that reason, it requires that the controller functions triggered by buttons and other widgets take zero arguments so they can all be called the same way. It is our job to figure out how to take the two-argument function we want to use and turn it into one that needs no arguments at all.

We *could* do this by writing a couple of wrapper functions:

```
def click_up():
    click(counter, 1)

def click_down():
    click(counter, -1)
```

But this gets us back to two nearly identical functions that rely on global variables. A better way is to use a *lambda function*, which allows us to create a one-line function anywhere we want without giving it a name. Here's a very simple example:

```
>>> lambda: 3
<function <lambda> at 0x00A89B30>
>>> (lambda: 3)()
3
```

The expression lambda: 3 on the first line creates a nameless function that always returns the number 3. The second expression creates this function and immediately calls it, which has the same effect as this:

```
>>> def f():
...     return 3
...
>>> f()
3
```

However, the lambda form does *not* create a new variable or change an existing one. Finally, lambda functions can take arguments, just like other functions:

```
>>> (lambda x: 2 * x)(3)
6
```

Why *Lambda*?

The name *lambda function* comes from lambda calculus, a mathematical system for investigating function definition and application that was developed in the 1930s by Alonzo Church and Stephen Kleene.

So how does this help us with GUIs? The answer is that it lets us write one controller function to handle different buttons in a general way and then wrap up calls to that function when and as needed. Here's the two-button GUI once again using lambda functions:

```python
import tkinter

window = tkinter.Tk()

# The model.
counter = tkinter.IntVar()
counter.set(0)

# General controller.
def click(var, value):
    var.set(var.get() + value)

# The views.
frame = tkinter.Frame(window)
frame.pack()
```

```
button = tkinter.Button(frame, text='Up', command=lambda: click(counter, 1))
button.pack()

button = tkinter.Button(frame, text='Down', command=lambda: click(counter, -1))
button.pack()

label = tkinter.Label(frame, textvariable=counter)
label.pack()

window.mainloop()
```

This code creates a zero-argument lambda function to pass into each button just where it's needed. Those lambda functions then pass the right values into click. This is cleaner than the preceding code because the function definitions are enclosed in the call that uses them—there is no need to clutter the GUI with little functions that are used only in one place.

Note, however, that it is a very bad idea to repeat the same function several times in different places—if you do that, the odds are very high that you will one day want to change them all but will miss one or two. If you find yourself wanting to do this, reorganize the code so that the function is defined only once.

16.4 Customizing the Visual Style

Every windowing system has its own *look and feel*—square or rounded corners, particular colors, and so on. In this section, we'll see how to change the appearance of GUI widgets to make applications look more distinctive.

A note of caution before we begin: the default styles of some windowing systems have been chosen by experts trained in graphic design and human-computer interaction. The odds are that any radical changes on your part will make things worse, not better. In particular, be careful about color (several percent of the male population has some degree of color blindness) and font size (many people, particularly the elderly, cannot read small text).

Changing Fonts

Let's start by changing the size, weight, slant, and family of the font used to display text. To specify the size, we provide the height as an integer in points. We can set the weight to either bold or normal and the slant to either italic (slanted) or roman (not slanted).

The font families we can use depend on what system the program is running on. Common families include Times, Courier, and Verdana, but dozens of others are usually available. One note of caution though: if you choose an unusual font, people running your program on other computers might not have it, so your GUI might appear different than you'd like for them. Every operating system has a default font that will be used if the requested font isn't installed.

The following sets the font of a button to be 14 point, bold, italic, and Courier.

```python
import tkinter

window = tkinter.Tk()
button = tkinter.Button(window, text='Hello',
                        font=('Courier', 14, 'bold italic'))
button.pack()
window.mainloop()
```

Here is the resulting GUI:

Using this technique, you can set the font of any widget that displays text.

Changing Colors

Almost all background and foreground colors can be set using the bg and fg keyword arguments, respectively. As the following code shows, we can set either of these to a standard color by specifying the color's name, such as white, black, red, green, blue, cyan, yellow, or magenta:

```python
import tkinter

window = tkinter.Tk()
button = tkinter.Label(window, text='Hello', bg='green', fg='white')
button.pack()
window.mainloop()
```

Here is the resulting GUI:

As you can see, white text on a bright green background is *not* particularly readable.

We can choose more colors by specifying them using the *RGB color model*. RGB is an abbreviation for "red, green, blue"; it turns out that every color can be created using different amounts of these three colors. The amount of each color is usually specified by a number between 0 and 255 (inclusive).

These numbers are conventionally written in hexadecimal (base 16) notation; the best way to understand them is to play with them. Base 10 uses the digits 0 through 9; base 16 uses those ten digits plus another six: A, B, C, D, E, and F. In base 16, the number 255 is written FF.

The following color picker does this by updating a piece of text to show the color specified by the red, green, and blue values entered in the text boxes; choose any two base-16 digits for the RGB values and click the Update button:

```python
import tkinter
def change(widget, colors):
    """ Update the foreground color of a widget to show the RGB color value
    stored in a dictionary with keys 'red', 'green', and 'blue'.  Does
    *not* check the color value.
    """

    new_val = '#'
    for name in ('red', 'green', 'blue'):
        new_val += colors[name].get()
    widget['bg'] = new_val

# Create the application.
window = tkinter.Tk()
frame = tkinter.Frame(window)
frame.pack()

# Set up text entry widgets for red, green, and blue, storing the
# associated variables in a dictionary for later use.
colors = {}
for (name, col) in (('red', '#FF0000'),
                    ('green', '#00FF00'),
                    ('blue', '#0000FF')):
    colors[name] = tkinter.StringVar()
    colors[name].set('00')
    entry = tkinter.Entry(frame, textvariable=colors[name], bg=col,
                          fg='white')
    entry.pack()

# Display the current color.
current = tkinter.Label(frame, text='      ', bg='#FFFFFF')
current.pack()

# Give the user a way to trigger a color update.
update = tkinter.Button(frame, text='Update',
                        command=lambda: change(current, colors))
update.pack()
tkinter.mainloop()
```

This is the most complicated GUI we have seen so far, but it can be understood by breaking it down into a model, some views, and a controller. The model is three StringVars that store the hexadecimal strings representing the current red, green, and blue components of the color to display. These three variables are kept in a dictionary indexed by name for easy access. The controller is function change, which concatenates the strings to create an RGB color and applies that color to the background of a widget. The views are the text-entry boxes for the color components, the label that displays the current color, and the button that tells the GUI to update itself.

This program works, but neither the GUI nor the code is very attractive. It's annoying to have to click the update button, and if a user ever types anything that isn't a two-digit hexadecimal value into one of the text boxes, it results in an error. The exercises will ask you to redesign both the appearance and the structure of this program.

Laying Out the Widgets

One of the things that makes the color picker GUI ugly is the fact that everything is arranged top to bottom. tkinter uses this layout by default, but we can usually come up with something better.

To see how, let's revisit the example from *Getting Information from the User with the Entry Type*, on page 322, placing the label and button horizontally. We tell tkinter to do this by providing a side argument to method pack:

```
import tkinter

window = tkinter.Tk()
frame = tkinter.Frame(window)
frame.pack()
label = tkinter.Label(frame, text='Name')
label.pack(side='left')
entry = tkinter.Entry(frame)
entry.pack(side='left')

window.mainloop()
```

Here is the resulting GUI:

Setting side to "left" tells tkinter that the leftmost part of the label is to be placed next to the left edge of the frame, and then the leftmost part of the entry field is placed next to the right edge of the label—in short, that widgets are to be packed using their left edges. We could equally well pack to the right, top, or bottom edges, or we could mix packings (though that can quickly become confusing).

For even more control of our window layout, we can use a different layout manager called grid. As its name implies, it treats windows and frames as grids of rows and columns. To add the widget to the window, we call grid instead of pack. Do not call both on the same widget; they conflict with each other. The grid call can take several parameters, as shown in Table 27, *grid() Parameters*

Parameter	Description
row	The number of the row to insert the widget into—row numbers begin at 0.
column	The number of the column to insert the widget into—column numbers begin at 0.
rowspan	The number of rows the widget occupies—the default number is 1.
columnspan	The number of columns the widget occupies—the default number is 1.

Table 27—grid() Parameters

In the following code, we place the label in the upper left (row 0, column 0) and the entry field in the lower right (row 1, column 1).

```
import tkinter

window = tkinter.Tk()
frame = tkinter.Frame(window)
frame.pack()
label = tkinter.Label(frame, text='Name:')
label.grid(row=0, column=0)
entry = tkinter.Entry(frame)
entry.grid(row=1, column=1)

window.mainloop()
```

Here is the resulting GUI; as you can see, this leaves the bottom-left and upper-right corners empty:

16.5 Introducing a Few More Widgets

To end this chapter, we will look at a few more commonly used widgets.

Using Text

The Entry widget that we have been using since the start of this chapter allows for only a single line of text. If we want multiple lines of text, we use the Text widget instead, as shown here:

```python
import tkinter

def cross(text):
    text.insert(tkinter.INSERT, 'X')

window = tkinter.Tk()
frame = tkinter.Frame(window)
frame.pack()

text = tkinter.Text(frame, height=3, width=10)
text.pack()

button = tkinter.Button(frame, text='Add', command=lambda: cross(text))
button.pack()

window.mainloop()
```

Here is the resulting GUI:

Text provides a much richer set of methods than the other widgets we have seen so far. We can embed images in the text area, put in tags, select particular lines, and so on. The exercises will give you a chance to explore its capabilities.

Using Checkbuttons

Checkbuttons, often called *checkboxes*, have two states: on and off. When a user clicks a checkbutton, the state changes. We use a tkinter mutable variable to keep track of the user's selection. Typically, an IntVar variable is used, and the values 1 and 0 indicate on and off, respectively. In the following code, we use three checkbuttons to create a simpler color picker, and we use method config to change the configuration of a widget after it has been created:

```python
import tkinter

window = tkinter.Tk()
frame = tkinter.Frame(window)
frame.pack()
red = tkinter.IntVar()
green = tkinter.IntVar()
blue = tkinter.IntVar()

for (name, var) in (('R', red), ('G', green), ('B', blue)):
    check = tkinter.Checkbutton(frame, text=name, variable=var)
    check.pack(side='left')

def recolor(widget, r, g, b):
    color = '#'
    for var in (r, g, b):
        color += 'FF' if var.get() else '00'
    widget.config(bg=color)

label = tkinter.Label(frame, text='[      ]')
button = tkinter.Button(frame, text='update',
                        command=lambda: recolor(label, red, green, blue))
button.pack(side='left')
label.pack(side='left')
window.mainloop()
```

Here is the resulting GUI:

Using Menu

The last widget we will look at is Menu.

The following code uses this to create a simple text editor:

```python
import tkinter
import tkinter.filedialog as dialog

def save(root, text):
  data = text.get('0.0', tkinter.END)
  filename = dialog.asksaveasfilename(
      parent=root,
      filetypes=[('Text', '*.txt')],
```

```
      title='Save as...')
  writer = open(filename, 'w')
  writer.write(data)
  writer.close()

def quit(root):
  root.destroy()

window = tkinter.Tk()
text = tkinter.Text(window)
text.pack()

menubar = tkinter.Menu(window)
filemenu = tkinter.Menu(menubar)
filemenu.add_command(label='Save', command=lambda : save(window, text))
filemenu.add_command(label='Quit', command=lambda : quit(window))

menubar.add_cascade(label = 'File', menu=filemenu)
window.config(menu=menubar)

window.mainloop()
```

The program begins by defining two functions: save, which saves the contents of a text widget, and quit, which closes the application. Function save uses tkFileDialog to create a standard "Save as..." dialog box, which will prompt the user for the name of a text file.

After creating and packing the Text widget, the program creates a menu bar, which is the horizontal bar into which we can put one or more menus. It then creates a File menu and adds two menu items to it called Save and Quit. We then add the File menu to the menu bar and run mainloop.

Here is the resulting GUI:

16.6 Object-Oriented GUIs

The GUIs we have built so far have not been particularly well structured. Most of the code to construct them has not been modularized in functions, and they have relied on global variables. We can get away with this for very small examples, but if we try to build larger applications this way, they will be difficult to understand and debug.

For this reason, almost all real GUIs are built using classes and objects that tie models, views, and controllers together in one tidy package. In the counter shown next, for example, the application's model is a member variable of class Counter, accessed using self.state, and its controllers are the methods up_click and quit_click.

```python
import tkinter

class Counter:
    """A simple counter GUI using object-oriented programming."""
    def __init__(self, parent):

        """Create the GUI."""

        # Framework.
        self.parent = parent
        self.frame = tkinter.Frame(parent)
        self.frame.pack()

        # Model.
        self.state = tkinter.IntVar()
        self.state.set(1)

        # Label displaying current state.
        self.label = tkinter.Label(self.frame, textvariable=self.state)
        self.label.pack()

        # Buttons to control application.
        self.up = tkinter.Button(self.frame, text='up', command=self.up_click)
        self.up.pack(side='left')

        self.right = tkinter.Button(self.frame, text='quit',
                                    command=self.quit_click)
        self.right.pack(side='left')

    def up_click(self):
        """Handle click on 'up' button."""

        self.state.set(self.state.get() + 1)
```

```
    def quit_click(self):
        """Handle click on 'quit' button."""

        self.parent.destroy()
if __name__ == '__main__':

    window = tkinter.Tk()
    myapp = Counter(window)
    window.mainloop()
```

16.7 Keeping the Concepts from Being a GUI Mess

In this chapter, you learned the following:

- Most modern programs provide a graphical user interface (GUI) for displaying information and interacting with users. GUIs are built out of widgets, such as buttons, sliders, and text panels; all modern programming languages provide at least one GUI toolkit.

- Unlike command-line programs, GUI applications are usually event-driven. In other words, they react to events such as keystrokes and mouse clicks when and as they occur.

- Experience shows that GUIs should be built using the model-view-controller pattern. The model is the data being manipulated; the view displays the current state of the data and gathers input from the user, while the controller decides what to do next.

- Lambda expressions create functions that have no names. These are often used to define the actions that widgets should take when users provide input, without requiring global variables.

- Designing usable GUIs is as challenging a craft as designing software. Being good at the latter doesn't guarantee that you can do the former, but dozens of good books can help you get started.

16.8 Exercises

Here are some exercises for you to try on your own. Solutions are available at http://pragprog.com/titles/gwpy2/practical-programming.

1. Write a GUI application with a button labeled "Goodbye." When the button is clicked, the window closes.
2. Write a GUI application with a single button. Initially the button is labeled 0, but each time it is clicked, the value on the button increases by 1.
3. What is a more readable way to write the following?

```
x = lambda: y
```

4. A DNA sequence is a string made up of *As*, *Ts*, *Cs*, and *Gs*. Write a GUI application in which a DNA sequence is entered, and when the Count button is clicked, the number of *As*, *Ts*, *Cs*, and *Gs* are counted and displayed in the window (see the image below).

5. In Section 3.3, *Defining Our Own Functions*, on page 35, we wrote a function to convert degrees Fahrenheit to degrees Celsius. Write a GUI application that looks like the image below.

   When a value is entered in the text field and the Convert button is clicked, the value should be converted from Fahrenheit to Celsius and displayed in the window, as shown in the image below.

6. Rewrite the text editor code from *Using Menu*, on page 333, as an object-oriented GUI.

## CHAPTER 17

Databases

In earlier chapters, we used files to store data. This is fine for small problems, but as our data sets become larger and more complex, we need something that will let us search for data in many different ways, control who can view and modify the data, and ensure that the data is correctly formatted. In short, we need a database.

Many different kinds of databases exist. Some are like a dictionary that automatically saves itself on disk, while others store backup copies of the objects in a program. The most popular by far, however, are *relational databases*, which are at the heart of most large commercial and scientific software systems. In this chapter, you will learn about the key concepts behind relational databases and how to perform a few common operations.

17.1 Overview

A relational database is a collection of *tables*, each of which has a fixed number of columns and a variable number of rows. Each column in a table has a name and contains values of the same data type, such as integer or string. Each row, or *record*, contains values that are related to each other, such as a particular patient's name, date of birth, and blood type.

Patients		
name	**birthday**	**blood_type**
Alice	1978/04/02	A
Bob	1954/03/10	AB
Carol	1963/09/29	A
Liz	1977/12/15	B
Wally	1949/07/05	O

← row

column

Superficially, each table looks like a spreadsheet or a file with one record per line (see *The Readline Technique*, on page 179), but behind the scenes, the database does a lot of work to keep track of which values are where and how different tables relate to one another.

Many different brands of databases are available to choose from, including commercial systems like Oracle, IBM's DB2, and Microsoft Access and open source databases like MySQL and PostgreSQL. Our examples use one called SQLite. It isn't fast enough to handle the heavy loads that sites like Amazon.com experience, but it is free, it is simple to use, and as of Python 3.3.0, the standard library includes a module called sqlite3 for working with it.

A database is usually stored in a file or in a collection of files. These files aren't formatted as plain text—if you open them in an editor, they will look like garbage, and any changes you make will probably corrupt the data and make the database unusable. Instead you must interact with the database in one of two ways:

- *By typing commands into a database GUI, just as you type commands into a Python interpreter.* This is good for simple tasks but not for writing applications of your own.

- *By writing programs in Python (or some other language).* These programs import a library that knows how to work with the kind of database you are using and use that library to create tables, insert records, and fetch the data you want. Your code can then format the results in a web page, calculate statistics, or do whatever else you like.

In the examples in this chapter, our programs all start with this line:

```
>>> import sqlite3
```

To put data into a database or to get information out, we'll write commands in a special-purpose language called SQL, which stands for Structured Query Language and is pronounced either as the three letters "S-Q-L" or as the word "sequel."

17.2 Creating and Populating

As a running example, we will use the predictions for regional populations in the year 2300, which is taken from http://www.worldmapper.org. The first table that we'll work with (Table 28, *Estimated World Population in 2300*, on page 341) has one column that contains the names of regions and another that contains the populations of regions, so each row of the table represents a region and its population.

Region	Population (in thousands)
Central Africa	330,993
Southeastern Africa	743,112
Northern Africa	1,037,463
Southern Asia	2,051,941
Asia Pacific	785,468
Middle East	687,630
Eastern Asia	1,362,955
South America	593,121
Eastern Europe	223,427
North America	661,157
Western Europe	387,933
Japan	100,562

Table 28—Estimated World Population in 2300

If the countries were sized by their estimated populations, they would look like this:

As promised earlier, we start by telling Python that we want to use sqlite3:

```
>>> import sqlite3
```

Next we must make a connection to our database by calling the database module's connect method. This method takes one string as a parameter, which identifies the database to connect to. Since SQLite stores each entire database in a single file on disk, this is just the path to the file. Since the database population.db doesn't exist, it will be created:

```
>>> con = sqlite3.connect('population.db')
```

Once we have a connection, we need to get a *cursor*. Like the cursor in an editor, this keeps track of where we are in the database so that if several programs are accessing the database at the same time, the database can keep track of who is trying to do what:

```
>>> cur = con.cursor()
```

We can now actually start working with the database. The first step is to create a database table to store the population data. To do this, we have to describe the operation we want using Structured Query Language (SQL). The general form of an SQL statement for table creation is as follows:

```
CREATE TABLE «TableName»(«ColumnName» «Type», ...)
```

The types of the data in each of the table's columns are chosen from the types the database supports:

Type	Python Equivalent	Use
NULL	NoneType	Means "know nothing about it"
INTEGER	int	Integers
REAL	float	8-byte floating-point numbers
TEXT	str	Strings of characters
BLOB	bytes	Binary data

Table 29—SQLite Data Types

To create a two-column table named PopByRegion to store region names as strings in the Region column and projected populations as integers in the Population column, we use this SQL statement:

```
CREATE TABLE PopByRegion(Region TEXT, Population INTEGER)
```

Now, we put that SQL statement in a string and pass it as an argument to a Python method that will execute the SQL command:

```
>>> cur.execute('CREATE TABLE PopByRegion(Region TEXT, Population INTEGER)')
<sqlite3.Cursor object at 0x102e3e490>
```

When method execute is called, it returns the cursor object that it was called on. Since cur refers to that same cursor object, we don't need to do anything with the value returned by execute.

The most commonly used data types in SQLite databases are listed in Table 29, *SQLite Data Types*, along with the corresponding Python data types. The BLOB type needs more explanation. The term BLOB stands for Binary Large OBject, which to a database means a picture, an MP3, or any other lump of bytes that isn't of a more specific type. The Python equivalent is a type we haven't seen before called bytes, which also stores a sequence of bytes that have no particular predefined meaning. We won't use BLOBs in our examples, but the exercises will give you a chance to experiment with them.

After we create a table, our next task is to insert data into it. We do this one record at a time using the INSERT command, whose general form is as follows:

```
INSERT INTO «TableName» VALUES(«Value», ...)
```

As with the arguments to a function call, the values are matched left to right against the columns. For example, we insert data into the PopByRegion table like this:

```
>>> cur.execute('INSERT INTO PopByRegion VALUES("Central Africa", 330993)')
<sqlite3.Cursor object at 0x102e3e490>
>>> cur.execute('INSERT INTO PopByRegion VALUES("Southeastern Africa", '
...             '743112)')
<sqlite3.Cursor object at 0x102e3e490>
...
>>> cur.execute('INSERT INTO PopByRegion VALUES("Japan", 100562)')
<sqlite3.Cursor object at 0x102e3e490>
```

Notice that the number and type of values in the INSERT statements matches the number and type of columns in the database table. If we try to insert a value of a different type than the one declared for the column, the library will try to convert it, just as it converts the integer 5 to a floating-point number when we do 1.2 + 5. For example, if we insert the integer 32 into a TEXT column, it will automatically be converted to "32"; similarly, if we insert a string into an INTEGER column, it is parsed to see whether it represents a number. If so, the number is inserted.

If the number of values being inserted doesn't match the number of columns in the table, the database reports an error and the data is not inserted. Surprisingly, though, if we try to insert a value that cannot be converted to the correct type, such as the string "string" into an INTEGER field, SQLite will actually do it (though other databases will not).

Another format for the INSERT SQL command uses placeholders for the values to be inserted. When using this format, method execute has two arguments: the first is the SQL command with question marks as placeholders for the values to be inserted, and the second is a tuple. When the command is executed, the items from the tuple are substituted for the placeholders from left to right. For example, the execute method call to insert a row with "Japan" and 100562 can be rewritten like this:

```
>>> cur.execute('INSERT INTO PopByRegion VALUES (?, ?)', ("Japan", 100562))
```

In this example, "Japan" is used in place of the first question mark, and 100562 in place of the second. This placeholder notation can come in handy when using a loop to insert data from a list or a file into a database, as shown in Section 17.6, *Using Joins to Combine Tables*, on page 349.

Saving Changes

After we've inserted data into the database or made any other changes, we must *commit* those changes using the connection's commit method:

```
>>> con.commit()
```

Committing to a database is like saving the changes made to a file in a text editor. Until we do it, our changes are not actually stored and are not visible to anyone else who is using the database at the same time. Requiring programs to commit is a form of insurance. If a program crashes partway through a long sequence of database operations and commit is never called, then the database will appear as it did before any of those operations were executed.

17.3 Retrieving Data

Now that our database has been created and populated, we can run *queries* to search for data that meets specified criteria. The general form of a query is as follows:

```
SELECT «ColumnName» , ... FROM «TableName»
```

The TableName is the name of the table to get the data from and the column names specify which columns to get values from. For example, this query retrieves all the data in the table PopByRegion:

```
>>> cur.execute('SELECT Region, Population FROM PopByRegion')
```

Once the database has executed this query for us, we can access the results one record at a time by calling the cursor's fetchone method, just as we can read one line at a time from a file using readline:

```
>>> cur.fetchone()
('Central Africa', 330993)
```

The fetchone method returns each record as a tuple (see Section 11.2, *Storing Data Using Tuples*, on page 204) whose elements are in the order specified in the query. If there are no more records, fetchone returns None.

Just as files have a readlines method to get all the lines in a file at once, database cursors have a fetchall method that returns all the data produced by a query that has not yet been fetched as a list of tuples:

```
>>> cur.fetchall()
[('Southeastern Africa', 743112), ('Northern Africa', 1037463), ('Southern
Asia', 2051941), ('Asia Pacific', 785468), ('Middle East', 687630),
('Eastern Asia', 1362955), ('South America', 593121), ('Eastern Europe',
223427), ('North America', 661157), ('Western Europe', 387933), ('Japan',
100562)]
```

Once all of the data produced by the query has been fetched, any subsequent
calls on fetchone and fetchall return None and the empty list, respectively:

```
>>> cur.fetchone()
>>> cur.fetchall()
[]
```

Like a dictionary or a set (Chapter 11, *Storing Data Using Other Collection
Types*, on page 199), a database stores records in whatever order it thinks is
most efficient. To put the data in a particular order, we could sort the list
returned by fetchall. However, it is more efficient to get the database to do the
sorting for us by adding an ORDER BY clause to the query like this:

```
>>> cur.execute('SELECT Region, Population FROM PopByRegion ORDER BY Region')
>>> cur.fetchall()
[('Asia Pacific', 785468), ('Central Africa', 330993), ('Eastern Asia',
1362955), ('Eastern Europe', 223427), ('Japan', 100562), ('Middle East',
687630), ('North America', 661157), ('Northern Africa', 1037463), ('South
America', 593121), ('Southeastern Africa', 743112), ('Southern Asia',
2051941), ('Western Europe', 387933)]
```

By changing the column name after the phrase ORDER BY, we can change the
way the database sorts. As the following code demonstrates, we can also
specify whether we want values sorted in ascending (ASC) or descending (DESC)
order:

```
>>> cur.execute('''SELECT Region, Population FROM PopByRegion
                      ORDER BY Population DESC''')
<sqlite3.Cursor object at 0x102e3e490>
>>> cur.fetchall()
[('Southern Asia', 2051941), ('Eastern Asia', 1362955), ('Northern Africa',
1037463), ('Asia Pacific', 785468), ('Southeastern Africa', 743112),
('Middle East', 687630), ('North America', 661157), ('South America',
593121), ('Western Europe', 387933), ('Central Africa', 330993), ('Eastern
Europe', 223427), ('Japan', 100562)]
```

As we've seen, we can specify one or more columns by name in a query. We
can also use * to indicate that we want all columns:

```
>>> cur.execute('SELECT Region FROM PopByRegion')
<sqlite3.Cursor object at 0x102e3e490>
>>> cur.fetchall()
[('Central Africa',), ('Southeastern Africa',), ('Northern Africa',),
```

```
('Southern Asia',), ('Asia Pacific',), ('Middle East',), ('Eastern
 Asia',), ('South America',), ('Eastern Europe',), ('North America',),
 ('Western Europe',), ('Japan',)]
>>> cur.execute('SELECT * FROM PopByRegion')
<sqlite3.Cursor object at 0x102e3e490>
>>> cur.fetchall()
[('Central Africa', 330993), ('Southeastern Africa', 743112),
 ('Northern Africa', 1037463), ('Southern Asia', 2051941), ('Asia
 Pacific', 785468), ('Middle East', 687630), ('Eastern Asia', 1362955),
 ('South America', 593121), ('Eastern Europe', 223427), ('North America',
 661157), ('Western Europe', 387933), ('Japan', 100562)]
```

Query Conditions

Much of the time, we want only some of the data in the database. (Think about what would happen if you asked Google for all of the web pages it had stored.) We can select a subset of the data by using the keyword WHERE to specify conditions that the rows we want must satisfy. For example, we can get the regions with populations greater than one million using the greater-than operator:

```
>>> cur.execute('SELECT Region FROM PopByRegion WHERE Population > 1000000')
<sqlite3.Cursor object at 0x102e3e490>
>>> cur.fetchall()
[('Northern Africa',), ('Southern Asia',), ('Eastern Asia',)]
```

These are the relational operators that may be used with WHERE:

Operator	Description
=	Equal to
!=	Not equal to
>	Greater than
<	Less than
>=	Greater than or equal to
<=	Less than or equal to

Table 30—SQL Relational Operators

Not surprisingly, they are the same as the ones that Python and other programming languages provide. As well as these relational operators, we can also use the AND, OR, and NOT operators. To get a list of regions with populations greater than one million that have names that come before the letter L in the alphabet, we would use this (we are using a triple-quoted string for the SQL statement so that it can span multiple lines):

```
>>> cur.execute('''SELECT Region FROM PopByRegion
                   WHERE Population > 1000000 AND Region < "L"''')
<sqlite3.Cursor object at 0x102e3e490>
>>> cur.fetchall()
[('Eastern Asia',)]
```

WHERE conditions are always applied row by row—they cannot be used to compare two or more rows. We will see how to do that in Section 17.6, *Using Joins to Combine Tables*, on page 349.

17.4 Updating and Deleting

Data often changes over time, so we need to be able to change the information stored in databases. To do that, we can use the UPDATE command, as shown in the following code:

```
>>> cur.execute('SELECT * FROM PopByRegion WHERE Region = "Japan"')
<sqlite3.Cursor object at 0x102e3e490>
>>> cur.fetchone()
('Japan', 100562)
>>> cur.execute('''UPDATE PopByRegion SET Population = 100600
                   WHERE Region = "Japan"''')
<sqlite3.Cursor object at 0x102e3e490>
>>> cur.execute('SELECT * FROM PopByRegion WHERE Region = "Japan"')
<sqlite3.Cursor object at 0x102e3e490>
>>> cur.fetchone()
('Japan', 100600)
```

We can also delete records from the database:

```
>>> cur.execute('DELETE FROM PopByRegion WHERE Region < "L"')
<sqlite3.Cursor object at 0x102e3e490>
>>> cur.execute('SELECT * FROM PopByRegion')
<sqlite3.Cursor object at 0x102e3e490>
>>> cur.fetchall()
[('Southeastern Africa', 743112), ('Northern Africa', 1037463),
 ('Southern Asia', 2051941), ('Middle East', 687630), ('South America',
 593121), ('North America', 661157), ('Western Europe', 387933)])]
```

In both cases, all records that meet the WHERE condition are affected. If we don't include a WHERE condition, then all rows in the database are updated or removed. Of course, we can always put records back into the database:

```
>>> cur.execute('INSERT INTO PopByRegion VALUES ("Japan", 100562)')
```

To remove an entire table from the database, we can use the DROP command:

```
DROP TABLE TableName
```

For example, if we no longer want the table PopByRegion, we would execute this:

```
>>> cur.execute('DROP TABLE PopByRegion');
```

When a table is dropped, all the data it contained is lost. You should be very, very sure you want to do this (and even then, it's probably a good idea to make a backup copy of the database before deleting any sizable tables).

17.5 Using NULL for Missing Data

In the real world, we often don't have all the data we want. We might be missing the time at which an experiment was performed or the postal code of a patient being given a new kind of treatment. Rather than leave what we *do* know out of the database, we may choose to insert it and use the value NULL to represent the missing values. For example, if there is a region whose population we don't know, we could insert this into our database:

```
>>> cur.execute('INSERT INTO PopByRegion VALUES ("Mars", NULL)')
```

On the other hand, we probably don't ever want a record in the database that has a NULL region name. We can prevent this from ever happening, stating that the column is NOT NULL when the table is created:

```
>>> cur.execute('CREATE TABLE Test (Region TEXT NOT NULL, '
...             'Population INTEGER)')
```

Now when we try to insert a NULL region into our new Test table, we get an error message:

```
>>> cur.execute('INSERT INTO Test VALUES (NULL, 456789)')
Traceback (most recent call last):
  File "<pyshell#45>", line 1, in <module>
    cur.execute('INSERT INTO Test VALUES (NULL, 456789)')
sqlite3.IntegrityError: Test.Region may not be NULL
```

Stating that the value must not be NULL is not always necessary, and imposing such a constraint may not be reasonable in some cases. Rather than using NULL, it may sometimes be more appropriate to use the value zero, an empty string, or false. You should do so in cases where you know something about the data and use NULL only in cases where you know nothing at all about it.

In fact, some experts recommend not using NULL at all because its behavior is counterintuitive (at least until you've retrained your intuition). The general rule is that operations involving NULL produce NULL as a result; the reasoning is that if the computer doesn't know what one of the operation's inputs is, it can't know what the output is either. Adding a number to NULL therefore produces NULL no matter what the number was, and multiplying by NULL also produces NULL.

Things are more complicated with logical operations. The expression NULL OR 1 produces 1, rather than NULL, because of the following:

- If the first argument was false (or 0, or the empty string, or some equivalent value), the result would be 1.

- If the first argument was true (or nonzero, or a nonempty string), the result would also be 1.

The technical term for this is *three-valued logic*. In SQL's view of the world, things aren't just true or false—they can be true, false, or unknown, and NULL represents the last. Unfortunately, different databases interpret ambiguities in the SQL standard in different ways, so their handling of NULL is not consistent. NULL should therefore be used with caution and only when other approaches won't work.

17.6 Using Joins to Combine Tables

When designing a database, it often makes sense to divide data between two or more tables. For example, if we are maintaining a database of patient records, we would probably want at least four tables: one for the patient's personal information (such as name and date of birth), a second to keep track of appointments, a third for information about the doctors who are treating the patient, and a fourth for information about the hospitals or clinics those doctors work at.

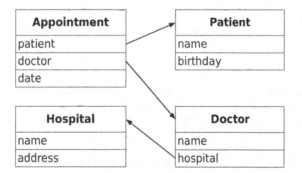

We could store all of this in one table, but then a lot of information would be needlessly duplicated:

Patient-Doctor-Appointment-Hospital					
patient	birthday	doctor	date	hospital	address
Alice	1978/04/02	Rajani	2008/09/01	Central	52 Walnut St.
Alice	1978/04/02	Nianiaris	2008/10/04	Central	52 Walnut St.
Alice	1978/04/02	Newton	2008/09/14	East	8 Elm St.
Zack	1964/12/15	Newton	2008/09/18	East	8 Elm St.
Zack	1964/12/15	Vaz	2008/11/01	East	8 Elm St.

If we divide information between tables, though, we need some way to pull that information back together. For example, if we want to know the hospitals at which a patient has had appointments, we need to combine data from all four tables to find out the following:

- Which appointments the patient has had
- Which doctor each appointment was with
- Which hospital/clinic that doctor works at

The right way to do this in a relational database is to use a *join*. As the name suggests, a join combines information from two or more tables to create a new set of records, each of which can contain some or all of the information in the tables involved.

To begin, let's add another table that contains the names of countries, the regions that they are in, and their populations:

```
>>> cur.execute('''CREATE TABLE PopByCountry(Region TEXT, Country TEXT,
                   Population INTEGER)''')
```

Then let's insert data into the new table:

```
>>> cur.execute('''INSERT INTO PopByCountry VALUES("Eastern Asia", "China",
                   1285238)''')
```

Inserting data one row at a time like this requires a lot of typing. It is simpler to make a list of tuples to be inserted and write a loop that inserts the values from these tuples one by one using the placeholder notation from Section 17.2, *Creating and Populating*, on page 340:

```
>>> countries = [("Eastern Asia", "DPR Korea", 24056), ("Eastern Asia",
"Hong Kong (China)", 8764), ("Eastern Asia", "Mongolia", 3407), ("Eastern
Asia", "Republic of Korea", 41491), ("Eastern Asia", "Taiwan", 1433),
("North America", "Bahamas", 368), ("North America", "Canada", 40876),
("North America", "Greenland", 43), ("North America", "Mexico", 126875),
("North America", "United States", 493038)]
>>> for c in countries:
...     cur.execute('INSERT INTO PopByCountry VALUES (?, ?, ?)', (c[0], c[1], c[2]))
...
>>> con.commit()
```

Now that we have two tables in our database, we can use joins to combine the information they contain. Several types of joins exist; you'll learn about *inner joins* and *self-joins*.

We'll begin with inner joins, which involve the following. (Note that the numbers in this list correspond to circled numbers in the following diagram.)

1. Constructing the cross product of the tables
2. Discarding rows that do not meet the selection criteria
3. Selecting columns from the remaining rows

1 Compute cross product

PopByRegion			PopByCountry		
Eastern Asia	1362955		Eastern Asia	Mongolia	3407
North America	661157		North America	Greenland	43

2a Keep rows where PopByRegion.Region = PopByCountry.Region

Eastern Asia	1362955	**Eastern Asia**	Mongolia	3407
North America	661157	**North America**	Greenland	43
Eastern Asia	1362955	North America	Greenland	43
North America	661157	Eastern Asia	Mongolia	3407

2b Keep rows where PopByRegion.Population > 1000000

Eastern Asia	**1362955**	Eastern Asia	Mongolia	3407
North America	661157	North America	Greenland	43

3 Keep columns PopByRegion.Region and PopByCountry.Country

Eastern Asia	1362955	Eastern Asia	**Mongolia**	3407

First, all combinations of all rows in the tables are combined, which makes the cross product. Second, the selection criteria specified by WHERE is applied, and rows that don't match are removed. Finally, the selected columns are kept, and all others are discarded.

In an earlier query, we retrieved the names of regions with projected populations greater than one million. Using an inner join, we can get the names of the countries that are in those regions. The query and its result look like this:

```
>>> cur.execute('''
SELECT PopByRegion.Region, PopByCountry.Country
FROM   PopByRegion INNER JOIN PopByCountry
WHERE  (PopByRegion.Region = PopByCountry.Region)
AND    (PopByRegion.Population > 1000000)
''')
<sqlite3.Cursor object at 0x102e3e490>
>>> cur.fetchall()
[('Eastern Asia', 'China'), ('Eastern Asia', 'DPR Korea'),
('Eastern Asia', 'Hong Kong (China)'), ('Eastern Asia', 'Mongolia'),
('Eastern Asia', 'Republic of Korea'), ('Eastern Asia', 'Taiwan')]
```

To understand what this query is doing, we can analyze it in terms of the three steps outlined earlier:

1. *Combine every row of PopByRegion with every row of PopByCountry.* PopByRegion has 2 columns and 12 rows, while PopByCountry has 3 columns and 11 rows, so this produces a temporary table with 5 columns and 132 rows:

Central Africa	330993	Eastern Asia	DPR Korea	24056
Southeastern Africa	743112	Eastern Asia	DPR Korea	24056
Northern Africa	1037463	Eastern Asia	DPR Korea	24056
Southern Asia	2051941	Eastern Asia	DPR Korea	24056
Asia Pacific	785468	Eastern Asia	DPR Korea	24056
Middle East	687630	Eastern Asia	DPR Korea	24056
Eastern Asia	1362955	Eastern Asia	DPR Korea	24056
South America	593121	Eastern Asia	DPR Korea	24056
Eastern Europe	223427	Eastern Asia	DPR Korea	24056
North America	661157	Eastern Asia	DPR Korea	24056
Western Europe	387933	Eastern Asia	DPR Korea	24056
Japan	100562	Eastern Asia	DPR Korea	24056
Central Africa	330993	Eastern Asia	Hong Kong (China)	8764
Southeastern Africa	743112	Eastern Asia	Hong Kong (China)	8764
Northern Africa	1037463	Eastern Asia	Hong Kong (China)	8764
Southern Asia	2051941	Eastern Asia	Hong Kong (China)	8764
Asia Pacific	785468	Eastern Asia	Hong Kong (China)	8764
Middle East	687630	Eastern Asia	Hong Kong (China)	8764
Eastern Asia	1362955	Eastern Asia	Hong Kong (China)	8764
South America	593121	Eastern Asia	Hong Kong (China)	8764
Eastern Europe	223427	Eastern Asia	Hong Kong (China)	8764
North America	661157	Eastern Asia	Hong Kong (China)	8764
Western Europe	387933	Eastern Asia	Hong Kong (China)	8764
Japan	100562	Eastern Asia	Hong Kong (China)	8764
...	...	...	...	...

2. *Discard rows that do not meet the selection criteria.* The join's WHERE clause specifies two of these: the region taken from PopByRegion must be the same as the region taken from PopByCountry, and the region's population must be greater than one million. The first criterion ensures that we don't look at records that combine countries in North America with regional populations in East Asia; the second filters out information about countries in regions whose populations are less than our threshold.

3. *Finally, select the region and country names from the rows that have survived.*

Removing Duplicates

To find the regions where one country accounts for more than 10 percent of the region's overall population, we would also need to join the two tables.

```
>>> cur.execute('''
SELECT PopByRegion.Region
FROM PopByRegion INNER JOIN PopByCountry
WHERE (PopByRegion.Region = PopByCountry.Region)
```

```
AND ((PopByCountry.Population * 1.0) / PopByRegion.Population > 0.10)''')
<sqlite3.Cursor object at 0x102e3e490>
>>> cur.fetchall()
[('Eastern Asia',), ('North America',), ('North America',)]
```

We use multiplication and division in our WHERE condition to calculate the percentage of the region's population by country as a floating-point number. The resulting list contains duplicates, since more than one North American country accounts for more than 10 percent of the region's population. To remove the duplicates, we add the keyword DISTINCT to the query:

```
>>> cur.execute('''
SELECT DISTINCT PopByRegion.Region
FROM PopByRegion INNER JOIN PopByCountry
WHERE (PopByRegion.Region = PopByCountry.Region)
AND ((PopByCountry.Population * 1.0) / PopByRegion.Population > 0.10)''')
>>> cur.fetchall()
[('Eastern Asia',), ('North America',)]
```

Now in the results above, 'North America' only appears once.

17.7 Keys and Constraints

Our query in the previous section relied on the fact that our regions and countries were uniquely identified by their names. A column in a table that is used this way is called a *key*. Ideally, a key's values should be unique, just like the keys in a dictionary. We can tell the database to enforce this constraint by adding a PRIMARY KEY clause when we create the table. For example, when we created the PopByRegion table, we should have specified the primary key:

```
>>> cur.execute('''CREATE TABLE PopByRegion (
                Region TEXT NOT NULL,
                Population INTEGER NOT NULL,
                PRIMARY KEY (Region))''')
```

Just as a key in a dictionary can be made up of multiple values, the primary key for a database table can consist of multiple columns.

The following code uses the CONSTRAINT keyword to specify that no two entries in the table being created will ever have the same values for region *and* country:

```
>>> cur.execute('''
    CREATE TABLE PopByCountry(
    Region TEXT NOT NULL,
    Country TEXT NOT NULL,
    Population INTEGER NOT NULL,
    CONSTRAINT CountryKey PRIMARY KEY (Region, Country))''')
```

In practice, most database designers don't use real names as primary keys. Instead, they usually create a unique integer ID for each "thing" in the database, such as a driver's license number or a patient ID. This is partly done for efficiency's sake—integers are faster to sort and compare than strings —but the real reason is that it is a simple way to deal with things that have the same name. There are a lot of Jane Smiths in the world; using that name as a primary key in a database is almost guaranteed to lead to confusion. Giving each person a unique ID, on the other hand, ensures that they can be told apart.

17.8 Advanced Features

The SQL we have seen so far is powerful enough for many everyday tasks, but other questions require more powerful tools. This section introduces a handful and shows when and how they are useful.

Aggregation

Our next task is to calculate the total projected world population for the year 2300. We will do this by adding up the values in PopByRegion's Population column using the SQL *aggregate* function SUM:

```
>>> cur.execute('SELECT SUM (Population) FROM PopByRegion')
<sqlite3.Cursor object at 0x102e3e490>
>>> cur.fetchone()
(8965762,)
```

SQL provides several other aggregate functions. All of these are *associative*; that is, the result doesn't depend on the order of operations. This ensures that the result doesn't depend on the order in which records are pulled out of tables.

Aggregate Function	Description
AVG	Average of the values
MIN	Minimum value
MAX	Maximum value
COUNT	Number of nonnull values
SUM	Sum of the values

Table 31—Aggregate Functions

Addition and multiplication are associative, since $1 + (2 + 3)$ produces the same results as $(1 + 2) + 3$, and $4 * (5 * 6)$ produces the same result as $(4 * 5) * 6$. By contrast, subtraction isn't associative: $1 - (2 - 3)$ is not the same thing as $(1 - 2) - 3$. Notice that there isn't a subtraction aggregate function.

Grouping

What if we only had the table PopByCountry and wanted to find the projected population for each region? We could get the table's contents into a Python program using SELECT * and then loop over them to add them up by region, but again, it is simpler and more efficient to have the database do the work for us. In this case, we use SQL's GROUP BY to collect results into subsets:

```
>>> cur.execute('SELECT SUM (Population) FROM PopByCountry GROUP BY Region')
<sqlite3.Cursor object at 0x102e3e490>
>>> cur.fetchall()
[(1364389,), (661200,)]
```

Since we have asked the database to construct groups by Region and there are two distinct values in this column in the table, the database divides the records into two subsets. It then applies the SUM function to each group separately to give us the projected populations of Eastern Asia and North America:

PopByCountry

North America	Bahamas	368
North America	Mexlco	126875
Eastern Asia	Mongolia	3407
Eastern Asia	Republic of Korea	41491

① Group by Region and compute SUM of Population

North America	Bahamas	368
North America	Mexico	126875
		127243

Eastern Asia	Mongolia	3407
Eastern Asia	Republic of Korea	41491
		44898

② Keep selected columns

North America	127243
Eastern Asia	44898

Self-Joins

Let's consider the problem of comparing a table's values to themselves. Suppose that we want to find pairs of countries whose populations are close to each other—say, within 1,000 of each other. Our first attempt might look like this:

```
>>> cur.execute('''SELECT Country FROM PopByCountry
                   WHERE (ABS(Population - Population) < 1000)''')
<sqlite3.Cursor object at 0x102e3e490>
>>> cur.fetchall()
[('China',), ('DPR Korea',), ('Hong Kong (China)',), ('Mongolia',),
('Republic of Korea',), ('Taiwan',), ('Bahamas',), ('Canada',),
('Greenland',), ('Mexico',), ('United States',)]
```

The output is definitely not what we want, for two reasons. First, the phrase SELECT Country is going to return only one country per record, but we want pairs of countries. Second, the expression ABS(Population - Population) is always going to return zero because we are subtracting each country's population from itself. Since every difference will be less than 1,000, the names of all the countries in the table will be returned by the query.

What we actually want to do is compare the population in one row with the populations in each of the other rows. To do this, we need to join PopByCountry with itself using an INNER JOIN:

PopByCountry

North America	Canada	40876
North America	United States	493038
Eastern Asia	Taiwan	1433

PopByCountry cross joined with itself

North America	Canada	40876	North America	Canada	40876
North America	United States	493038	North America	United States	493038
Eastern Asia	Taiwan	1433	Eastern Asia	Taiwan	1433
North America	Canada	40876	North America	United States	493038
North America	United States	493038	Eastern Asia	Taiwan	1433
Eastern Asia	Taiwan	1433	North America	Canada	40876
North America	Canada	40876	Eastern Asia	Taiwan	1433
North America	United States	493038	North America	Canada	40876
Eastern Asia	Taiwan	1433	North America	United States	493038

This will result in the rows for each pair of countries being combined into a single row with six columns: two regions, two countries, and two populations. To tell them apart, we have to give the two instances of the PopByCountry table temporary names (in this case, A and B):

```
>>> cur.execute('''
SELECT A.Country, B.Country
FROM    PopByCountry A INNER JOIN PopByCountry B
WHERE   (ABS(A.Population - B.Population) <= 1000)
AND     (A.Country != B.Country)''')
<sqlite3.Cursor object at 0x102e3e490>
>>> cur.fetchall()
[('Republic of Korea', 'Canada'), ('Bahamas', 'Greenland'), ('Canada',
'Republic of Korea'), ('Greenland', 'Bahamas')]
```

Notice that we used ABS to get the absolute value of the population difference. Let's consider what would happen without ABS:

```
(A.Population - B.Population) <= 1000
```

Omitting ABS would result in pairs like ('Greenland', 'China') being included, because every negative difference is less than 1,000. If we want each pair of countries to appear only once (in any order), we could rewrite the second half of the condition as follows:

```
A.Country < B.Country
```

By changing the condition above, each pair of countries only appears once.

Nested Queries

Up to now, our queries have involved only one SELECT command. Since the result of every query looks exactly like a table with a fixed number of columns and some number of rows, we can run a second query on the result—that is, run a SELECT on the result of another SELECT, rather than directly on the database's tables. Such queries are called *nested queries* and are analogous to having one function called on the value returned by another function call.

To see why we would want to do this, let's write a query on the PopByCountry table to get the regions that do *not* have a country with a population of 8,764,000. Our first attempt looks like this (remember that the units are in thousands of people):

```
>>> cur.execute('''SELECT DISTINCT Region
                   FROM PopByCountry
                   WHERE (PopByCountry.Population != 8764)''')
<sqlite3.Cursor object at 0x102e3e490>
>>> cur.fetchall()
[('Eastern Asia',), ('North America',)]
```

This result is wrong—Hong Kong has a projected population of 8,764,000, so eastern Asia shouldn't have been returned. Because other countries in eastern Asia have populations that are not 8,764,000, though, eastern Asia was included in the final results.

Let's rethink our strategy. What we have to do is find out which regions include countries with a population of 8,764,000 and then exclude those regions from our final result—basically, find the regions that *fail* our condition and subtract them from the set of all countries (Figure 15, *Nested negation*, on page 358).

The first step is to get those regions that have countries with a population of 8,764,000, as shown in the following code:

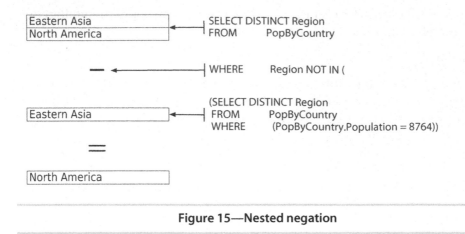

Figure 15—Nested negation

```
>>> cur.execute('''
SELECT DISTINCT Region
FROM PopByCountry
WHERE (PopByCountry.Population = 8764)
''')
<sqlite3.Cursor object at 0x102e3e490>
>>> cur.fetchall()
[('Eastern Asia',)
```

Now we want to get the names of regions that were not in the results of our first query. To do this, we will use a WHERE condition and NOT IN:

```
>>> cur.execute('''
SELECT DISTINCT Region
FROM PopByCountry
WHERE Region NOT IN
    (SELECT DISTINCT Region
     FROM PopByCountry
     WHERE (PopByCountry.Population = 8764))
''')
<sqlite3.Cursor object at 0x102e3e490>
>>> cur.fetchall()
[('North America',)]
```

This time we got what we were looking for. Nested queries are often used for situations like this one, where negation is involved.

Transactions

A *transaction* is a sequence of database operations that are interdependent. No operation in a transaction can be committed unless every single one can be successfully committed in sequence. For example, if an employer is paying an employee, there are two interdependent operations: withdrawing funds from the employer's account and depositing funds in the employee's account. By grouping the operations into a single transaction, it is guaranteed that either both operations occur or neither operation occurs. When executing the operations in a transaction, if one operation fails, the transaction must be *rolled back*. That causes all the operations in the transaction to be undone. Using transactions ensures the database doesn't end up in an unintended state (such as having funds withdrawn from the employer's account but not deposited in the employee's account).

Databases create transactions automatically. As soon as you try to start an operation (such as by calling the execute method), it becomes part of a transaction. When you commit the transaction successfully, the changes become permanent. At that point, a new transaction begins.

Imagine a library that may have multiple copies of the same book. It uses a computerized system to track its books by their ISBN numbers. Whenever a patron signs out a book, a query is executed on the Books table to find out how many copies of that book are currently signed out, and then the table is updated to indicate that one more copy has been signed out:

```
cur.execute('SELECT SignedOut FROM Books WHERE ISBN = ?', isbn)
signedOut = cur.fetchone()[0]
cur.execute('''UPDATE Books SET SignedOut = ?
            WHERE ISBN = ?''', signedOut + 1, isbn)
cur.commit()
```

When a patron returns a book, the reverse happens:

```
cur.execute('SELECT SignedOut FROM Books WHERE ISBN = ?', isbn)
signedOut = cur.fetchone()[0]
cur.execute('''UPDATE Books SET SignedOut = ?
            WHERE ISBN = ?''', signedOut - 1, isbn)
cur.commit()
```

What if the library had two computers that handled book signouts and returns? Both computers connect to the same database. What happens if one patron tried to return a copy of *Gray's Anatomy* while another was signing out a different copy of the same book at the exact same time?

One possibility is that computers A and B would each execute queries to determine how many copies of the book have been signed out, then computer A would add one to the number of copies signed out and update the table without computer B knowing. Computer B would decrease the number of copies (based on the query result) and update the table.

Here's the code for that scenario:

```
Computer A: cur.execute('SELECT SignedOut FROM Books WHERE ISBN = ?', isbn)
Computer A: signedOut = cur.fetchone()[0]
Computer B: cur.execute('SELECT SignedOut FROM Books WHERE ISBN = ?', isbn)
Computer B: signedOut = cur.fetchone()[0]
Computer A: cur.execute('''UPDATE Books SET SignedOut = ?
                           WHERE ISBN = ?''', signedOut + 1, isbn)
Computer A: cur.commit()
Computer B: cur.execute('''UPDATE Books SET SignedOut = ?
                           WHERE ISBN = ?''', signedOut - 1, isbn)
Computer B: cur.commit()
```

Notice that computer B counts the number of signed-out copies before computer A updates the database. After computer A commits its changes, the value that computer B fetched is no longer accurate. If computer B were allowed to commit its changes, the library database would account for more books than the library actually has!

Fortunately, databases can detect such a situation and would prevent computer B from committing its transaction.

17.9 Some Data Based On What You Learned

In this chapter, you learned the following:

- Most large applications store information in relational databases. A database is made up of tables, each of which stores logically related information. A table has one or more columns—each of which has a name and a type—and zero or more rows, or records. In most tables, each row can be identified by a unique key, which consists of one or more of the values in the row.

- Commands to put data into databases, or to get data out, can be written in a specialized language called SQL.

- SQL commands can be sent to databases interactively from GUIs or command-line tools; but for larger jobs, it is more common to write programs that create SQL and process the results.

- Changes made to a database don't actually take effect until they are committed. This ensures that if two or more programs are working with a database at the same time, it will always be in a consistent state. However, it also means that operations in one program can fail because of something that another program is doing.

- SQL queries must specify the table(s) and column(s) that values are to be taken from. They may also specify Boolean conditions those values must satisfy and the ordering of results.

- Simple queries work on one row at a time, but programs can join tables to combine values from different rows. Queries can also group and aggregate rows to calculate sums, averages, and other values.

- Databases can use the special value NULL to represent missing information. However, it must be used with caution, since operations on NULL values don't behave in the same way that operations on "real" values do.

17.10 Exercises

Here are some exercises for you to try on your own. Solutions are available at http://pragprog.com/titles/gwpy2/practical-programming.

1. In this exercise, you will create a table to store the population and land area of the Canadian provinces and territories according to the 2001 census. Our data is taken from http://www12.statcan.ca/english/census01/home/index.cfm.

Province/Territory	Population	Land Area
Newfoundland and Labrador	512930	370501.69
Prince Edward Island	135294	5684.39
Nova Scotia	908007	52917.43
New Brunswick	729498	71355.67
Quebec	7237479	1357743.08
Ontario	11410046	907655.59
Manitoba	1119583	551937.87
Saskatchewan	978933	586561.35
Alberta	2974807	639987.12
British Columbia	3907738	926492.48
Yukon Territory	28674	474706.97
Northwest Territories	37360	1141108.37
Nunavut	26745	1925460.18

Table 32—2001 Canadian Census Data

Write Python code that does the following:

a. Creates a new database called census.db

b. Makes a database table called Density that will hold the name of the province or territory (TEXT), the population (INTEGER), and the land area (REAL)

c. Inserts the data from Table 32, *2001 Canadian Census Data*, on page 361

d. Retrieves the contents of the table

e. Retrieves the populations

f. Retrieves the provinces that have populations of less than one million

g. Retrieves the provinces that have populations of less than one million or greater than five million

h. Retrieves the provinces that do not have populations of less than one million or greater than five million

i. Retrieves the populations of provinces that have a land area greater than 200,000 square kilometers

j. Retrieves the provinces along with their population densities (population divided by land area)

2. For this exercise, add a new table called Capitals to the database. Capitals has three columns—province/territory (TEXT), capital (TEXT), and population (INTEGER)—and it holds the data shown here:

Province/Territory	Capital	Population
Newfoundland and Labrador	St. John's	172918
Prince Edward Island	Charlottetown	58358
Nova Scotia	Halifax	359183
New Brunswick	Fredericton	81346
Quebec	Quebec City	682757
Ontario	Toronto	4682897
Manitoba	Winnipeg	671274
Saskatchewan	Regina	192800
Alberta	Edmonton	937845
British Columbia	Victoria	311902
Yukon Territory	Whitehorse	21405
Northwest Territories	Yellowknife	16541
Nunavut	Iqaluit	5236

Table 33—2001 Canadian Census Data: Capital City Populations

Write SQL queries that do the following:

a. Retrieve the contents of the table

b. Retrieve the populations of the provinces and capitals (in a list of tuples of the form [province population, capital population])

c. Retrieve the land area of the provinces whose capitals have populations greater than 100,000

d. Retrieve the provinces with land densities less than two people per square kilometer and capital city populations more than 500,000

e. Retrieve the total land area of Canada

f. Retrieve the average capital city population

g. Retrieve the lowest capital city population

h. Retrieve the highest province/territory population

i. Retrieve the provinces that have land densities within 0.5 persons per square kilometer of on another—have each pair of provinces reported only once

3. Write a Python program that creates a new database and executes the following SQL statements. How do the results of the SELECT statements differ from what you would expect Python itself to do? Why?

```
CREATE TABLE Numbers(Val INTEGER)
INSERT INTO Numbers Values(1)
INSERT INTO Numbers Values(2)
SELECT * FROM Numbers WHERE 1/0
SELECT * FROM Numbers WHERE 1/0 AND Val > 0
SELECT * FROM Numbers WHERE Val > 0 AND 1/0
```

Bibliography

[DEM02]   Allen Downey, Jeff Elkner, and Chris Meyers. *How to Think Like a Computer Scientist: Learning with Python.* Green Tea Press, Needham, MA, 2002.

[GE13]   Mark J. Guzdial and Barbara Ericson. *Introduction to Computing and Programming in Python: A Multimedia Approach.* Prentice Hall, Englewood Cliffs, NJ, Third, 2013.

[GL07]   Michael H. Goldwasser and David Letscher. *Object-Oriented Programming in Python.* Prentice Hall, Englewood Cliffs, NJ, 2007.

[Hoc04]   Roger R. Hock. *Forty Studies That Changed Psychology.* Prentice Hall, Englewood Cliffs, NJ, 2004.

[Hyn06]   R. J. Hyndman. *Time Series Data Library.* http://www.robjhyndman.com, http://www.robjhyndman.com, 2006.

[Lak76]   Imre Lakatos. *Proofs and Refutations.* Cambridge University Press, Cambridge, United Kingdom, 1976.

[Lut13]   Mark Lutz. *Learning Python.* O'Reilly & Associates, Inc., Sebastopol, CA, Fifth, 2013.

[Pyt11]   Python EDU-SIG. *Python Education Special Interest Group (EDU-SIG).* Python EDU-SIG, http://www.python.org/community/sigs/current/edu-sig, 2011.

[Win06]   Jeannette M. Wing. Computational Thinking. *Communications of the ACM.* 49[3]:33–35, 2006.

[Zel03]   John Zelle. *Python Programming: An Introduction to Computer Science.* Franklin Beedle & Associates, Wilsonville, OR, 2003.

Index

programming style guide (website), 26

programs
  defined, 2
  profiling, 232
  Python, 27
  running, 7, 59
  writing, 59

prompt, 9, 87

Protein Data Bank (PDB) format, 191

Python
  = in, 16
  about, 4
  computer memory, 15–16
  describing code, 25
  dividing integers, 11
  error messages, 22
  exercises, 27
  exponentials, 11
  expressions, 9, 27
  functions, 31
  installing, 5, 9
  integers, 14
  keywords, 38
  making code readable, 26
  modulo, 11
  online tutor, 17
  programs, 27
  running programs in, 7
  statement spanning multiple lines, 23
  statements, 27
  tracking values in, 34
  types, 10, 12
  values, 9, 16
  variables, 15–16, 27
  website, 26

Python interpreter, 8

Python syntax, 280

Q

QA (quality assurance), 297

queries, 344, 357

query conditions, 346

quotes, 47, 65

R

ragged lists, 157

RAISED value, 322

range function, 151

ranges of numbers, looping over, 150

Read technique, 176

reading files, see files

Readline technique, 179, 183

Readlines technique, 177

REAL data type, 342

real numbers, precision of, 14

reassigning to variables, 19

records, 179, 191, 339

relational databases, see databases

relational operators, 80, 82

relative path, 175

relief attribute, 322

remove method, 201

removing duplicates, 352

repeating code, see loops

replace method, 120

repr method, 281

restoring modules, 103

retrieving data, 344

return statement, 39, 60

reusing variable names, 41

reversed function, 177

RGB color model, 328

RIDGE value, 322

rolled back transactions, 358

root window, 318, 321

round function, 33

rounding numbers, 14

rstrip method, 121

running programs, 7, 59

running times, measuring algorithms, 257
  binary search, 245
  linear search, 244

running_sum function, 305

S

saving changes to databases, 344

Scheme programming language, 4

searching
  about, 237, 265
  binary search, 245
  exercises, 266
  lists, 237
  for smallest values, 224
  timing searches, 243

SELECT command, 357

selection sort, 251

self parameter, 274

self-joins, 350, 355

semantic errors, 22

sentinel search, 242

set type, 199

sets
  about, 218
  defined, 199
  exercises, 219
  in operator, 217
  operations on, 201

Shannon, Claude, 77

shell, defined, 8

short-circuit evaluation, 84

side argument, 330

single quote, 68

skipping headers, 183

slicing lists, 137

sort method, 259

sorted function, 178

sorting
  about, 237, 249, 265
  algorithms, 259
  exercises, 266
  insertion sort, 255
  mergesort, 261
  selection sort, 251

sparse vectors, 221

special characters, using in strings, 68

split method, 120

SQL (Structured Query Language), 340

SQLite, 340

sqrt function, 101

square brackets []
  about, 5
  for dictionary values, 211
  empty list, 132

startswith function, 121

statements
  assignment, 15, 18, 72, 134, 148, 213
  break, 161
  choosing which to execute, 86
  continue, 163
  control flow, 77
  CREATE TABLE, 342
  defined, 7
  if, 87, 92
  Import, 100
  import math, 101
  Python, 27
  return, 39, 60

Long Live the Command Line!

Use tmux and Vim for incredible mouse-free productivity.

Your mouse is slowing you down. The time you spend context switching between your editor and your consoles eats away at your productivity. Take control of your environment with tmux, a terminal multiplexer that you can tailor to your workflow. Learn how to customize, script, and leverage tmux's unique abilities and keep your fingers on your keyboard's home row.

Brian P. Hogan
(88 pages) ISBN: 9781934356968. $16.25
http://pragprog.com/book/bhtmux

Vim is a fast and efficient text editor that will make you a faster and more efficient developer. It's available on almost every OS, and if you master the techniques in this book, you'll never need another text editor. In more than 120 Vim tips, you'll quickly learn the editor's core functionality and tackle your trickiest editing and writing tasks. This beloved bestseller has been revised and updated to Vim 7.4 and includes three brand-new tips and five fully revised tips.

Drew Neil
(354 pages) ISBN: 9781680501278. $29
http://pragprog.com/book/dnvim2

Tinker, Tailor, Solder, and DIY!

Get into the DIY spirit with Raspberry Pi or Arduino. Who knows what you'll build next...

The Raspberry Pi is one of the most successful open source hardware projects ever. For less than $40, you get a full-blown PC, a multimedia center, and a web server—and this book gives you everything you need to get started. You'll learn the basics, progress to controlling the Pi, and then build your own electronics projects. This new edition is revised and updated with two new chapters on adding digital and analog sensors, and creating videos and a burglar alarm with the Pi camera. *Printed in full color.*

Maik Schmidt
(176 pages) ISBN: 9781937785802. $22
http://pragprog.com/book/msraspi2

Arduino is an open-source platform that makes DIY electronics projects easier than ever. Gone are the days when you had to learn electronics theory and arcane programming languages before you could even get an LED to blink. Now, with this new edition of the best-selling *Arduino: A Quick-Start Guide*, readers with no electronics experience can create their first gadgets quickly. This book is up-to-date for the latest Arduino boards and for Arduino 1.x, with step-by-step instructions for building a universal remote, a motion-sensing game controller, and many other fun, useful projects.

Maik Schmidt
(324 pages) ISBN: 9781941222249. $34
http://pragprog.com/book/msard2

Kick your Career up a Notch

Ready to blog or promote yourself for real? Time to refocus your personal priorities? We've got you covered.

Technical Blogging is the first book to specifically teach programmers, technical people, and technically-oriented entrepreneurs how to become successful bloggers. There is no magic to successful blogging; with this book you'll learn the techniques to attract and keep a large audience of loyal, regular readers and leverage this popularity to achieve your goals.

Antonio Cangiano
(288 pages) ISBN: 9781934356883. $33
http://pragprog.com/book/actb

It's your first day on the new job. You've got the programming chops, you're up on the latest tech, you're sitting at your workstation... now what? *New Programmer's Survival Manual* gives your career the jolt it needs to get going: essential industry skills to help you apply your raw programming talent and make a name for yourself. It's a no-holds-barred look at what *really* goes on in the office—and how to not only survive, but thrive in your first job and beyond.

Josh Carter
(256 pages) ISBN: 9781934356814. $29
http://pragprog.com/book/jcdeg

Seven in Seven

You need to learn at least one new language every year. Here are fourteen excellent suggestions to get started.

You should learn a programming language every year, as recommended by *The Pragmatic Programmer*. But if one per year is good, how about *Seven Languages in Seven Weeks*? In this book you'll get a hands-on tour of Clojure, Haskell, Io, Prolog, Scala, Erlang, and Ruby. Whether or not your favorite language is on that list, you'll broaden your perspective of programming by examining these languages side-by-side. You'll learn something new from each, and best of all, you'll learn how to learn a language quickly.

Bruce A. Tate
(330 pages) ISBN: 9781934356593. $34.95
http://pragprog.com/book/btlang

Great programmers aren't born—they're made. The industry is moving from object-oriented languages to functional languages, and you need to commit to radical improvement. New programming languages arm you with the tools and idioms you need to refine your craft. While other language primers take you through basic installation and "Hello, World," we aim higher. Each language in *Seven More Languages in Seven Weeks* will take you on a step-by-step journey through the most important paradigms of our time. You'll learn seven exciting languages: Lua, Factor, Elixir, Elm, Julia, MiniKanren, and Idris.

Bruce Tate, Fred Daoud, Jack Moffitt, Ian Dees
(318 pages) ISBN: 9781941222157. $38
http://pragprog.com/book/7lang

Seven in Seven

From Web Frameworks to Concurrency Models, see what the rest of the world is doing with this introduction to seven different approaches.

Whether you need a new tool or just inspiration, *Seven Web Frameworks in Seven Weeks* explores modern options, giving you a taste of each with ideas that will help you create better apps. You'll see frameworks that leverage modern programming languages, employ unique architectures, live client-side instead of server-side, or embrace type systems. You'll see everything from familiar Ruby and JavaScript to the more exotic Erlang, Haskell, and Clojure.

Jack Moffitt, Fred Daoud
(302 pages) ISBN: 9781937785635. $38
http://pragprog.com/book/7web

Your software needs to leverage multiple cores, handle thousands of users and terabytes of data, and continue working in the face of both hardware and software failure. Concurrency and parallelism are the keys, and *Seven Concurrency Models in Seven Weeks* equips you for this new world. See how emerging technologies such as actors and functional programming address issues with traditional threads and locks development. Learn how to exploit the parallelism in your computer's GPU and leverage clusters of machines with MapReduce and Stream Processing. And do it all with the confidence that comes from using tools that help you write crystal clear, high-quality code.

Paul Butcher
(296 pages) ISBN: 9781937785659. $38
http://pragprog.com/book/pb7con

Put the "Fun" in Functional

Elixir puts the "fun" back into functional programming, on top of the robust, battle-tested, industrial-strength environment of Erlang.

You want to explore functional programming, but are put off by the academic feel (tell me about monads just one more time). You know you need concurrent applications, but also know these are almost impossible to get right. Meet Elixir, a functional, concurrent language built on the rock-solid Erlang VM. Elixir's pragmatic syntax and built-in support for metaprogramming will make you productive and keep you interested for the long haul. This book is *the* introduction to Elixir for experienced programmers.

Maybe you need something that's closer to Ruby, but with a battle-proven environment that's unrivaled for massive scalability, concurrency, distribution, and fault tolerance. Maybe the time is right for the Next Big Thing. Maybe it's *Elixir*.

Dave Thomas
(340 pages) ISBN: 9781937785581. $36
http://pragprog.com/book/elixir

Write code that writes code with Elixir macros. Macros make metaprogramming possible and define the language itself. In this book, you'll learn how to use macros to extend the language with fast, maintainable code and share functionality in ways you never thought possible. You'll discover how to extend Elixir with your own first-class features, optimize performance, and create domain-specific languages.

Chris McCord
(128 pages) ISBN: 9781680500417. $17
http://pragprog.com/book/cmelixir

The Joy of Mazes and Math

Rediscover the joy and fascinating weirdness of mazes and pure mathematics.

A book on mazes? Seriously?

Yes!

Not because you spend your day creating mazes, or because you particularly like solving mazes.

But because it's fun. Remember when programming used to be fun? This book takes you back to those days when you were starting to program, and you wanted to make your code do things, draw things, and solve puzzles. It's fun because it lets you explore and grow your code, and reminds you how it feels to just think.

Sometimes it feels like you live your life in a maze of twisty little passages, all alike. Now you can code your way out.

Jamis Buck
(286 pages) ISBN: 9781680500554. $38
http://pragprog.com/book/jbmaze

Mathematics is beautiful—and it can be fun and exciting as well as practical. *Good Math* is your guide to some of the most intriguing topics from two thousand years of mathematics: from Egyptian fractions to Turing machines; from the real meaning of numbers to proof trees, group symmetry, and mechanical computation. If you've ever wondered what lay beyond the proofs you struggled to complete in high school geometry, or what limits the capabilities of the computer on your desk, this is the book for you.

Mark C. Chu-Carroll
(282 pages) ISBN: 9781937785338. $34
http://pragprog.com/book/mcmath

The Pragmatic Bookshelf

The Pragmatic Bookshelf features books written by developers for developers. The titles continue the well-known Pragmatic Programmer style and continue to garner awards and rave reviews. As development gets more and more difficult, the Pragmatic Programmers will be there with more titles and products to help you stay on top of your game.

Visit Us Online

This Book's Home Page
http://pragprog.com/book/gwpy2
Source code from this book, errata, and other resources. Come give us feedback, too!

Register for Updates
http://pragprog.com/updates
Be notified when updates and new books become available.

Join the Community
http://pragprog.com/community
Read our weblogs, join our online discussions, participate in our mailing list, interact with our wiki, and benefit from the experience of other Pragmatic Programmers.

New and Noteworthy
http://pragprog.com/news
Check out the latest pragmatic developments, new titles and other offerings.

Save on the eBook

Save on the eBook versions of this title. Owning the paper version of this book entitles you to purchase the electronic versions at a terrific discount.

PDFs are great for carrying around on your laptop—they are hyperlinked, have color, and are fully searchable. Most titles are also available for the iPhone and iPod touch, Amazon Kindle, and other popular e-book readers.

Buy now at *http://pragprog.com/coupon*

Contact Us

Online Orders:	*http://pragprog.com/catalog*
Customer Service:	*support@pragprog.com*
International Rights:	*translations@pragprog.com*
Academic Use:	*academic@pragprog.com*
Write for Us:	*http://pragprog.com/write-for-us*
Or Call:	+1 800-699-7764

CPSIA information can be obtained at www.ICGtesting.com
Printed in the USA
BVOW09s1123150316

440395BV00008B/40/P